Getting Great Results with Excel® Pivot Tables, PowerQuery, and PowerPivot®

Getting Great Results with Excel® Pivot Tables, PowerQuery, and PowerPivot®

Thomas Fragale
Microsoft Certified Trainer

WILEY

*To the strongest, bravest, most courageous person I've ever met, Josephine Basta.
Fly free, now, and forever. Much love.*

Acknowledgments

I have been very fortunate to be given the opportunity to work with professionals from Wiley to help me create this book.

Jim Minatel, associate publisher at John Wiley & Sons, first reached out to me in the summer of 2023. Thank you for the opportunity, Jim, and to your assistant, Sara Deichman. It was an absolute pleasure to work with editors Brad Jones, Joyce Neilsen, Magesh Elangovan, Pavithra Sankar, Satish Gowrishankar, and everybody else at Wiley. Thank you all for helping me produce a much better book than I would have on my own. I am eternally grateful to everybody at Wiley. A special thank you to Brad and Joyce, who put up with me and my hard head and really pushed me to write a better book.

To my very good friend Media Baldwin, who was gracious enough to write the foreword of this book, even though she had her hands quite full, I am very thankful. Much love.

To my immediate family, Mary Caviston, Vincent Fragale, Jeanne Keller, Melissa Caviston, Jim and Carol Brill, John Caviston, Sean, Emily, Teddy, Louis and Rose Caviston, much love.

To all other friends and family, much love.

I am thankful for the computer classes I took at Central High School (class 241) in Philadelphia and LaSalle University in Philadelphia way back in the late 70s and 80s. I was hooked right from the beginning.

Thank you to all of you who are reading this book. I appreciate every one of you.

—Tom Fragale

About the Author

Thomas Fragale is a Microsoft Certified Trainer with more than 40 years of experience in the IT profession, 24 of which have been spent as a corporate trainer. He has trained more than 50,000 businesspeople in online webinars, public seminars, and on-site training. His clients include many Fortune 500 companies, government agencies, military bases, and companies large and small across many industries, including insurance, manufacturing, banking, pharmaceutical, education, retail, etc. His topics of expertise include Access, Excel, Word, PowerPoint, Outlook, Crystal Reports, SQL Server, Power BI, Teams, Visio, QuickBooks, and SharePoint, among others. His passion is training people and helping people get the most out of their computers. He graduated in 1988 from LaSalle University in Philadelphia, Pennsylvania, with a BA in computer science. He currently lives in Cherry Hill, New Jersey, and still teaches many live webinars and seminars all across the United States of America and the world. He is also a part-time professor at Fordham University.

About the Technical Editor

Joyce J. Nielsen has worked in the publishing industry for more than 30 years as an author, technical editor, development editor, and project manager. Prior to her work in publishing, Joyce was a research analyst for Simon Property Group in Indianapolis. She earned a BS degree in quantitative business analysis from Indiana University's Kelley School of Business in Bloomington. Joyce currently resides in Arizona.

Contents at a Glance

Contents

Foreword

In 2002, Steven Spielberg released the film *Minority Report*. I watched mesmerized as the lead detective swiped and shifted data midair from one holographic screen to another. He used this technology to find the would-be killer *before* he committed the crime.

Obviously, this was science fiction, but the film's premise left me wondering: can the speed of technology allow businesses to prevent potential disasters *before* they happen?

I began my career providing technical training. As I worked with more and more organizations across the United States and globally, I realized that software skills training was helpful and important but didn't really solve what I saw as the larger problem: employees needed a way to make *data-based decisions* that would drive positive outcomes. The data needed to be current and easy to access.

As a solution, I created the "efficiency audit," which helped teams look at information in fresh ways. We identified what data was important now and what might be important in the future. We located and eliminated inefficient duplications of effort. Data warehouses were built. Using customized dashboards, users accessed fact-based analysis from this shared treasure trove of up-to-date data, tailored to their needs. Decision-making became easier, faster, and more accurate.

This is when I first met Tom Fragale. Introduced by a mutual friend, we quickly connected over our shared passion for all things tech and teaching. It was an easy decision to collaborate with Tom on training and database design projects. That business relationship morphed into a strong friendship that I'm proud to say continues some 20 years later.

When Tom reached out to share the news that he had been asked to write this book, I was thrilled.

New data becomes available constantly. For data analytics to be successful, employees need to be able to access data and data models on their own—easily and quickly.

Enter Microsoft pivot tables. Microsoft Excel is accessible, familiar, and relatively easy to use. Pivot tables are the hidden powerhouse of the program. If you know how, you can quickly analyze large and small bodies of data. This data can reside inside or outside of Excel. Pivot tables are flexible and interactive. You can flip, swipe, and move data as easily as it was done in that scene in *Minority Report* (minus the holographic screens!).

In *Getting Great Results with Excel Pivot Tables, PowerQuery, and PowerPivot*, Tom shares his specialized knowledge of data modeling and design. He understands the powerful applications for this tool. Additionally, he is a highly experienced and skilled instructor. Tom thoughtfully includes the example files he uses in the book. Download them to practice hands-on as you go through each chapter. *Getting Great Results with Excel Pivot Tables, PowerQuery, and PowerPivot* methodically walks you through each step of the "how-to" while explaining the "why" and sharing best practices. Before you know it, you will be able quickly access the stories your data wants to tell you.

I'm glad his book has found its way into your hands. It's a resource you'll refer to over and over.

—*Media Baldwin*
CEO of Diversified Seminars

Introduction

There used to be a time when a company's IT team would manage all of the data and create the necessary charts and reports from that data, based on the user's needs. But now, for most companies, those days are long gone!

In today's world, we are all overwhelmed by huge amounts of data from many different sources. On top of that, our co-workers, bosses, vendors, and customers are asking us for all kinds of reports and charts from that data. They also want it to be flexible so they can change the parameters and have it produce instant results. Oh, and by the way, they needed it all yesterday! Sort it this way, filter it that way, show it month by month, etc. It is a daunting and time-consuming task, to say the least! Plus, you have all the other responsibilities for your job as well.

Microsoft Excel has great tools to help you manage your data and to report on that data the way you want to see it. Using pivot tables, Power Query, and PowerPivot, you can pull in data from many sources. You can also clean up and prepare your data, summarize your data in many ways, analyze your data by adding formulas, create visually appealing and interactive dashboards, and get real results from your data. You can do all of this without having to be a programmer. This book will show how to use these tools in an easy-to-follow step-by-step format, backed up with screenshots and real-life examples.

What Does This Book Cover?

An Excel pivot table is an amazing tool that helps you summarize your data just about any way you want. I tried to make this book as thorough as possible so you can really see the depth of the pivot tables, and you can use them to help summarize your own data.

This book has been made to be as easy to follow as possible. Each chapter has specific topics, step-by-step instructions, and screenshots to guide you along.

All the sample files that are mentioned in this book and featured in the screenshots are accessible online so that you can learn the skills using the downloadable sample files and then apply the skills to your own data.

Each chapter has its own sample files and is independent of the other chapters so you can go right to the chapter you want and start to benefit from its information right away.

Chapter 1: Preparing the Data for an Excel Pivot Table   This chapter shows you how to structure your data so that you can create a pivot table from your data. You will see how to import data from other data sources such as text/CSV files, Access databases, websites, ODBC databases, and others. You will also learn how to clean up your data using Power Query.

Chapter 2: Summarizing and Presenting Data with a Pivot Table   This chapter will show you how to get your pivot table started so you can start summarizing your data.

Chapter 3: Using Calculations in Pivot Tables   This chapter teaches you how to use the many built-in calculations of a pivot table and how to create your own calculations in a pivot table.

Chapter 4: Sorting and Filtering the Pivot Table   This chapter demonstrates the many ways that a pivot table can be sorted and filtered, including slicers and timelines, so you can get the exact results you are looking for.

Chapter 5: Making the Pivot Table More Visual with Charts   This chapter will show you how to create and manage charts that come from a pivot table.

Chapter 6: Summarizing Data by Date and Time   This chapter teaches you how to summarize your data by year, quarter, month, day, hour, minute, second, or any combination. It will also show you how to use Excel's built-in calculations to summarize the pivot table by other date and time ranges.

Chapter 7: Creating a Pivot Table from Multiple Spreadsheets   This chapter displays how to make a consolidated pivot table from multiple sheets that are structured in a similar way, and it will also show you how to make a pivot table from sheets that can be linked together on common fields, creating a data model.

Chapter 8: Improving the Pivot Table with Power Pivot   This chapter will demonstrate how to take the data model even further with Power Pivot. It will also show you how to create Data Analysis Expression (DAX) formulas when the pivot table is created from the data model.

Chapter 9: Pulling It All Together: Creating a Dashboard from Pivot Tables   This chapter will show how you can use charts, slicers, timelines, calculations, and form controls to create user-friendly, dynamic, interactive dashboards from pivot tables.

Who Should Read This Book

This book is great for anybody who has tons of raw data and needs to summarize and report on the data in many ways and is looking for quick and easy ways to do that. This can include managers, salespeople, administrative staff, office workers, and people who work in the following professions: accounting, finance, marketing, billing, teaching, purchasing, government, inventory, medical, scientific, engineering, advertising, education, banking, military, and really any other profession that uses huge amounts of data. Anybody who would benefit from the reports made from the pivot tables would also benefit from reading this book.

Reader Support for This Book

If you need help, refer to the following sections.

Companion Download Files

The example files used in this book can be found at and downloaded from `www.wiley.com/go/GGRXL_PivotTables`. Each chapter of the book indicates which workbook to use from the sample files.

How to Contact the Author

We appreciate your input and questions about this book or about possible speaking/training engagements. Email me at `tom@pcwebinars.com` or find me on LinkedIn at `www.linkedin.com/in/tomfragale`.

Preparing the Data for an Excel Pivot Table

If you are like most office workers, you probably have tons of data coming from all directions that you somehow must summarize and make it all make sense. Maybe it is endless lists of sales, bills, invoices, customers, vendors, employees, benefits, payments, orders, products, inventory, collections, books, charges, or countless other possible lists. Additionally, it seems that the lists of information come from all different sources, and it never ends.

When I started in IT a long time ago, it was pretty much up to the IT team to gather all the data and then make reports and charts from the data. At the time, programming languages such as COBOL, Fortran, Basic, Pascal, ColdFusion, VBA, dBase, FoxPro, and others were used to write long, complex programs that would open the data file, go through the file record by record, clean up the data if necessary, accumulate totals, and then finally generate the reports or charts that were asked for. It was a time-consuming process that was prone to errors and many other challenges.

For most companies, those days are long gone. Now it is up to you, the individual, or the people you work with to gather all the data from different sources and make some kind of sense out of it. Somehow you are expected to know how to sort, filter, summarize, chart, and report on the data for the next staff meeting to show something meaningful from the data. Oh, and, by the way, the meeting is this afternoon! No pressure. It's only your job, your career, your life!

What are you going to do?

Relax, it's going to be OK. This whole book is designed to help you make sense of all that data, and you don't even have to be a programmer to get great results from your data. This book will show how to create and manage a pivot table, which is a powerful reporting tool built into Excel. A pivot table can take in huge amounts of data, and it allows you to summarize your data just about any way you want, all without you having to be on the IT team. By using the steps in this book, you really should be able to get great results from your data by using pivot tables.

NOTE   This chapter will present a number of examples. To get the most from these examples, you can download sample files from www.wiley.com/go/GGRXL_ PivotTables. The examples throughout the chapter will note which book file is being used.

What Is Data?

For the purposes of this book, *data* can be defined as a list of rows of information or transactions that have a common theme. The data itself could represent any number of lists of information. It could be names of customers, employees, teachers, students, grades, bills, invoices, inventory, sales, credits, debits, investments, addresses, cities, countries, and so on and so on. The data could be any list of items that people keep track of. It could be a short list with just a few rows, or it could be a long list with hundreds of thousands of rows. Microsoft Excel spreadsheets can hold more than 1,048,000 rows down and more than 16,000 columns across. Larger databases, going into the hundreds of millions of rows, can be managed in Power Pivot, which is discussed in Chapter 8, "Improving Your Pivot Table with Power Pivot." Each row in the list within the Excel worksheet list is a separate transaction or record. Each column is a different field of information.

What the Data Should Look Like

For the data to be used in a pivot table, the data has to be set up in a certain way so it will be optimized for the pivot table. If necessary, Power Query, which is discussed later in this chapter, along with other traditional Excel techniques, can be used to clean the data. Figure 1.1 shows an example of "good" data, and Figure 1.2 shows an example of "bad" data. The following is a list of ways the data should be structured so it is ready to be made into a pivot table:

- It is important that the column headings or field names appear on the top row of the data. The row that contains the field names is also called the *header row*.

- There should be only one row for the column headings. Excel will use the top row of the list as the headers.

- If the data you want to use does not have a header row, then you should take the time to manually insert a row at the top of the data and give each column a meaningful name.

- The header row does not necessarily have to be row 1 of the Excel spreadsheet, but it does have to be the first row of the list of data. Similarly, the first column of information does not have to be in column A of the Excel spreadsheet; it just has to be the first column of the list.

- If there is anything above the header row, then there has to be at least one completely blank row before the header row, and if there is anything before the first column of data in the list, there has to be at least one blank column before the first column of data in the list.

- After the header row, there should be no entirely blank rows until the bottom of the data, and there should be no entirely blank columns until the right side of the list. The reason for this is when the pivot table is first made, Excel will automatically select a range of data, and it will stop at the next completely blank row it finds above the current cell and also below the current cell, and the next completely blank column it finds to the left of the current cell and to the right of the current cell.

- There can be blank cells here and there, but an entire row or column should not be blank within the list of data.

- Each separate transaction should take up only one row of the Excel spreadsheet.

- Each column should have just one piece of information, and it should be consistent all the way up and down the column. A column called Country, for example, should contain only names of countries.

- The column should have the same data type, for example being all text, numbers, or dates within the same column.
- The list of data should not contain any merged cells. A merged cell is when more than one cell is combined into one big cell. These merged cells really get in the way of a successful pivot table.

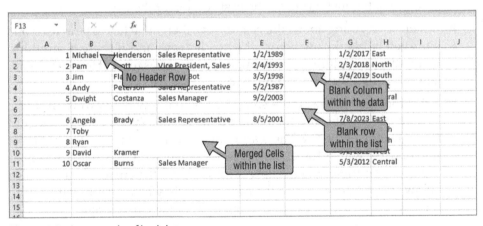

Figure 1.1: An example of good data

Figure 1.2: An example of bad data

NOTE   Checking for Merged Cells

The following is a quick way to see if your list of data has any merged cells:

1. Click one of the cells within the data range.

2. Use the Ctrl+A keyboard shortcut to select the entire range of data.

3. Click the Home tab.

4. Click the Find icon, as shown in Figure 1.3.

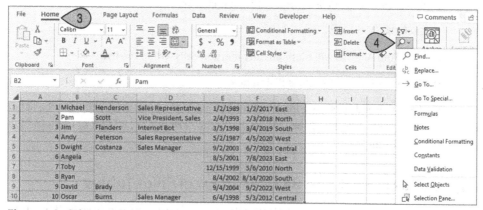

Figure 1.3: Selecting the Find icon

5. In the Find And Replace dialog box, click Options. This will show a list of options, as shown in Figure 1.4.

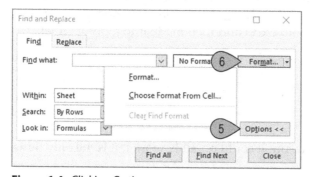

Figure 1.4: Clicking Options

6. Click Format. This will display the Find Format dialog box, as shown in Figure 1.5.

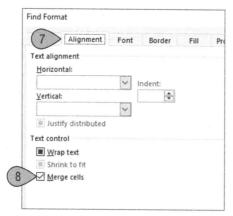

Figure 1.5: The Alignment tab in the Find Format dialog box

7. Click the Alignment tab.

8. Select the Merge Cells option so that it is checked.

9. Click OK.

10. Click Find All. This will highlight any merged cells within the list.

11. Close the Find And Replace dialog box.

12. If any merged cells were found within the list of the data, then highlight the list of data, right-click the range, and then use the Format Cells option to unmerge the cells within the list.

Types of Data That Can Be Used in Excel Pivot Tables

The data for a pivot table can potentially come from many sources. The data can already be in Excel, or it can come from external sources. Data external to Excel would eventually have to be imported into an Excel worksheet. If there are more than 1,048,000 rows in the table, however, it would have to be imported into Power Pivot instead, which will be discussed in Chapter 8, "Improving Your Pivot Table with Power Pivot". The following are the most popular data sources that can be imported into Excel and then made into a pivot table:

- An Excel workbook
- A text or CSV file
- An XML dataset
- A JSON dataset
- A PDF file (not preferable, but it could possibly work if it is the only thing available)
- A SQL Server database
- An Access database
- An Oracle database
- An IBM DB2 database
- A MySQL database
- A PostgreSQL database
- A Sybase database
- A Teradata database
- A SAP HANA database
- Data from Azure
- Data from PowerBI
- Data from Dataverse

- Data from Dataflows
- A SharePoint list
- Microsoft Exchange
- Microsoft Dynamics 365
- Salesforce
- A website that has a table of data
- An OData feed
- A Hadoop file
- An ODBC data source
- An OLEDB data source

There are other possible data sources, but these are the main ones that are being used. Additionally, most of the widely used databases are ODBC compliant, OLE compliant, or both, so that almost every popular database can be a source of data that can be imported into Excel and then used as the main data for a pivot table. If the database you are using is not listed here and it is not ODBC compliant or OLE compliant, there's a pretty good chance that the database program you are using has a way to export the data either into a text/CSV file or even an Excel spreadsheet, so there should still be a way to get that data into Excel so that you can use it for your pivot tables. By using the newly improved Power Query, you can import data directly from all of the previous data sources into Excel. Power Query is an excellent tool that is built into Excel that allows you to import data from other sources, clean the data, and also enhance the data in many ways, some of which will be demonstrated in this chapter.

Using Excel Data

It is likely that you already have data in your existing Excel workbooks that is ready to be made into a pivot table. That's a great start! The data can be just plain, unformatted data, also called *raw data*, or it can be a formatted table, also called a table in Excel. Figure 1.6 shows an example of plain, unformatted data. Figure 1.7 shows an example of a formatted table in Excel.

Either one will be a great source for your pivot table, although there are advantages to using a formatted table as the source for your pivot table such as the following:

- A formatted table automatically expands to include the new columns or rows when they are added. These new columns and rows would then carry over to the pivot table as well. On the other hand, if more rows or columns were added to a list of data that is not a formatted table, the data range that the pivot table uses may have to be manually expanded.

	A	B	C	D	E	F	G	H
1	EmployeeID	FirstName	LastName	JobTitle	BirthDate	HireDate	Region	
2	1	Michael	Henderson	Sales Representative	1/2/1989	1/2/2017	East	
3	2	Pam	Scott	Vice President, Sales	2/4/1993	2/3/2018	North	
4	3	Jim	Flanders	Internet Bot	3/5/1998	3/4/2019	South	
5	4	Andy	Peterson	Sales Representative	5/2/1987	4/5/2020	West	
6	5	Dwight	Costanza	Sales Manager	9/2/2003	6/7/2023	Central	
7	6	Angela	Brady	Sales Representative	8/5/2001	7/8/2023	East	
8	7	Toby	Kramer	Sales Representative	12/15/1999	5/6/2010	North	
9	8	Ryan	Pierce	Sales Coordinator	8/4/2002	8/14/2020	South	
10	9	David	Honeycut	Sales Representative	9/4/2004	9/2/2022	West	
11	10	Oscar	Burns	Sales Manager	6/4/1998	5/3/2012	Central	
12				Plain Unformatted data				
13								

Figure 1.6: Nonformatted data

	A	B	C	D	E	F	G	H
1	EmployeeID	FirstName	LastName	JobTitle	BirthDate	HireDate	Region	
2	1	Michael	Henderson	Sales Representative	1/2/1989	1/2/2017	East	
3	2	Pam	Scott	Vice President, Sales	2/4/1993	2/3/2018	North	
4	3	Jim	Flanders	Internet Bot	3/5/1998	3/4/2019	South	
5	4	Andy	Peterson	Sales Representative	5/2/1987	4/5/2020	West	
6	5	Dwight	Costanza	Sales Manager	9/2/2003	6/7/2023	Central	
7	6	Angela	Brady	Sales Representative	8/5/2001	7/8/2023	East	
8	7	Toby	Kramer	Sales Representative	12/15/1999	5/6/2010	North	
9	8	Ryan	Pierce	Sales Coordinator	8/4/2002	8/14/2020	South	
10	9	David	Honeycut	Sales Representative	9/4/2004	9/2/2022	West	
11	10	Oscar	Burns	Sales Manager	6/4/1998	5/3/2012	Central	
12								
13				Formatted Table				

Figure 1.7: Formatted table

- Formatted tables can be used to make a pivot table from more than one sheet by joining the tables on common fields, a technique that is covered in Chapter 7, "Creating a Pivot Table from Multiple Spreadsheets," and in Chapter 8, "Improving Your Pivot Table with Power Pivot".

- A formatted table is already structured to be used in a pivot table in almost all cases. A list of data that is not a formatted table may have to be cleaned up before being used in a pivot table.

- A formatted table will automatically eliminate any merged cells that were previously within the data and will not allow any new merged cells to be placed within the table.

- Sort and filter are facilitated in formatted tables by having a drop-down list on the top of each column.

- The headers on the formatted table will stay on the top of each column as you scroll down. This does not happen in unformatted lists unless you use Excel's Freeze Panes command, which can be found on the View tab within Excel.

▪ A formatted table is ready to be used with Power Pivot.

▪ The formatted table will assist when you create formulas.

You can create a formatted table from unformatted data by doing the following:

1. Click a cell within your data.
2. Click the Home tab.
3. Click the Format as Table icon on the ribbon. This will display a gallery of table styles, as shown in Figure 1.8.

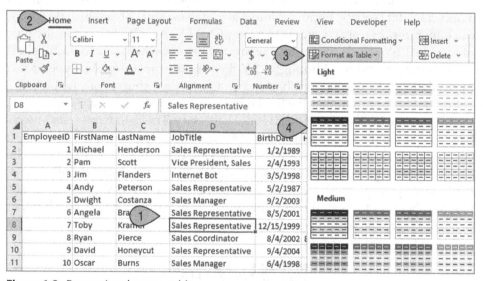

Figure 1.8: Formatting data as a table

4. Choose one of the styles. A Create Table dialog box will be displayed.
5. Make sure the My table has headers check box is selected.
6. Click OK.

Your list is now a formatted table.

Importing Data from External Data Sources into Excel

It is also possible that you will have to import data from other external data sources into Excel. Power Query is set up to import data from many different file types and database formats. The good news is that when the data is imported, it automatically creates a refreshable formatted table from that data, which then can be easily made into a pivot table. In the following section, we will walk through the steps to import data from the most popular data sources. Other data sources that are not specifically shown here will work similarly.

> **NOTE**   You may need the help of your IT team to provide access to an external data source. Please follow your company's procedures when trying to get access to data sources that are external to the Excel workbook.

Importing Data from a Text/CSV File

A text/CSV file is just a plain, unformatted text file. It is considered to be almost a universal data source, because almost all database and spreadsheet programs can either import from or export to a text/CSV file. A CSV file is a specific type of text file. CSV stands for comma-separated values, which means each field is separated by a comma. Although CSV files are the most popular type of text files, other text files could also be used as a good data source for pivot tables.

While it is important that the field names or column headers are included in the first line of the actual text file, it is not necessary. The field names can always be added manually once the data has been successfully imported into Excel. It is also important that the text file has some kind of recognizable structure. The data fields should be delimited, or separated, by some character, usually one of the following: a space, a comma, a semicolon, a colon, or a tab, among others. On the other hand, a text file containing free-form text, like text from a book or a magazine article, would probably not be a good candidate for reliable data that could be used in a pivot table.

> **NOTE**   You can download sample files for this book from www.wiley.com/ go/GGRXL_PivotTables. For the following example, you can use the file *ProductDescriptions.csv* included with the sample files.

The following are the steps for importing data from a text/CSV file:

1. Open a new, blank workbook and click the Data tab.

2. Select Get Data ⇨ From File ⇨ From Text/CSV from the menu, as shown in Figure 1.9. This will display the Import Data dialog box.

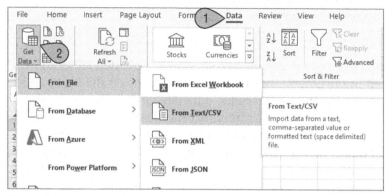

Figure 1.9: Importing data

3. Browse to the folder where your text/CSV file is located and click the filename.

4. Click Import. A new screen will display the data from the file you selected, as shown in Figure 1.10.

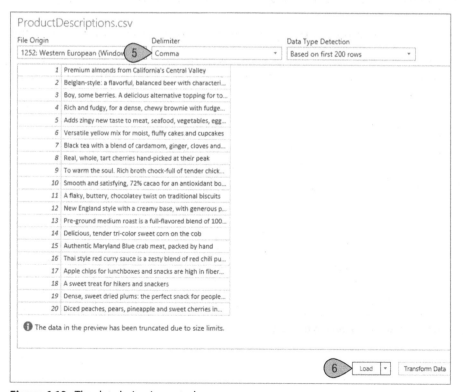

Figure 1.10: The data being imported

5. You may have to change the delimiter, but usually Excel guesses that for you properly. If you have to change the delimiter, try each one on the list of delimiters until the data looks like usable columns of data. A CSV file will always have a comma as the delimiter.

6. Click Load.

The data should be imported into its own sheet as a formatted table. You will see the table listed in the Queries & Connections window on the right, which could be used to clean up or to enhance the data table using Power Query.

Sometimes when importing data from a text file, Excel does not recognize the first row of data from the text file as headers. If you see the field headers on the first row of data, you can use the following steps to create headers from that data. Alternatively, you might notice that the first row of the sheet that was imported has column headings like "Column 1" and "Column 2," while the real field names are on the next row, or even several rows down. If this is the case and you see the field headers a few rows down, you may have to first delete the rows above the row containing the column headers. You can then make that row the header row for the imported data by using the following steps.

NOTE   If you have trouble getting the column names on the first row, you can refer to the section "Removing Columns and Rows" later in this chapter.

To make the first row of data become the actual field names, do the following:

1. Right-click the table in the Queries & Connections window and click Edit from the menu. This will display the Power Query Editor window, as shown in Figure 1.11.

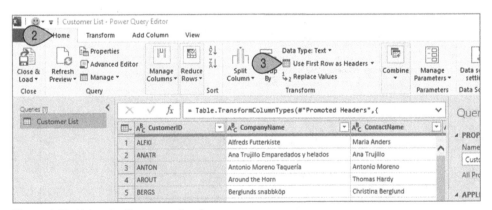

Figure 1.11: Using the first row as headers

2. In the Power Query Editor window, click the Home tab.

3. Click the Use First Row As Headers icon. You now see the much better field names.

4. Close the Power Query Editor window and keep your changes.

Importing Data from an Access Database

Microsoft Access has been Microsoft's standard database on the PC for many years. It is part of the Microsoft 365 suite. Many people still use Access databases to track all kinds of information. An Access database is an outstanding source of data that could be used in pivot tables. An Access database file will contain the tables and the queries/views for that database, among other database objects. Both the tables and the queries can be imported into Excel. Any Access database files created from Access 2000 or later should work just fine. Access databases created on older versions of Access might not work, but you should be able to use Access itself to convert these into the newer file format.

> **NOTE** There is an Access database called *States.accdb* that is included in the sample files for this book that you can use for this example.

To import data from an Access database, you can use the following steps:

1. Click the Data tab.

2. On the left side of the ribbon, select Get Data ⇨ From Database ⇨ From Microsoft Access Database. This will display the Import Data dialog box.

3. Browse to the folder where your Access database file is and click the file you want to import.

4. Click Import. As shown in Figure 1.12, you will see the Navigator window that will display the tables and queries in that database.

5. Click the table or query that you would like to import and then click Load.

The data should be imported into its own sheet, and it will be a formatted table. You will see the table listed in the Queries & Connections window on the right, which could be used to clean up or to enhance the data table using Power Query.

Importing Data from a Web Page

In today's world, there are many websites that have vast amounts of data that can be successfully imported into Excel and then made into a pivot table. The amount of available data on the Internet grows by leaps and bounds every day.

Maybe it is sales data, online catalogs, financial data, sports statistics, or any number of possible lists. Not every website is going to work, of course. The website has to have a table of data that Excel will actually recognize as a table of data.

Figure 1.12: The Navigator window when importing data from an Access database

Maybe you have tried to copy and paste the data from a website into Excel in the past. I know I have. The results are usually disastrous, and even if it does work, a lot of time can be spent trying to reformat the data into something that is usable.

 Here's a better way to import that data from a web page:

1. Open a web browser, like Google Chrome, Edge, Safari, or whichever you choose, and open the website you want to get the data from. For this example, I will use `https://finance.yahoo.com/gainers`.

2. Highlight the website name (the URL) and copy it.

3. Open either an existing or a new Excel workbook.

4. Click the Data tab.

5. On the left side of the ribbon, select Get Data ➪ From Other Sources ➪ From Web. This will display the dialog box for importing data, as shown in Figure 1.13.

Figure 1.13: Importing data from a web page

6. Paste or enter the website URL from step 2 and click OK. If you do not paste it, you will have to enter the website name exactly right. I prefer to paste it. Microsoft Excel will now try to connect to the website and the tables of data on that website, if there are any.

7. If you get an Access Web Content window, just click Connect. You will see the Navigator window, which will show the tables it found, if any.

8. Select the tables on the left side of the Navigator window until you find the one you want to use, and then click Load.

The data should be imported into its own sheet, and it will be a formatted table. You will see the table listed in the Queries & Connections window on the right, which could be used to clean up or to enhance the data table using Power Query.

Connecting to an ODBC Database

Most popular databases are ODBC compliant. ODBC means Open Data Base Connectivity. It is a protocol that is used so that different database management systems can share data with each other. Some examples of ODBC-compliant databases are SQL Server, Oracle, MYSQL, dBase, Paradox, IBM DB2, and Sybase.

In my experience, most IT teams will not grant you direct access to the company's database. Understandably, the IT team is going to be very protective of the important company data. There's a much better chance of getting them to give you access through the ODBC connection because it allows your IT team the flexibility to provide the exact access the end user needs to the data, while at the same time keeping everything secure. You will have to get your IT team to set up an ODBC driver on the computer where you are using Excel. Tell your IT team what you need, and make sure you use the phrase "Read Only" when you make the request. Your company may have specific procedures that you need to follow for such requests, and I strongly recommend that you follow your company's procedures when trying to access the company's data.

Once you have this access from your IT team, you can import data from the ODBC Database by doing the following:

1. From the left side of the Data tab, select Get Data ⇨ From Other Sources ⇨ From ODBC. This will display the From ODBC dialog box, as shown in Figure 1.14.

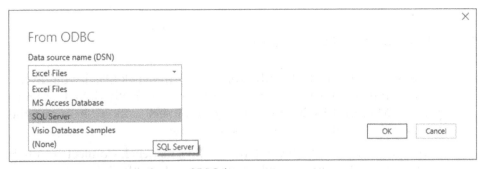

Figure 1.14: Importing data from an ODBC data source

2. Click the drop-down list that displays the data source names. Select the one that your IT team has set up for you and then click OK. Microsoft Excel will now try to connect to the server.

3. Fill in the ODBC Driver info, and then click Connect. Excel will then attempt to connect to your data source. Once connected, you will see the Navigator window, which will show the databases and tables on the server. Check with your IT team, and they will tell you which databases, tables, and views are necessary for your needs.

4. Select the table or view you want to import and click Load.

The data should be imported into its own sheet, and it will be a formatted table. You will see the table listed in the Queries & Connections window on the right, which could be used to clean up or to enhance the data table using Power Query.

Importing Data from a Different Excel Workbook

It is definitely possible to import data from one Excel workbook to another. There are multiple reasons why you would want to do this. For example, sometimes you want to pull all of your data into one workbook.

This is especially important if you plan to link the sheets together on common fields. Each data table that you want to import into the new Excel workbook should be on its own separate sheet. The field names should be on row 1 of that sheet unless the data is a formatted table. The data should also follow the rules for acceptable data listed at the beginning of this chapter.

> **NOTE** There is an Excel workbook included in the sample files that comes with the book called *Pivot Table Book sample data.xlsx* that you can use for this example.

To import one sheet from an existing Excel workbook, follow these steps:

1. From the left side of the Data tab, select Get Data ⇨ From File ⇨ From Excel Workbook. This will display the Import Data dialog box for you to select a file from.

2. Browse to the folder where your Excel workbook is, select the file, and then click Import. You will see the Navigator window that will display the sheets from that workbook. It will show the sheets that are formatted tables at the top, and then the sheets that are not formatted tables below them.

3. Select the sheet you would like to import and click Load.

The data should be imported into its own sheet, and it will be a formatted table. You will see the table listed in the Queries & Connections window on the right, which could be used to clean up or to enhance the data table using Power Query.

Sometimes when importing data from an Excel sheet that was not a formatted table in the original workbook, Excel does not recognize the first row of data from the Excel sheet file as headers. You might notice that the first row of the sheet that was imported from the Excel file has column headings like "Column 1," "Column 2," and so on. Then you might see the real field names on the next row. Refer to the earlier "Importing Data from a Text/CSV File" section to help rectify this issue, if necessary.

If you want to import more than one sheet from the other workbook, there are some important additional steps. Let's look at an example. There is an Excel workbook included with the files that come with the book called *Pivot Table Book sample data.xlsx* that you can use for this example. You can import multiple sheets from an existing Excel workbook by doing the following:

1. Click the Data tab.
2. Select Get Data ⇨ From File ⇨ From Excel Workbook on the left side of the ribbon.
3. Browse to the folder where your Excel workbook is located.
4. Click the file.
5. Click Import. This will open the Navigator window that will display the sheets from that workbook. It will show the sheets that are formatted tables at the top and then the sheets that are not formatted tables below them.
6. Check the Select multiple Items check box on the top of the window, as shown in Figure 1.15.
7. Check all of the sheets you would like to import.
8. Click the drop-down to the right of the word Load.
9. Click Load To.
10. In the Import Data dialog box, make sure Table is selected.
11. Make sure New Worksheet is also selected.
12. Click OK.

Each sheet you selected should be imported as a separate sheet, and they will all be formatted tables. They will be listed in the Queries & Connections window on the right, which could be used to further manage the data using Power Query.

Refreshing the Data

Typically, people want to make sure they are looking at the most recent data. In many cases, the data is being updated every minute or maybe even every second of the day. The tables from any of the data sources can be refreshed so that you are always looking at the most recent data. The data can be refreshed manually, or it can be automated.

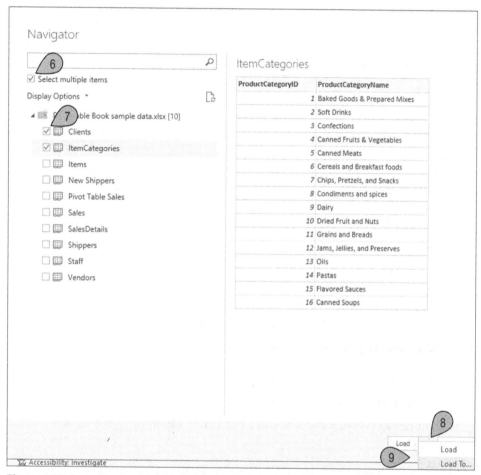

Figure 1.15: Importing multiple sheets from a different Excel workbook

To refresh a table manually, first click a cell within the table that you want to refresh. You can then click the Refresh All icon on the Data tab, or you can right-click the cell and select Refresh from the menu. If the data has changed since the last time you imported or refreshed the table, you will now see the changes.

To refresh a table automatically, follow these steps:

1. Click a cell within the table you want to refresh.

2. Click the Data tab.

3. Click the down arrow on the Refresh All icon.

4. Select Connection Properties. This will open the Query Properties dialog box, as shown in Figure 1.16.

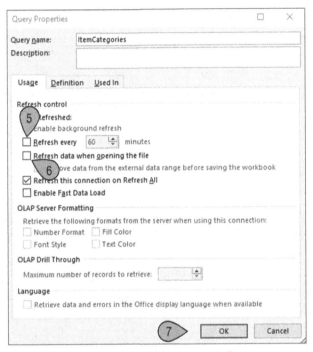

Figure 1.16: Refreshing the table automatically

5. Check the box to the left of Refresh Every. Then you can set the number of minutes between refreshes.

6. You can also check the Refresh Data When Opening The File box.

7. Click OK.

The table will now automatically update either every so many minutes or whenever you open the Excel workbook, or both.

Using Power Query to Clean the Data

Now you have data in your Excel workbook that you want to use in your pivot table. It could have been already in Excel, or maybe you just imported the data from other sources, as described earlier. You still may have to do some things to the data to make it ready to be made into a pivot table. This is where Power Query can help. The following are just some of the ways that Power Query can help you clean up your data:

■ Analyzing your data for errors and blanks

- Splitting columns
- Merging columns
- Changing data types
- Replacing data
- Removing rows and columns
- Sorting
- Filtering
- Calculating the age based on a date field
- Parsing dates and times
- Creating standard calculations
- Trimming spaces from the beginning or end of a column
- Creating conditional columns, similar to an IF function in Excel
- Combining tables
- Generating subtotals
- Reformatting a column

Even though many of these tasks can also be done in Excel without using Power Query, Power Query can do a lot more than standard Excel tasks, and many of these tasks are done quicker and easier in Power Query than by just using Excel itself.

Using the Queries & Connections Window

To use Power Query, you will want to open a window called Queries & Connections. The Queries & Connections window allows you to access the Power Query Editor and other features of Power Query. If it is not already opened on the right side of your Excel window, then click the Queries & Connections icon near the left side of the Data tab, as shown in Figure 1.17.

Once the Queries & Connections window is open on the right side of the Excel screen, you should see your tables from the workbook listed there.

> **NOTE** The Power Query examples presented in the next few sections will use the data file called *Pivot Table Book sample data-formatted tables.xlsx* that can be downloaded from the Wiley site as mentioned earlier in this chapter. Of course, these steps will work with your data as well. When you open the sample file or your own Excel workbook, you might need to display the Queries & Connections window if you do not see it on the right side of the screen.

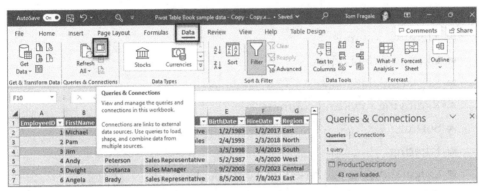

Figure 1.17: Displaying the Queries & Connections window

If the table that you want to use does not appear in the Queries & Connections window, then follow these steps:

1. Right-click a cell within the list you want to use and select Click Get Data From Table/Range.

2. If you see the Create Table dialog box and your data has a header row, select the My Data Has Headers check box.

3. Click OK.

4. This will take you to the Power Query Editor window, as shown in Figure 1.18.

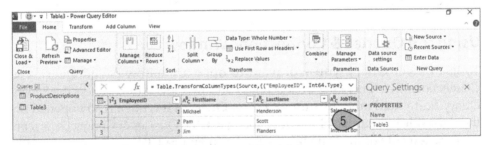

Figure 1.18: Allowing Power Query to see normal Excel data

5. In the Query Settings window on the right side of the window, give the table a better name.

6. Close the Power Query Editor window.

7. Click Keep to save your changes.

8. You will see the new table on its own sheet, and it will now appear in the Queries & Connection window.

Analyzing the Table

Power Query can help you analyze your table. It can show how many cells in a column are valid, how many are in error, how many are empty, and other relevant information about your table.

To analyze your data, follow these steps:

1. Right-click a table in the Queries & Connections window.

2. Click Edit. This will open the Power Query Editor window.

3. Click the View tab.

4. Check the Column Quality, Column Distribution, and Column Profile boxes. This will show information about each column in the table, as shown in Figure 1.19.

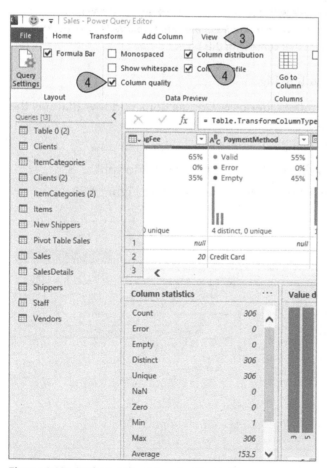

Figure 1.19: Analyzing the data using Power Query

5. Uncheck the Column Quality, Column Distribution, and Column Profile boxes.

6. Close the Power Query Editor window and keep your changes.

Splitting a Column

There will be times when you have to split a column. An example would be if the first name and the last name are in the same column. You would want to split that column so that you would be able to sort on either column. There are many other reasons to split a column. This would be similar to using the Text to Columns feature in Excel. Power Query has an easy and flexible way to split columns.

> **NOTE** You can try this example with the Contact Name column in the Vendors table from the Excel workbook called *Pivot Table Book sample data-formatted tables.xlsx* that is included with the sample files that come with this book.

To split columns, do the following:

1. Right-click the table in the Queries & Connections window that has the field you want to split.

2. Click Edit. This will open the Power Query Editor window.

3. Click the column heading of the column you want to split.

4. On the Home tab, click Split Column, as shown in Figure 1.20.

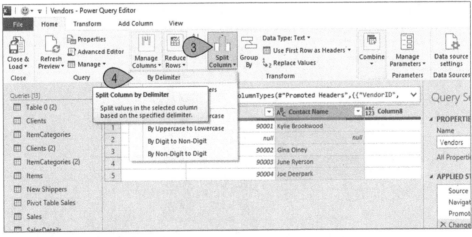

Figure 1.20: Splitting a column

5. Click By Delimiter. This will open a window called Split Column by Delimiter.

6. Usually, it will guess the correct delimiter, but if it does not, click the drop-down list for the delimiter and select the proper one.

7. Click OK.

8. The column is now split.

9. Close the Power Query Editor window and keep your changes.

Merging Columns

Sometimes you might want to put fields back together again rather than split them. Maybe you want to put the first name and the last name back together into a full name column, for example. In Excel, you would use a function called Concatenate. Power Query can easily merge the columns.

> **NOTE** You can try this example with the Manager First Name and Manager Last Name columns in the Vendors table from the Excel workbook called *Pivot Table Book sample data-formatted tables.xlsx* that is included with the sample files that come with this book.

To merge columns, do the following:

1. Right-click the table in the Queries & Connections window that has the fields you want to merge.

2. Click Edit. This will open the Power Query Editor window.

3. Click the first column you want to merge, hold down the Shift key, and click the column headings of the additional columns you want to merge.

4. Click the Add Column tab.

5. Click Merge Columns. This will open a new window called Merge Columns, as shown in Figure 1.21.

Merge Columns   ×

Choose how to merge the selected columns.

Separator

| Space   ▾ |

New column name (optional)

| Manager Full Name |

                                                  [OK]   [Cancel]

Figure 1.21: Merging columns

6. Click the Separator drop-down list and choose the separator you want to use between each field.

7. Give the new column a good name.

8. Click OK.

9. Scroll all the way to the right to see the new column.

10. Close the Power Query Editor window and keep your changes.

Changing Data Types

There will be times when you will need to change the data type of a column, maybe from a text field to a number or a text field to a date or vice versa. This process will be especially important if you plan to use a field in number or date calculations. Power Query makes it easy to change the data type of a column.

> **NOTE** You can try this example with the Vendor Since Date column in the Vendors table from the Excel workbook called *Pivot Table Book sample data–formatted tables. xlsx* that is included with the sample files that come with this book. Right now, it is a text data type. Change it to a date data type.

To change data types, you do the following:

1. Right-click the table in the Queries & Connections window that has the fields you want to change.

2. Click Edit. This will open the Power Query Editor window.

3. Observe the column headings of each field. Notice the little icon to the left of the column name.

4. Click the icon to the left of the column you want to change, as shown in Figure 1.22.

5. Click the data type you want to use.

6. Close the Power Query Editor window and keep your changes.

Removing Columns and Rows

There may be columns and rows that need to be removed because they are extraneous, they are blank, or there might be other reasons to omit them. Remember, extraneous blank rows and blank columns may get in the way of creating a pivot table. Removing rows and columns is easily accomplished in Power Query.

> **NOTE** You can try this example with the blank column that appears to the right of the Contact Name column in the Vendors table from the Excel workbook called *Pivot Table Book sample data-formatted tables.xlsx* that is included with the sample files that come with this book.

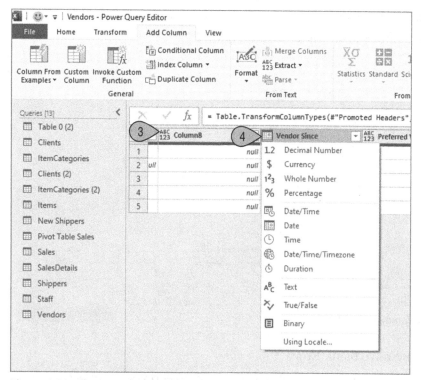

Figure 1.22: Changing data types

To remove columns, do the following:

1. Right-click the table in the Queries & Connections window that has the columns you want to remove.

2. Click Edit. This will open the Power Query Editor window.

3. Right-click the column you want to delete.

4. Click Remove.

5. Close the Power Query Editor window and keep your changes.

> **NOTE** You can try this example with the blank row that appears in the Vendors table from the Excel workbook called *Pivot Table Book sample data-formatted tables.xlsx* that is included with the sample files that come with this book.

To remove blank rows, do the following:

1. Right-click the table in the Queries & Connections window that has the rows you want to remove.

2. Click Edit. This will open the Power Query Editor window.

3. Click the Home tab.

4. Click Remove Rows, as shown in Figure 1.23.

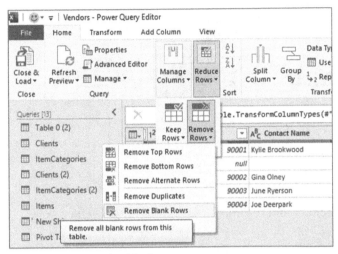

Figure 1.23: Removing blank rows

5. Click Remove Blank Rows.

6. Close the Power Query Editor window and keep your changes.

Undoing Steps in Power Query

It is inevitable that all of us are going to want to undo something in the Power Query Editor window. However, when you go through the tabs of the Power Query Editor, you will not find an Undo icon on any of the ribbons. Nonetheless, there is a way to undo steps in Power Query.

A powerful feature of Power Query is that it maintains the entire history of all the steps that have been done to the table within the Applied Steps window, which can be found on the right side of the Power Query Editor window. These steps can be changed and deleted.

WARNING If steps are deleted from the Applied Steps, it could cause other steps further down in the list to no longer work. You may have to also delete these steps and then redo the steps. Also, once you keep the changes in the Power Query Editor window, the deleted steps cannot be retrieved.

To undo steps in the Power Query Editor window, do the following:

1. Right-click the table in the Queries & Connections window that has the steps you want to undo.

2. Click Edit. This will open the Power Query Editor window.

3. The applied steps on the right side of the window accumulate for the history of the table, as shown in Figure 1.24.

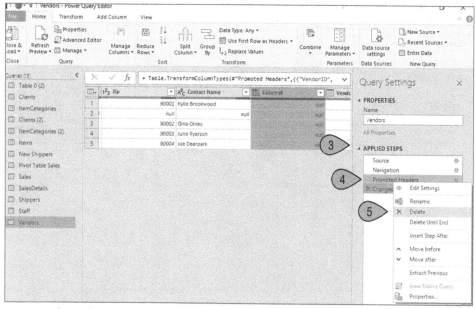

Figure 1.24: Undoing steps in Power Query

4. Right-click the step you want to delete.

5. Click Delete. If you click Delete Until End, then all of the steps after the step you are on will also be deleted. Click Delete again to confirm the deletion.

6. That will take that step away, which will undo that step, and then you can take it from there.

7. Close the Power Query Editor window and keep your changes.

Replacing Values

There will be times when values in a field have to be replaced with other values. Power Query makes this task easy.

To replace values, follow these steps:

1. Right-click the table in the Queries & Connections window that has the fields you want to replace.

2. Click Edit. This will open the Power Query Editor window.

3. Click the column header of the column where you want to replace the data.

4. Click the Home tab of the Power Query Editor.

5. Click Replace Values. This will open a new window, as shown in Figure 1.25.

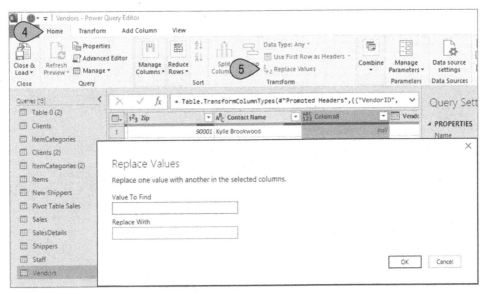

Figure 1.25: Replacing values using Power Query

6. Type in the text you want to replace in the Value To Find text box.

7. Type in the text you want to replace it with in the Replace With text box.

8. Click OK.

9. Close the Power Query Editor window and keep your changes.

Trimming Spaces from the Beginning and End of the Data in a Column

Sometimes, especially when data is imported from other sources, there can be spaces before the first main character of the field, spaces after the last main character of the field, and sometimes both. These are called *leading* and *trailing spaces*, which can both cause issues with other Excel functions and formulas. Power Query has an easy way to remove the leading and trailing spaces from your data.

To trim leading and trailing spaces in a column, do the following:

1. Right-click the table in the Queries & Connections window that has the fields you want to trim.

2. Click Edit. This will open the Power Query Editor window.

3. Click the column header of the column that you want to trim.

4. Click the Transform tab of the Power Query Editor.

5. Click the Format icon, as shown in Figure 1.26.

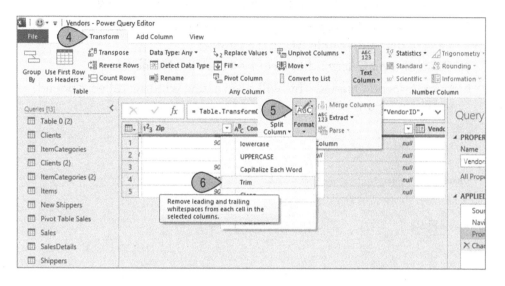

Figure 1.26: Trimming leading and trailing spaces

6. Click Trim.

7. Close the Power Query Editor window and keep your changes.

Combining Tables Using the Append Query

Let's say you have a main list of data, maybe customers, transactions, or what-ever information that table contains. This main list is also called the *master list*. Many times, new data will come in from various sources that have the same structure as the main list. These new records need to be added or appended to the master list. Perhaps, like me, you have used Copy and Paste to accomplish this task. If you have ever tried that method, you know it can be time-consuming, prone to errors, cumbersome, and not always reliable. Power Query has a more efficient way to add the records from the new list into the master list that is called the Append Query.

NOTE   You can use the New Shippers and Shippers tables in the sample Excel file called *Pivot Table Book sample data-formatted tables.xlsx* that is included with the files that come with this book for this example. Shippers is the main list, and New Shippers is the list to be appended. These steps would also work with your own tables, of course.

To combine tables using the Append Query, do the following:

1. Right-click the table in the Queries & Connections window that contains your current records. If you are using the sample data, this would be the Shippers table.

2. Click Edit. This will open the Power Query Editor window.

3. Notice the number of records that are currently in the table. The Shippers table in the sample data has two records.

4. On the Power Query Editor window, click the Home tab.

5. Click Append Queries. This will open a new window called Append, as shown in Figure 1.27.

Figure 1.27: Using the Append Query

6. Click Two Tables.

7. Click the drop-down list and click the table with the new records. In the sample data, this would be the New Shippers table.

8. Click OK.

9. Notice there are now additional records.

10. Close the Power Query Editor window and keep your changes.

Combining Tables Using the Merge Query

There are many times when one table needs to look up information in another table. Maybe a table containing the orders for a company has only the customer number for each customer but needs to retrieve the other information about the customer from a different table and then include the field from the other table into the original table. In Excel, maybe you would use formulas containing the XLOOKUP, VLOOKUP, HLOOKUP, MATCH, or INDEX functions, or different combinations of these functions. Each column that you would want to retrieve from the other table would need to have its own formula. These formulas can be cumbersome and confusing. Power Query can actually retrieve all of the fields from the second table into the first table in one step using the Merge Query.

> **NOTE** You can use the Vendors and Items tables in the sample Excel file called *Pivot Table Book sample data-formatted tables.xlsx* that is included with the files that come with this book for this example. Items is the main list, and Vendors is the list to be merged. The common field is VendorID. These steps would also work with your own tables, of course.

To combine tables using the Merge Query, do the following:

1. Right-click the table in the Queries & Connections window that you want to merge with another table. If you are using the sample data, this would be the Items table.

2. Click Edit. This will open the Power Query Editor window.

3. On the Power Query Editor window, click the Home tab.

4. Click Merge Queries. This will open a new window called Merge as shown in Figure 1.28.

5. Click the drop-down list in the middle of the window.

6. Choose the table you would like to merge with. In the sample data, this would be the Vendors table.

7. Choose the common field from the top table. In the sample data, this would be the VendorID.

8. Click the common field on the table in the middle of the screen. On the sample data, this is also called VendorID. When you do this with your data, it is not necessary that the two fields have the same field name. It is more important that they both have the same type of data.

9. Click OK.

10. Click the icon to the right of the Vendors field in the second table, as shown in Figure 1.29.

11. Choose the fields you want to merge. Choose all of the fields if you are using the sample data.

12. Click OK.

13. All the columns from the second table are now on the right side of the fields from the first table. Excel knows which records from the second table go with which records from the first table because of the common field you chose on the previous window.

14. Close the Power Query Editor window and keep your changes.

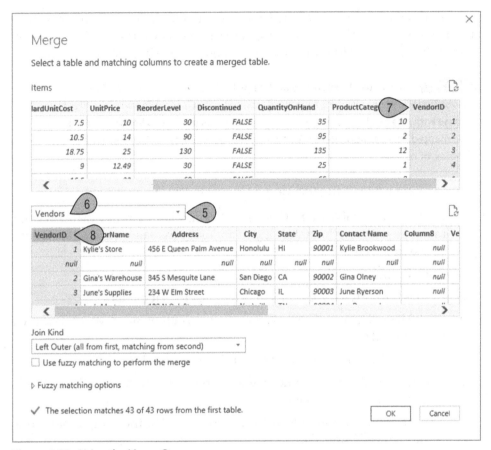

Figure 1.28: Using the Merge Query

Creating Subtotals in Your Data Using the GroupBy Query

I think it is fair to say that if you are reading this book, you probably have tons and tons of data to deal with. I know you are anxious to learn how to summarize that data with the pivot table, which is coming up in Chapter 2, "Summarizing and Presenting Data with a Pivot Table." Power Query has a great way to give you subtotals from your tables, even before we make the pivot table. You can generate subtotals from your data in Power Query using a GroupBy Query.

> **NOTE** You can use the pivot table Sales table in the sample Excel file called *Pivot Table Book sample data-formatted tables.xlsx* that is included with the files that come with this book for this example. These steps would also work with your own tables, of course.

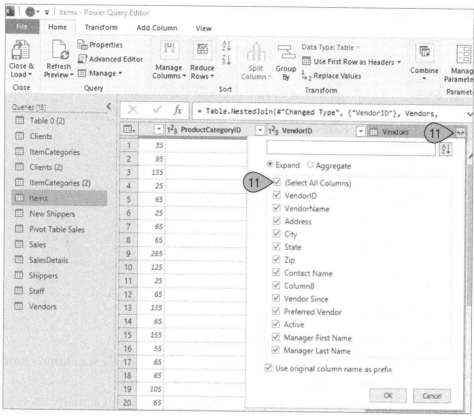

Figure 1.29: Completing the Merge Query

To create subtotals in your data using the GroupBy query, do the following:

1. Right-click the table in the Queries & Connections window that has the fields you want to subtotal. In the sample data, this would be the Pivot Table Sales table.

2. Click the word Duplicate. This will display the Power Query Editor window.

3. Notice the number of rows on the bottom-left corner of the window. The sample table has 306 rows, for example.

4. Click the Home tab.

5. Click the GroupBy icon. This will open a new window called Group By, as shown in Figure 1.30.

6. Click the first drop-down list and click the field that you want to subtotal on. In the sample data, this would be the Customer Name field so that it will produce a subtotal for each different customer name.

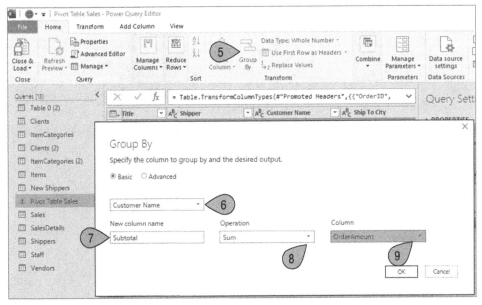

Figure 1.30: Using the GroupBy Query to create subtotals

7. Type in **Subtotal** for the new column name.

8. Click the Operation drop-down list to the right of the new column name and click Sum, or the one you want to use.

9. Click the next drop-down list and choose the field you actually want to summarize. For the sample data, this would be the OrderAmount field.

10. Click OK.

11. Notice the new number of rows on the bottom left. The sample table would now have eight rows, which is one row for each customer, and there is a subtotal for each customer.

12. Close the Power Query Editor window and keep your changes.

13. You may want to rename the new table in the Queries & Connections window.

Using Power Query to Create Calculations

Another great feature of Power Query is the ability to add your own calculations to your data directly in the Power Query Editor window. Power Query formulas use the M language. You can build simple formulas or complicated formulas using the M language. There are even built-in functions in the M language, which can even go further than Excel functions. The examples in the following sections will show you how to build a formula and demonstrate some popular formulas.

To use the Age and the other date and time functions in the following examples, the column must be seen by Power Query as a Date or a Date/Time data type. For calculations involving number fields, the field must be one of the number data types. If necessary, see the earlier "Changing Data Types" section that shows you how to convert the data type in a column to make sure it is the appropriate data type.

NOTE You can find a complete reference of the M language at `learn` `.microsoft.com/en-us/PowerQuery-m`.

Calculating Age/Years of Service

It is likely that at least one of your tables has a date field of some kind. Maybe it is a birth date, a hire date, or an order date. There may be times you want to be able to calculate the age based on this date. In Excel, you would have to build a formula to calculate the age. In Power Query, the age is built right in.

NOTE To calculate age or years of service, we'll use the Staff table from the Excel workbook called *Pivot Table Book sample data-formatted tables.xlsx* that is included with the downloadable sample files. The Staff table has a field called BirthDate and another field called HireDate.

To calculate age or years of service, do the following:

1. Right-click the table in the Queries & Connections window that has a date field. In the sample data, it would be the Staff table.
2. Click Edit. This will open the Power Query Editor window.
3. Click the column heading of the date column you want to use.
4. Click the Add Column tab.
5. Click the Date icon on the right side of the ribbon, as shown in Figure 1.31.

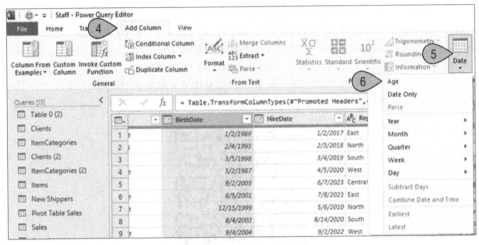

Figure 1.31: Calculating age using Power Query

6. Choose Age from the list. This will create a new column called Age on the right side of the table. Right now, the age is showing the number of days.

7. Right-click the Age column.

8. Click Transform and then Total Years. The age is now in years, but you may want to round it down.

9. Right-click the Age column.

10. Click Transform and then Round and then Round Down.

11. Close the Power Query Editor window and keep your changes.

Using the Built-in Date Functions

When you calculated the age from the date field in the previous section, you may have noticed that there were many more ways to break down a date field. Power Query can quickly and easily separate parts of the data and provide other meaningful results from a date column. You can break down a date field into year, quarter, month, week, and day. These options can be found when you click the Date icon of the Add Column tab in the Power Query Editor window, similar to the steps used in calculating the age in the previous section. Table 1.1 shows all the ways you can break down a date. The examples use the date 11/24/2025.

Table 1.1: Ways to break down a date field

DATE ELEMENT	BREAKOUT	EXAMPLE
Year	Year	2025
	Start of Year	1/1/2025 12:00:00 AM
	End of Year	1/1/2026 12:00:00 AM

DATE ELEMENT	BREAKOUT	EXAMPLE
Month	Month	11
	Start of Month	11/01/2025
	End of Month	11/30/2025
	Days in Month	30
	Name of Month	November
Quarter	Quarter of Year	4
	Start of Quarter	10/01/2025
	End of Quarter	12/31/2025
Week	Week of Year	48
	Week of Month	5
	Start of Week	11/23/2025
	End of Week	11/30/2025
Day	Day	24
	Day of Week	2
	Day of Year	329
	Start of Day	11/24/2025 12:00:00 AM
	End of Day	11/25/2025 12:00:00 AM
	Name of Day	Tuesday

Using the Built-In Time Functions

Similar to breaking down a date field, Power Query can also quickly and easily separate parts of a time field and provide other meaningful results from a time column. You can break down a time field into hour, minute, and second. To get to these time functions, use the same first few steps from calculating an age in the previous section, but click Time on the Add Column tab of the Power Query Editor window, instead of Date. Table 1.2 shows all the ways you break down a time field using the Power Query Editor. This table shows the results for 2:35 p.m.

Table 1.2: Ways to break down a time field

TIME ELEMENT	BREAKOUT	EXAMPLE
Hour	Hour	14
	Start of Hour	2:00:00 PM
	End of Hour	3:00:00 PM
Minute	Minute	35
Second	Second	0

Using a Custom Column for Other Calculations

Power Query can be used to create many other calculations as well. As mentioned earlier, the M language is robust and can be used for simple formulas or for more complex formulas, including functions.

Examples of some of the other calculations you can do using M include doing line totals, calculating days to ship, and creating a new total. Let's look at each of these.

Calculating a Line Total

> **NOTE**   You can use the SalesDetails table that is in the Excel workbook called *Pivot Table Book sample data-formatted tables.xlsx* that is included with the book's sample files for this example.

To calculate a line total, do the following:

1. Right-click the table in the Queries & Connections window where you want to create a new calculation. In the sample data, this would be the SalesDetails table.

2. Click Edit. This will open the Power Query Editor window.

3. Click the Add Column tab.

4. Click the Custom Column icon on the left side of the ribbon. This will open a new window called Custom Column, as shown in Figure 1.32.

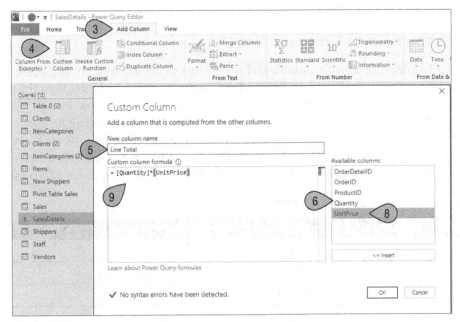

Figure 1.32: Line total calculation

5. For the column name, type Line Total.

6. Double-click the Quantity field on the right side of the window. This will add the Quantity field to the formula.

7. Type * for multiplication.

8. Double-click the UnitPrice field on the right side of the window. This will add the UnitPrice field to the formula.

9. The formula will now display `= [Quantity] * [UnitPrice]`.

10. Click OK. The Line Total column should be on the right side of the table.

11. Close the Power Query Editor window and keep your changes.

Calculating the Days to Ship

> **NOTE** You can use the Sales table that is in the Excel workbook called *Pivot Table Book sample data-formatted tables.xlsx* that is included in the sample files that come with this book for the next two examples.

To calculate the days to ship, do the following:

1. Right-click the Sales table in the Queries & Connections window.

2. Click Edit. This will open the Power Query Editor window.

3. In the Power Query Editor window, click the Add Column tab.

4. Click the Custom Column icon on the left side of the ribbon. This will open a new window called Custom Column, as shown in Figure 1.33.

5. For the new column name, type **Days to Ship**.

6. Double-click the ShippedDate field on the right side of the window.

7. Type the – for subtraction.

8. Double-click the OrderDate field on the right side of the window.

9. The formula should now say `= [ShippedDate] - [OrderDate]`.

10. Click OK. You should now see the ShippedDate column on the right side of the table.

11. Close the Power Query Editor window and keep your changes.

Calculating the New Total

To calculate the new total, do the following:

1. Right-click the Sales table in the Queries & Connections window.

2. Click Edit. This will open the Power Query Editor window.

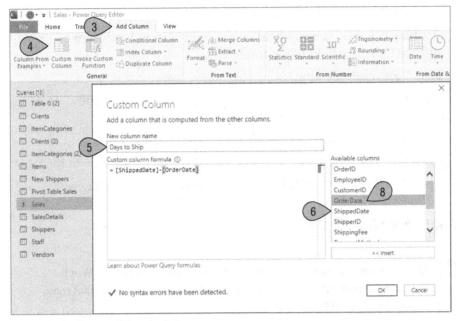

Figure 1.33: Days to Ship calculation

3. Click the Add Column tab.

4. Click the Custom Column icon on the left side of the ribbon. This will open a window called Custom Column, as shown in Figure 1.34.

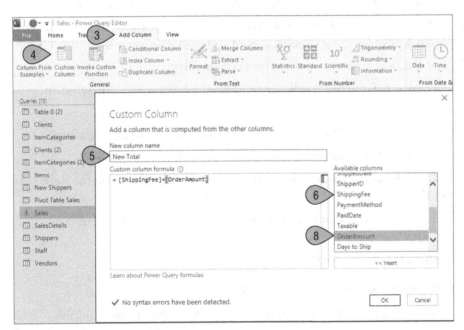

Figure 1.34: New total calculation

5. For the new column name, type **New Total**.

6. Double-click the ShippingFee field on the right side of the window.

7. Type the + for addition.

8. Double-click the OrderAmount field on the right side of the window.

9. The formula should now display `=[ShippingFee] + [OrderAmount]`.

10. Click OK.

11. You should now see the New Total column on the right side of the table.

12. Close the Power Query Editor window and keep your changes.

Changing or Viewing an Existing Custom Column

If you need to change or view a formula that was made using a custom column, you can perform these steps:

1. Right-click the table you want to change in the Queries & Connections window and click Edit. This will open the Power Query Editor window.

2. Look at the Applied Steps window on the right side of the Power Query Editor.

3. Find a step that says "Added Custom" or "Added Custom1" or something similar.

4. Move your mouse to the right of that step and click the settings wheel, as shown in Figure 1.35.

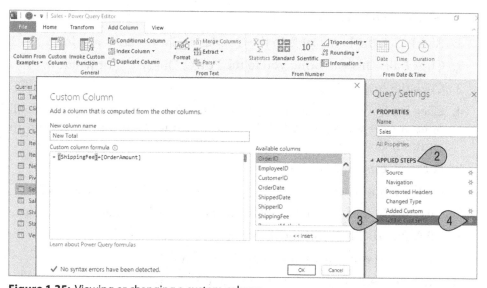

Figure 1.35: Viewing or changing a custom column

5. You can now view or change the formula for the custom column.

6. Click OK.

7. Close the Power Query Editor window and keep your changes.

Using a Conditional Column for Calculations

In Excel, a popular function is the IF function, which is used to perform one action if a condition is true and another action if the condition is not true. More conditions can be added by adding more IF statements inside the original IF formula. When this happens, it is called a *nested if*.

You can create something similar in Power Query by using a conditional column. The "nested if" can be accomplished in a conditional column by adding more clauses. This is shown in the following example, and you can have as many clauses as you need to make, using either a simple formula or a more complicated formula, similar to a "nested if."

Calculating a Reorder

Let's look at an example. In this case, we want to see if an item in our inventory needs to be reordered or not.

> **NOTE**   You can use the Items table that is in the Excel workbook called *Pivot Table Book sample data-formatted tables.xlsx* that is included in the sample files that come with this book for this example.

To calculate a reorder, do the following:

1. Right-click the Items table in the Queries & Connections window.

2. Click Edit. This will bring you to the Power Query Editor window.

3. Click the Add Column tab.

4. Click the Conditional Column icon on the left side of the ribbon. This will open a new window called Add Conditional Column, as shown in Figure 1.36.

5. For the New column name, type **Reorder**.

6. On the If line, click the first drop-down list and click QuantityOnHand.

7. Click the Equals drop-down list and click Is Greater Than Or Equal To.

8. Click the ABC 123 icon and click Select A Column.

9. On the next drop-down list, click ReorderLevel.

10. Click the field at the end of the row and type **No**.

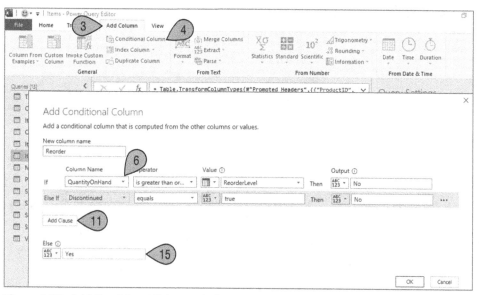

Figure 1.36: Add Conditional Column window

11. Click Add Clause.

12. On the Else If line, click the first drop-down list and click Discontinued.

13. Click the space after the ABC 123 icon and type **true**.

14. Click the space at the end of the row and type **No**.

15. Click the space below the word Else and type **Yes**.

16. Click OK. You will now see the reorder column on the right side of the table.

17. Close the Power Query Editor window and keep your changes.

Changing or Viewing an Existing Conditional Column

If you need to change or view a formula that was made using a conditional column, you can perform these steps:

1. Right-click the table you want to change in the Queries & Connections window and click Edit. This will open the Power Query Editor window.

2. Look at the Applied Steps window on the right side of the Power Query Editor.

3. Find the Added Conditional Column step (or something similar).

4. Move your mouse to the right of that step and click the settings wheel, as shown in Figure 1.37.

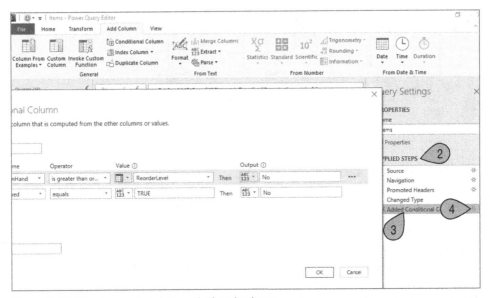

Figure 1.37: Viewing or changing a calculated column

5. You can now view or change the formula for the conditional column.

6. Click OK.

7. Close the Power Query Editor window and keep your changes.

Summary

In this chapter, you learned about what data is and how it should be structured if you want to use that data in a pivot table. You saw how to import data from other sources into Excel. Of course, you can also use the data that is already in your existing Excel spreadsheets. Then, the chapter showed many examples of using Power Query to help you analyze your data, clean your data, and even add your own calculations.

In the next chapter, we will use your data to create the pivot table, which can summarize, sort, and filter your data just about any way you want.

Summarizing and Presenting Data with a Pivot Table

So, you have your data ready from the previous chapter. Maybe you have a list of data that was already in Excel or a list of data that you imported from another data source. You might have a few rows of data or maybe thousands of rows of data or maybe even a lot more than that. Your data might be on one sheet or spread across multiple sheets. Now, it is time to summarize that data with a pivot table.

What Is a Pivot Table?

A *pivot table* is a powerful reporting tool that allows you to summarize your data just about any way you want. A pivot table can provide subtotals, subcounts, and many other calculations. It can be one-dimensional, giving you subtotals for just one field, or it can be multidimensional, allowing you to do a cross tab or a cross reference for two fields, where one field comprises the rows of the pivot table and the other field comprises the columns.

In the pivot table, each row will automatically have a total on the right, each column will automatically have a total at the bottom, and there will be a grand total on the right side of the bottom row. The rows and columns can contain multiple fields to provide more layers of detail for your table and more subtotals. The pivot table can be sorted and filtered the way you want, and that can be changed dynamically, which will be covered in Chapter 4, "Sorting and

Filtering the Pivot Table." It can also summarize your data by second, minute, hour, day, month, quarter, or year, or any combination thereof, when you have a date/time column in your data, which will be covered in Chapter 6, "Summarizing Your Data by Date and Time." The pivot table can be made to be more interactive by adding slicers, timelines, charts, and form controls so that you can create dashboards to visually summarize your data. These topics will be covered in Chapter 4, as well as in Chapter 5, "Making the Pivot Table More Visual with Charts," and Chapter 9, "Pulling It All Together: Creating a Dashboard from Your Pivot Tables."

Most pivot tables come from a list of data in one sheet in an Excel workbook, but they can come from multiple sheets as well. The pivot tables that come from more than one sheet will be covered in Chapter 7, "Creating a Pivot Table from Multiple Spreadsheets," and Chapter 8, "Improving Your Pivot Table with Power Pivot."

> **NOTE**   The steps and figures in this book were made using the PC desktop version of Excel that comes with Microsoft 365. Although most of the steps and figures should be relatively similar to what you see on your screen, your own experience may be different if you have an older version of Excel, the online version of Excel, or Excel for Mac.

Making a Pivot Table from Scratch

Let's start by using data from one sheet. I'll assume that the data has a header row at the top and is one consistent block of data. I'll also assume there are no completely blank rows until the bottom of the data, and that there are no completely blank columns until the right side of the data The sheet should also meet all of the other characteristics of acceptable data listed at the beginning of Chapter 1, "Preparing the Data for an Excel Pivot Table."

> **NOTE**   For this and the examples presented in the rest of this chapter, you can use the Pivot Table Sales sheet from the sample file called *Pivot Table Book sample data.xls*

that is included with this book. You can find the sample files at www.wiley
.com/go/GGRXL_PivotTables.

To create your pivot table, start by doing the following:

1. Click a cell within your data.

2. Click the Insert tab.

3. Click the PivotTable icon on the far-left side of the ribbon and then select
    From Table/Range, if you see the submenu. You will now see the PivotTable
    from table or range dialog box, as shown in Figure 2.1.

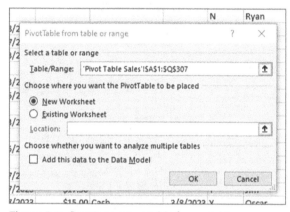

Figure 2.1: Creating a pivot table from a table or range

If you are making a pivot table from a formatted table, then the Table/
Range field should display the table's name, which comes from the name
of the formatted table, not the sheet name. If you are making the pivot table
from data that is not a formatted table, Excel will automatically select a
range for the pivot table. This range will start at the next completely blank
row it finds above the data, at row 1 of the sheet if there are no blank rows
above the current cell and will stop at the next completely blank row it
finds below the current cell, or at the last row of data if there are no blank
rows below the current cell.

Similarly, the selected range will start at the next completely blank column
it finds to the left of the data, or column A of the sheet if there are no blank
columns to the left of the current cell, and will stop at the next completely
blank column it finds to the right of the current cell, or the last column
of data if there are no blank columns to the right of the current cell. Excel
usually selects the correct range for you, but you could select a different
range, if necessary.

Typically, I place the pivot table on a new sheet, but you could also place it on an existing sheet by clicking the field to the right of the word Location and then clicking a cell of an existing sheet. This is where the upper-left corner of the new pivot table will appear.

4. Click OK.

You should now be in a new sheet that looks similar to Figure 2.2.

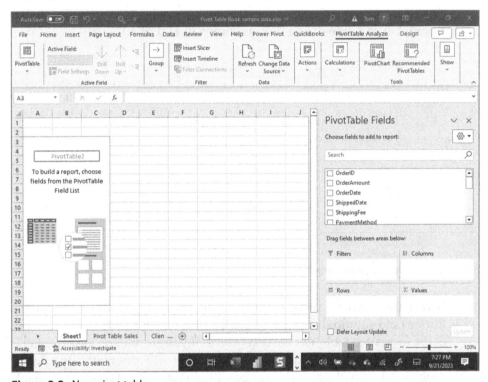

Figure 2.2: New pivot table

Notice the two new tabs on the right side of the Excel menu at the top of the page. One is called PivotTable Analyze, and the other is called Design. These will appear only when you click the pivot table. The PivotTable Analyze tab will help you add features to and manage the pivot table. The Design tab will help you change the look and feel of the pivot table. These two tabs will be explored in further detail later in this chapter and in other chapters of the book.

NOTE   In older versions of Excel, the PivotTable Analyze tab was called Analyze.

The PivotTable Fields Window

When your pivot table was created, you should have noticed the PivotTable Fields window displayed on the right side of the screen. This window displays the column headers from the sheet where the data is on the PivotTable Fields window. That's why it is so critical to have the field names on the top of the data. The PivotTable Fields window is where you dynamically control what fields actually appear on the pivot table. This window appears only when you click a pivot table.

> **NOTE**   Displaying and Hiding the PivotTable Fields Window
>
> The PivotTable Fields window is important in building your pivot table. Sometimes, it disappears from the screen. When this happens, don't panic! You can always get it back. If you click a blank cell outside of the pivot table, the field list will go away. If you click anywhere on the pivot table, then the PivotTable Fields window should reappear. If this window does not reappear when you click the pivot table, then right-click a cell in the pivot table, and choose Show Field List, as shown in Figure 2.3.

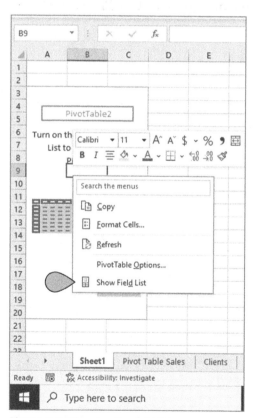

Figure 2.3: Showing the field list

If you look closely at the PivotTable Fields window, you'll see there are several sections. Table 2.1 describes the different sections.

Table 2.1: The PivotTable Fields window sections

SECTION	DESCRIPTION
Filters	This is a way to filter the data that will be displayed. This section will be explored in Chapter 4.
Columns	These are the fields that make up the columns going across the pivot table.
Rows	These are the fields that make up the rows in the pivot table.
Values	This section lists the fields that are used for calculations in the pivot table.

Each section can remain empty or can contain as many fields as you want. When a section contains more than one field, the fields will be displayed in top-down order on the pivot table. This topic is discussed later in this chapter.

You can rearrange and manage the sections within the PivotTable Fields window by clicking the settings wheel on the right side of the PivotTable Fields window, as shown in Figure 2.4.

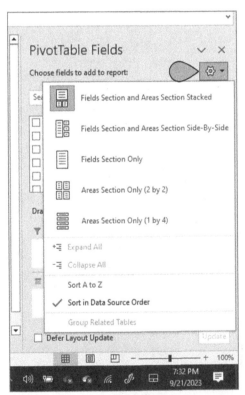

Figure 2.4: Rearranging the PivotTable Fields window

Many people who use pivot tables prefer to show the sections to the right of the fields, instead of below the fields, as displayed in Figure 2.5.

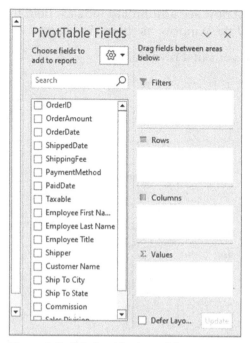

Figure 2.5: Side-by-side view of the PivotTable Fields window

To display the PivotTable Fields window with the sections to the right of the fields, click the settings wheel on the top right of the PivotTable Fields window and then select Field Sections And Areas Section Side-By-Side.

Summarizing Data on One Field

Let's start with a simple pivot table that will summarize one field. What if you wanted to get a summary by salesperson, region, office, or any field within your data. The pivot table can summarize by any of these fields in two steps:

1. Within the PivotTable Fields window, drag the field you want to summarize from the fields section to the Rows section of the PivotTable Fields. If you are using the sample data, drag the Customer Name field to the Rows section. You will see the name listed in the Rows box and also see that the pivot table on the left side of the screen now includes the customer names. Each row will be a different value of the field you moved to the Rows section, as shown in Figure 2.6.

2. Drag a field to the Values section of the PivotTable Fields window. Usually, you move a numeric field to the Values section, so you will have more possibilities of different calculations you can do with that field. The available calculations will be further discussed in Chapter 3, "Using Calculations in Pivot Tables." If you are using the sample data, drag the OrderAmount

field to the Values section. You will now see a summary for each field in the Rows section on the left side of the window, as shown in Figure 2.7.

Congratulations, you have just made your first pivot table!

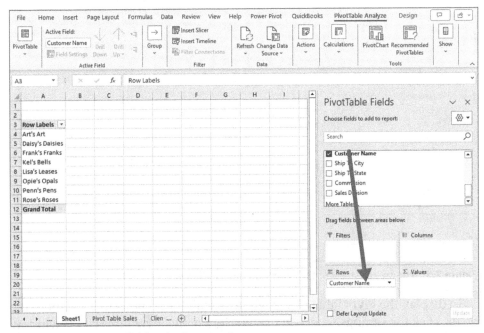

Figure 2.6: Dragging a field to the Rows section

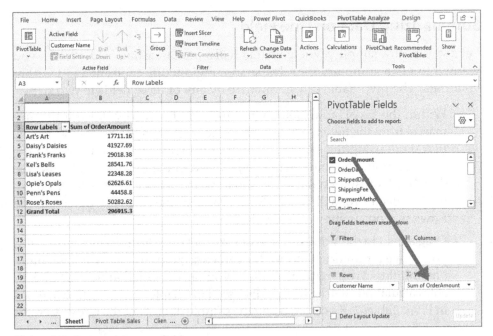

Figure 2.7: Summarizing one field

The Default Calculation in the Values Section

When you move a field to the Values section of the PivotTable Fields window, sometimes the calculation defaults to a sum. Other times, it defaults to a count. The calculation type can be changed, as described in Chapter 3. The default calculation is based on the data type for that column back in the data sheet. If Excel sees any text data in that column, it will default to a count calculation in the Values section. Date fields also default to a count. If Excel sees all numbers in that column, it will default to a sum calculation. Refer to Chapter 1 to change the data type of the column, if necessary.

Showing the Detail with a Drill Down

What you see on the pivot table is a summary of each different value of the field that you put in the Rows section. The number you see is either the sum or the count of all the records from the original sheet that have the same value in that field. There are many more calculations available, and these will be discussed further in Chapter 3. Maybe you want to see the actual detail records that make up that summary number. This is called a *drill down*. It is also called "showing the detail."

To create a drill down, double-click any number within the pivot table. This will take you to a new sheet that shows all the detail transactions associated with that number, as shown in Figure 2.8.

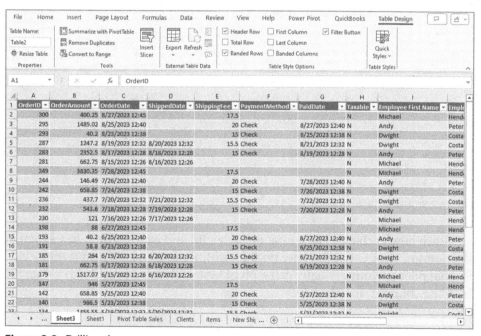

Figure 2.8: Drilling down

This is a great feature, and it is built right in. Every time you double-click any number on the pivot table, the drill down for that number will be presented in a new sheet. You can simply click back on the sheet where the pivot table is to return to the pivot table.

Creating a Cross Tab or Cross Reference

What we are looking at now is technically a pivot table, but usually the pivot table also has the columns going across, which would further summarize and categorize the field in the rows by the field in the columns going across. Let's say you wanted to summarize your data by office by airline, by employee, by division, or by some other combination of two different fields. When one field is in the Rows section of the PivotTable Fields window and another field is in the Columns section of the PivotTable Fields window, this is called a *cross reference*, or a *cross tab*.

To make a cross reference or cross tab, drag a different field from the Pivot-Table Fields list to the Column section. If you are using the sample data, drag the Employee Last Name field to the Columns section. You will now see a cross reference or a cross tab of the fields you used in the Rows section and the Columns section, as shown in Figure 2.9.

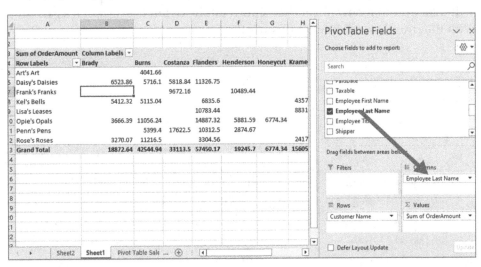

Figure 2.9: A cross reference

Notice how each row has a total on the right, and each column has a total at the bottom. On the bottom row on the right, there is even a grand total. This is what people would usually call a pivot table, when it has summary data for both the columns and the rows.

When you move your fields to different sections of the PivotTable Fields window, or even back to the fields list, you will get different pivot tables. It all depends on how you want to display the data.

Adding More Layers of Detail to the Pivot Table

Each section in the PivotTable Fields window can have multiple fields, really as many as you want. Adding fields is how you can add more layers of detail into your pivot table. When a section has more than one field, the fields are going to be displayed in top-down order.

To add more fields to your pivot table, simply drag another field from the fields section to the Rows section of the PivotTable Fields window. If you are using the sample data, drag the Shipper field to the Rows section and drop it below Customer Name.

Notice the pivot table on the left side of the screen. As shown in Figure 2.10, notice how the first field you have in the Rows section is the upper field, and then that field is broken down by the second field.

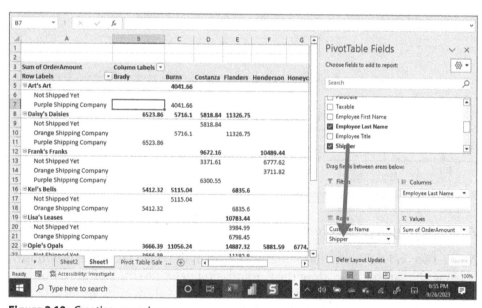

Figure 2.10: Creating groupings

Creating and Managing Groups

Also notice the minus sign to the left of some values in the pivot table. If you click the minus sign to the left of the values, it will collapse that section. If you then click the plus sign to the left of the values, it will expand that section. This is called a *group*. This occurs automatically when you have more than one field in the Rows section or the Columns section of the PivotTable Fields window.

Changing the Grouping Order

To change the order of the fields in the Rows section, drag a field in the Rows section above or below another field in the Rows section. When you do this, you will see that the grouping order has changed on the pivot table. Using the sample data, you can drag the Shipper field above the Customer Name field in the Rows section. Figure 2.11 shows the updated results shown immediately within the pivot table. This action would work on the other sections of the PivotTable Fields window the same way.

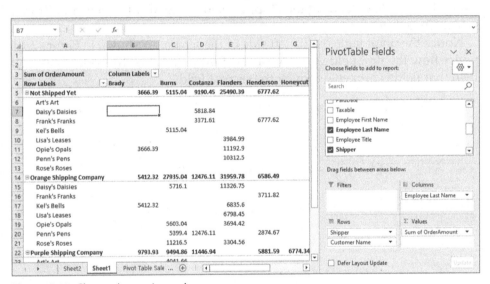

Figure 2.11: Changed grouping order

Adding Groupings to Columns

Move a second field into the Columns section of the PivotTable Fields window. If using the sample data, drag the Commission field into the Columns box and place it below the Employee Last Name. Notice as shown in Figure 2.12 that the columns are now broken down into the next level of detail, and now the column groups can be collapsed or expanded.

Creating Your Own Group

The groups are created automatically when you have more than one field in either the Rows section or the Columns section of the PivotTable Fields window. But sometimes you want to create your own group. You can do the following steps to create your own grouping. You should do this when you just have one field in the Rows section and one field in the Columns section of the PivotTable Fields list. If you have more than one field in either the Rows section or the Columns section of the PivotTable Fields window, then you can remove the extra fields by dragging the extra fields from the Rows section or the Columns section back to the list of field names in the PivotTable Fields window. If you are using the sample data, drag the Commission field from the Columns section to the field list and the Shipper field from the Rows section to the fields list on the PivotTable Fields window.

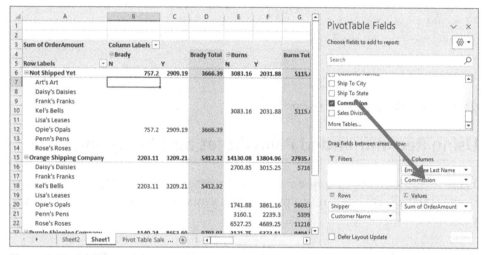

Figure 2.12: Adding a column grouping

To create your own group, do the following:

1. Click a value in the first column or the first row of the pivot table.

2. Hold down the Ctrl key and select another value in the first column or the first row.

3. While still holding down the Ctrl key, continue to select as many items from the first column or the first row as you want in your group.

4. Release the Ctrl key.

5. Right-click one of the selected values.

6. Click Group.

Your selected items are now in their own group, as shown in Figure 2.13.

Removing Your Own Group

To remove the group that you added, right-click the group name in the pivot table, and then click Ungroup. You will now see the pivot table without the group.

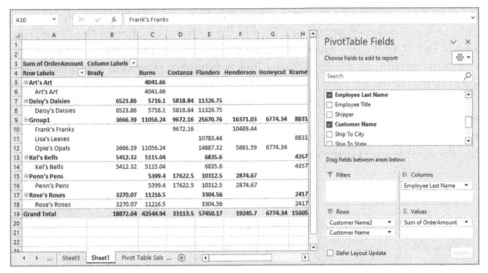

Figure 2.13: Creating your own group

Using Recommended PivotTables and Analyzing Data

There are other ways to create a pivot table, other than making the pivot table from scratch. Excel has built-in pivot tables you can use to quickly summarize your data.

Creating a Pivot Table Using Recommended PivotTables

Excel has a feature called Recommended PivotTables that can give you a head start in creating your pivot tables. The Recommended PivotTables feature gets you results even quicker than a pivot table made from scratch. The recommended pivot tables will show you some pivot tables and what the pivot tables would look like with your own data. Once you choose one of the recommended pivot tables, Excel will create that pivot table for you. You can then manage that pivot table like any other pivot table. You will want to go back to the sheet that contains your list of data to use the Recommended PivotTables.

To use the Recommended PivotTables feature, do the following:

1. Click a cell within your data of the Pivot Table Sales sheet.

2. Select the Insert tab, followed by clicking the Recommended PivotTables icon on the left side of the ribbon. The Recommended PivotTables dialog box displays, as shown in Figure 2.14. Notice how the pivot tables that are shown in the Recommended PivotTables window are displaying the same data from your data sheet.

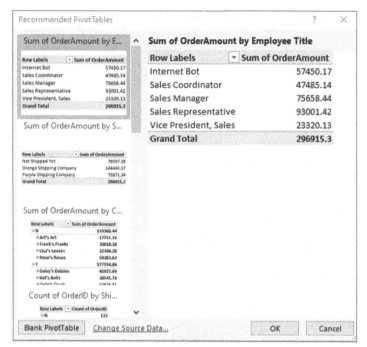

Figure 2.14: Recommended PivotTables feature

3. Browse through the suggestions, choose the one you like, and click OK.

4. You will see the pivot table you selected on a new sheet.

Creating a Pivot Table Using Analyze Data

You can find even more recommended pivot tables and pivot charts by using another built-in Excel feature called Analyze Data, which can quickly and easily summarize your data in many ways. You will want to go back to the sheet that contains your list of data to use the Analyze Data feature.

To use the Analyze Data tool, do the following:

1. Click a cell within your data of the Pivot Table Sales sheet.

2. Select the Home tab.

3. Click the Analyze Data icon on the right side of the ribbon. This will display the Analyze Data window to the right of your spreadsheet, as shown in Figure 2.15. As you scroll down this list, notice how the suggested charts and pivot tables are displaying your data.

4. Click the Insert icon below the suggestion you like, and Excel will create that pivot table or pivot chart for you on a new sheet.

5. Close the Analyze Data window when you are done with it.

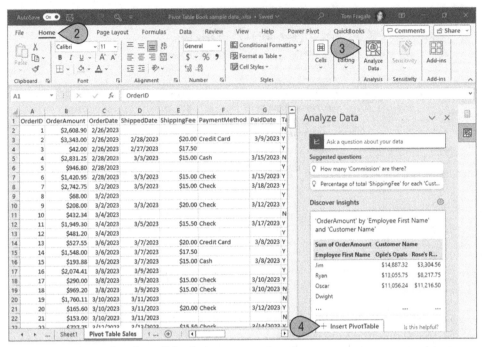

Figure 2.15: The Analyze Data dialog box

Making the Pivot Table Look Better

The pivot table is definitely starting to come together. You can see how the pivot table summarizes your data. However, you probably will have to change some things about the pivot table to make it look better before you show it to other people. Think about who is going to see the pivot table. Is it for your boss, or your boss's boss? Is it for a vendor, client, employee, or investor? There are numerous ways to make the pivot table look better. This includes the following:

- Formatting numbers
- Adding subtotals
- Calculating grand totals
- Working with blank rows
- Changing the layout
- Applying styles
- Replacing spaces
- Using conditional formatting

Formatting Numbers

As a default, the pivot table will display numbers without any formatting. Some of the numbers will show with different numbers of decimal places. You will almost always want to change the number format. The pivot table can display the number formats in many ways. Changing the number formats in the pivot table is easy.

1. Right-click any number in the pivot table and select Number Format.

2. You will see the classic Format Cells dialog box, as shown in Figure 2.16.

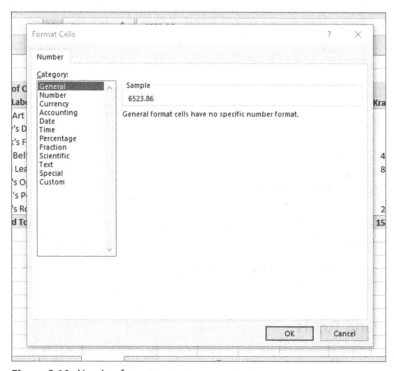

Figure 2.16: Number formats

3. Choose the formatting style you want to apply and click OK. The numbers in the pivot table display the number format you chose.

Managing Subtotals

When you have more than one field in the Rows section of the PivotTable Fields window, you will see subtotals for each group on the pivot table. The subtotals might be on the top of each group. You may want to display the subtotals on the bottom of each group, or even not show them at all. Let's see how we can show the subtotals at the bottom of the group or make it so the subtotals do not show at all.

To change how the subtotals display, do the following:

1. Click the pivot table.

2. Select the Design tab.

3. Click the Subtotals icon on the left side of the ribbon. This will show the options displayed in Figure 2.17.

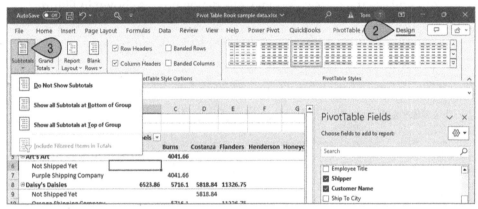

Figure 2.17: Displaying or modifying subtotals

4. Pick the option you want. The location or display of the subtotals should be immediately adjusted in the pivot table based on your selection.

These choices work only when there is more than one field in the Rows section of the PivotTable Fields window.

Calculating Grand Totals

As a default, the pivot table will show grand totals on the right side of each row and at the bottom of each column. You may or may not want to display these totals in your pivot table. The grand totals can be turned on or off by doing the following:

1. Click the pivot table.

2. Select the Design tab.

3. Click the Grand Totals icon on the left side of the ribbon. This will show the options displayed in Figure 2.18.

4. Pick the option you want. The location or display of the grand totals should be immediately adjusted in the pivot table based on your selection.

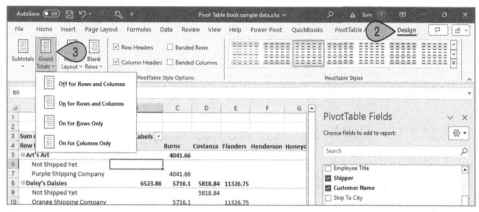

Figure 2.18: Displaying or hiding grand totals

Working with Blank Rows

When you have more than one field in the Rows section of the PivotTable Fields window, you may want to add a space between each group, to make the pivot table easier to read. Here's a quick way to add or remove blank rows between each group:

1. Click the pivot table.
2. Select the Design tab.
3. Click the Blank Rows icon on the left side of the ribbon. This will show the options displayed in Figure 2.19.
4. Pick the option you want. The display of your pivot table should immediately change based on your selection.

These choices work only when there is more than one field in the Rows section of the PivotTable Fields window.

Changing the Layout

When you first make the pivot table, you will see the words "Row Headings" and "Column Headings" at the top of the pivot table. Personally, I would rather see the actual field names instead. Changing the pivot table layout will fix this issue and change the pivot table in other ways as well.

To change the layout of the pivot table you can do the following:

1. Click the pivot table.
2. Select the Design tab.
3. Click the Report Layout icon on the left side of the ribbon. This will present the options displayed in Figure 2.20.

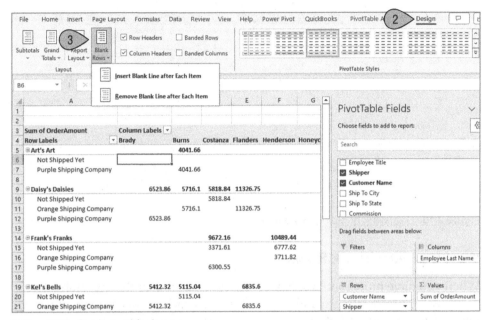

Figure 2.19: Displaying blank rows

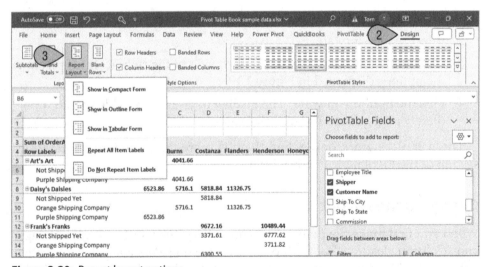

Figure 2.20: Report layout options

4. Pick the one you want. Personally, I prefer Tabular Form. Once selected, your pivot table's display should update accordingly.

Table 2.2 describes the choices on the Report Layout menu.

Table 2.2: Report Layout menu options

MENU CHOICE	DESCRIPTION
Show in Compact Form	This is the default layout of the pivot table. If it is already in Compact Form, nothing will change. The field names will revert to "Row Headings" and "Column Headings" in the pivot table.
Show in Outline Form	This changes the field names to the actual field names in the pivot table. It moves each field in the Rows section of the PivotTable Fields window to its own column in the pivot table.
Show in Tabular Form	This changes the field names to the actual field names in the pivot table. It moves each field in the Rows section of the PivotTable Fields window to its column. It displays the subtotal for each group at the bottom of each group.
Repeat All Item Labels	When there is more than one field in the Rows section of the PivotTable Fields window, this option will show the values for each row for the group field, even if it repeats.
Do Not Repeat Item Labels	When there is more than one field in the Rows section of the PivotTable Fields window, this option will show only the first occurrence of each group and then will show blanks in that column until the next group.

Applying Styles

When you first make the pivot table, it just appears in plain black and white. A great way to change the overall appearance of the pivot table is to change the style. There are many built-in styles that can quickly add color, borders, and other formatting features to the pivot table.

To change the pivot table style, you can do the following:

1. Click the pivot table.

2. Select the Design tab.

3. Click the pull-down to the right of the PivotTable Styles on the right side of the ribbon, as shown in Figure 2.21.

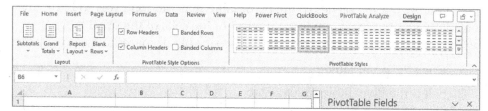

Figure 2.21: Pivot table styles

4. Choose a style that you like by clicking it. Note that as your mouse cursor hovers over the styles in the gallery, they will be reflected on your current pivot table.

The pivot table will now display the style you chose. For more variety, try the PivotTable Style options in the middle of the Design tab. A popular choice, for example, is Banded Rows, which would make the pivot table look like Figure 2.22 when used with certain styles.

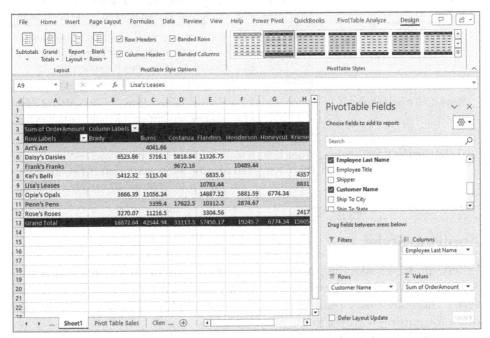

Figure 2.22: A pivot table with banded rows

Replacing Spaces and Other Options

You may see blank spaces in the pivot table. If you try to click a cell that is empty within the pivot table and try to type in that cell, you will get a message that says, "We can't change this part of the PivotTable." There are many things going on behind the scenes of the pivot table that we don't see, so Excel does not allow you to type in anything in most of the cells of the pivot table.

The following shows how you can replace the blank spaces in the pivot table:

1. Click the pivot table.

2. Select the PivotTable Analyze tab.

3. Click the Options icon on the left side of the ribbon. You will now see the PivotTable Options dialog box, as displayed in Figure 2.23.

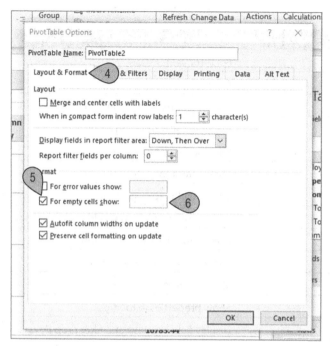

Figure 2.23: PivotTable Options dialog box

4. Select the Layout & Format tab.

5. Select the For Empty Cells Show box.

6. In the space to the right of the words "For empty cells show," type in what you want displayed in the empty cell. I usually enter a **0**.

7. Click OK.

What used to be the blank spaces in the pivot table have now been replaced with whatever you typed in step 7.

The PivotTable Options dialog box contains a number of other items that you can also set or change. Table 2.3 shows a list of all such options.

Table 2.3: PivotTable Options

TAB	MENU ITEM
Top	PivotTable name.
Layout & Format	Merge and center cells with labels.
Layout & Format	When in compact form indent row labels *n* characters.
Layout & Format	Display fields in report filter area.
Layout & Format	Report filter fields per column.

Continues

Table 2.3 (*continued*)

TAB	MENU ITEM
Layout & Format	For error values show.
Layout & Format	For empty cells show.
Layout & Format	Autofit column widths on update.
Layout & Format	Preserve cell formatting on update.
Totals & Filters	Show grand totals for rows.
Totals & Filters	Show grand totals for columns.
Totals & Filters	Subtotal filtered page items.
Totals & Filters	Allow multiple filters per field.
Totals & Filters	Use Custom Lists when sorting.
Display	Show expand/collapse buttons.
Display	Show contextual tooltips.
Display	Show properties in tooltips.
Display	Display field captions and filter drop downs.
Display	Classic pivot table layout.
Display	Show the Values row.
Display	Show Items with no data on rows.
Display	Show items with no data on columns.
Display	Display item labels when no fields are in the values area.
Display	Sort A to Z.
Display	Sort in data source order.
Printing	Print expand/collapse buttons when displayed on PivotTable.
Printing	Repeat row labels on each printed page.
Printing	Set print titles.
Data	Save source data with file.
Data	Enable show details.
Data	Refresh data when opening the file.
Data	Number of items to retain per field.
Data	Enable cell editing in the values area.
Alt Text	Title.
Alt Text	Description.

Using Conditional Formatting

There may be times when you want certain values in the pivot table to stand out if a certain condition is met. Maybe you want all the numbers that are at least $500 to be in green and the numbers that are less than $500 to be in red. The Conditional Formatting feature that is built into Excel will work on pivot tables. You can apply as many conditional formats in your pivot table as you need.

The following steps show you how to display all the numbers that are less than $500 in red. This uses Excel's Conditional Formatting in a pivot table:

1. Click the pivot table.

2. Use the Ctrl+A keyboard shortcut to highlight the entire pivot table.

3. Select the Home tab.

4. Click the Conditional Formatting icon on the ribbon. You will now see the options for Conditional Formatting, as shown in Figure 2.24. All of these should work on a pivot table.

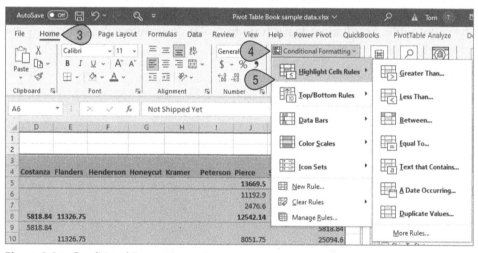

Figure 2.24: Conditional Formatting options

5. Select Highlight Cell Rules ⇨ Less Than.

6. On the left side of the Less Than dialog box, type **500**, as shown in Figure 2.25.

7. On the right side of the dialog box, click the pull-down to choose a format.

8. Click OK.

The cells that meet the condition should now be formatted.

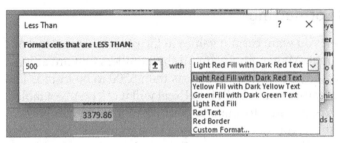

Figure 2.25: Conditional Formatting settings

Summary

In this chapter, you built a pivot table. You then added more fields to the Rows section and the Columns section of the PivotTable Fields window to add more layers of detail. You then learned many ways to make your pivot table look better. You should practice moving your fields back and forth to the different sections of the PivotTable Fields list to get different pivot tables.

In the next chapter, we will explore the many calculations that are built into the pivot table. You'll even learn how to make your own calculations on the pivot table.

CHAPTER 3

Using Calculations in Pivot Tables

In Chapter 2, "Summarizing and Presenting Data with a Pivot Table," the pivot table you built displays either a sum or a count for the field you have in the Values section of the PivotTable Fields window. If the field being used in the Values section of the PivotTable Fields window contains any text or date values in the column from the original data, the calculation will default to a count. If the field being used in the Values section of the PivotTable Fields window contains all numbers in the column from the original data, the calculation will default to a sum. You can see the calculation that is used by looking at the Values section of the PivotTable Fields window or by looking at the top-left corner of the pivot table. Of course, as you will learn in this chapter, you can add more calculations to the pivot table or change the calculations that are already there.

Using Built-In Calculations in Your Pivot Table

It is time to explore the many other calculations that are available in pivot tables. These calculations allow you to summarize and analyze your data in many ways. There are numerous calculations that are built in, and there are calculations that you can create. Let's start with the calculations that are already part of the pivot table.

NOTE For the examples presented in this section of the chapter, you can use the sample file called *Calculations.xlsx* that is included with this book. You can find the sample files at www.wiley.com/go/GGRXL_PivotTables. Most sections of this part of the chapter will use the sheet called MainPivotTable, except for the "Changing the Way Errors Display in the Pivot Table" section, which will use the sheet called Errors.

Adding Calculation Fields to the Pivot Table

As you continue to use pivot tables, there will be many times when you want the pivot table to display multiple calculations at the same time. For example, you might want to display both the sum and the count of a field. The pivot table can display as many calculations as you want.

To add additional calculations to the pivot table, you can do the following:

1. Click the pivot table.

2. Drag another field from the list of fields to the Values section of the PivotTable Fields window. You can either use the same field that you used before or use a different field. If you are using the sample data, drag the OrderAmount field to the Values section.

You will now see the additional column in the pivot table, as shown in Figure 3.1.

You may notice that the pivot table is displaying two sums or two counts. If you used the same field in the Values section of the PivotTable Fields window that you used previously, the pivot table could now be displaying duplicate data. Of course, you want to change the calculation type of one of those fields, maybe from a sum to a count or from a count to a sum. Excel provides several ways to easily change the calculation type of a field.

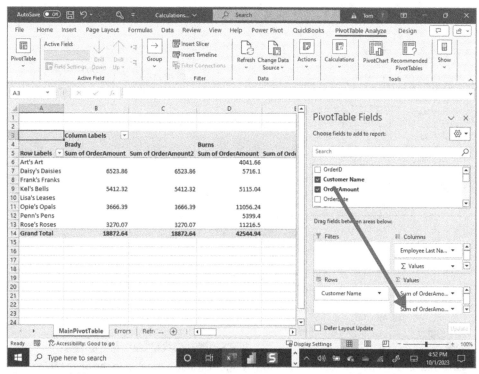

Figure 3.1: Adding another calculation to a pivot table

Changing the Calculation Type of a Field

A quick way to change the calculation type of a number in the pivot table is to right-click a number in the pivot table and then click Summarize Values By, as shown in Figure 3.2. In the resulting menu, click the type of calculation you want to use.

There is a different way to change the type of calculation, which I prefer. The Value Field Settings dialog box gives you more types of calculations and more flexibility when managing a calculation in the pivot table. The Value Field Settings dialog box also allows you to change the name of the field and the number format of the field. The following steps show you how to change a sum calculation to a count using the Value Field Settings dialog box.

1. Click the field you want to change in the Values section of the PivotTable Fields window. If you are using the sample data, click the second OrderAmount field you see in the Values section.

2. Click Value Field Settings, which will appear right above the field name. You will now see the Value Field Settings dialog box, as shown in Figure 3.3.

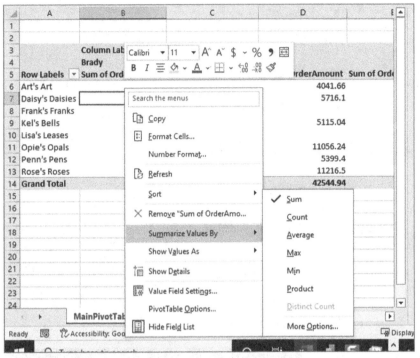

Figure 3.2: Changing a number's calculation by right-clicking a number in the pivot table

Figure 3.3: The Value Field Settings dialog box

3. Click the Summarize Values By tab.

4. Choose the calculation you want. For this example, I will choose Count.

5. Click the space to the right of Custom Name and type **Count**. Whatever you type into the Custom Name box will show up as the column header for the field in the pivot table and also in the Values section of the PivotTable Fields window.

6. Click OK to save your changes.

You will now see the new results in the pivot table for the field that you changed, as shown in Figure 3.4.

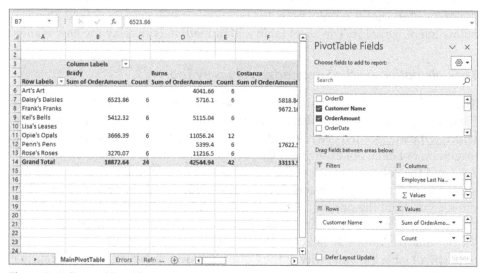

Figure 3.4: Pivot table with a sum and a count

NOTE   If you get a message that states "Averages, standard deviations, and variances are not supported when a PivotTable report has calculated items," it is because your pivot table already contains at least one calculated item, which will be covered later in this chapter.

Although it is better to use a number field in the Values section of the Pivot-Table Fields window, a number field is not required. All the available calculations from the Value Field Settings window will work with a number field. A text field, on the other hand, will display meaningful results only if you use the count calculation. Some of the numeric calculations, like average, will give you an error if you try to use them with a text field.

Similarly, only the count, min, and max calculations will give you any meaningful results with a date field. When the min or max calculations are used with a date field, the pivot table will display either the earliest date or the most recent date in the pivot table. The value displayed in the pivot table for the min or max date will probably be displayed in numeric format, so you will likely need to reformat the column as a date field.

Changing the Order of the Calculations

Just like in the Rows section or the Columns section of the PivotTable Fields window, the order of the fields matters in the Values section. The pivot table will display the fields going across left to right based on the top-down order in the Values section. You can have as many fields in the Values section as you need. To change the order of the fields within the Values section, simply drag each field above or below the other fields. The pivot table will immediately display the new results.

The Calculations in the Summarize Values By Tab

The calculations that are available in the Summarize Values By tab of the Value Field Settings dialog box are all mathematical summaries of a particular data point, which is the intersection of a row and column in the pivot table that is based on the original list of data. For example, if the row header of the pivot table shows "Art's Art" and the column header of the pivot table shows "Brady," then the number shown in the cell that intersects the row and column would be the summary of the records from the original data that have "Art's Art" in the Customer Name column and "Brady" in the Employee Last Name column. All the calculations in the Summarize Values By tab of the Value Field Settings dialog box can be added to the pivot table the same way as the Count. Table 3.1 shows the calculations that are available in the Summarize Values By tab of the Value Field Settings dialog box.

Table 3.1: Calculations available to summarize values

CALCULATION TYPE	DESCRIPTION
Sum	The sum of the values for a data point.
Count	The number of rows for a data point. It is similar to the COUNTA function in Excel.
Average	The average of the values for a data point.
Max	The largest value for the data point.
Min	The smallest value for the data point.
Product	The product of the values for the data point.
Count Numbers	The number of cells that contain numbers for a data point. It is similar to the COUNT function in Excel.
Stddev	An estimate of the standard deviation of a population, where the sample is a subset of the entire population.

CALCULATION TYPE	DESCRIPTION
Stddevp	The standard deviation of a population, where the population is all of the values to be summarized.
Var	An estimate of the variance of a population, where the sample is a subset of the entire population.
Varp	The variance of a population, where the population is all of the values to be summarized.
Distinct Count	The number of different values in the column. This calculation is available only when you use the data model, as described in Chapter 7, "Creating a Pivot Table from Multiple Spreadsheets," and Chapter 8, "Improving Your Pivot Table with Power Pivot."

The Calculations in the Show Values As Tab

The calculations within the Summarize Values By tab of the Value Field Settings dialog box allow you to summarize your data in various ways and are widely used. Using these calculations will allow you to start getting great results from your data in the pivot table. The good news is that there are even more calculations available in the Show Values As tab of the Value Field Settings dialog box, including the popular percent of total. Table 3.2 displays the calculations of the Show Values As tab and what they do.

Table 3.2: The Calculations in the Show Values As tab of the Value Field Settings dialog box

CALCULATION TYPE	DESCRIPTION
No Calculation	The normal summary from the Summarize Values By tab of the Value Field Settings dialog box.
% of Grand Total	The value of the field divided by the overall grand total of the pivot table.
% of Column Total	The value of the field divided by the total of the column the value is in.
% of Row Total	The value of the field divided by the total of the row the value is in.
% Of	The value of the field divided by the number of your choice.
% of Parent Row Total	When there is more than one field in the Rows section of the PivotTable Fields window, a field above another field is called the *parent field*. This calculation shows the value of the field divided by the total of the parent row the value belongs to.
% of Parent Column Total	When there is more than one field in the Columns section of the PivotTable Fields window, a field above another field is called the parent field. This calculation shows the value of the field divided by the total of the parent column the value belongs to.

Continues

Table 3.2 (continued)

CALCULATION TYPE	DESCRIPTION
% of Parent Total	When there is more than one field in the Rows section of the PivotTable Fields window, a field above another field is called the parent field. This calculation shows the value of the field divided by the grand total of the parent field the value belongs to.
Difference From	This shows the difference from the same column either in the record before the current row, the record after the current row, or the row that you choose.
% of Difference From	This shows the percent of change from the same column either in the record before the current row, the record after the current row, or the row that you choose.
Running Total In	Displays the value of the current row added to the values of all the rows above the current row for the field that you choose.
% Running Total In	Displays the value of the current row divided by the total of the current row added to the values of all the rows above the current row for the field that you choose.
Rank Smallest to Largest	Displays the rank of the current value compared to the other values of the column. The lowest number in the list would have the value of 1.
Rank Largest to Smallest	Displays the rank of the current value compared to the other values of the column. The highest number in the list would have the value of 1.
Index	Displays something similar to a weighted average. When displayed, the rows with the higher numbers in the index will be impacted the most if changes are made in the original data. The calculation is (the value * grand total of the pivot table) / (row total of the current row * column total of the current column).

There are a number of ways you can show values using the settings in the Show Values As tab. Let's look into a few of them.

Displaying the Percent of Total

A pivot table can display a value as the percent of a total. The total used can be for the row the value is in, the column it is in, the overall grand total of the pivot table, or any other value you choose.

To add a percent of total into the pivot table, you can do the following:

1. Click the pivot table to select it.
2. Click the field in the Values section of the PivotTable Fields window for which you want to display a percentage of total. You can click the Count field if using the sample data for the book.

3. Select the Value Field Settings icon. You will now see the Value Field Settings dialog box.

4. Choose the Show Values As tab.

5. Click the Show Values As pull-down list to show the list of options, as shown in Figure 3.5.

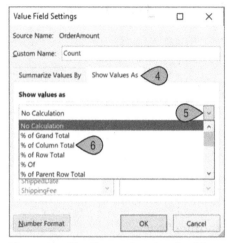

Figure 3.5: The Show Values As tab of the Value Field Settings dialog box

6. Select % of Column Total.

7. Enter **% of Total** for the Custom Name field.

8. Click OK to apply your changes.

You will now see the % of Total column in your pivot table, as shown in Figure 3.6.

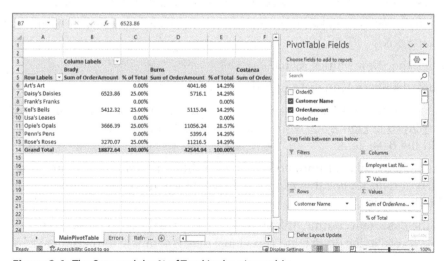

Figure 3.6: The Sum and the % of Total in the pivot table

The calculations on the Show Values As tab of the Value Field Settings dialog box are based on the calculation type selected in the Summarize Values By tab of the Value Field Settings dialog box. For example, the % of Column Total calculation from the Show Values As tab will show different results for the Sum calculation on the Summarize Values By tab as it does for the Count calculation on the Summarize Values By tab.

The following calculations can be added to the pivot table the same way as the % of Total:

- % of Grand Total
- % of Row Total
- % of Column Total
- % of Parent Row Total
- % of Parent Column Total
- % of Parent Total
- Index

Displaying the Difference from One Row to Another Row

The Difference From calculation will show the change from one record to the next. Either it can show the change from the previous record in the pivot table, the next record, or you can pick any record to be the baseline and all other records would be compared to that baseline. The % Difference From calculations can be added to the pivot table in the same way as the Difference From calculation.

Here are the steps on how to add the Difference From calculation in the pivot table:

1. Click a field in the Values section of the PivotTable Fields window.
2. Click the Value Field Settings icon. You will now see the Value Field Settings dialog box.
3. Click the Show Values As tab.
4. Click the Show Values As pull-down.
5. Select Difference From from the list. You will now see the dialog box displayed in Figure 3.7. Notice the dialog box now contains the Base field and the Base item.
6. In the Base field column, you can pick a different field to compare your current field to. For this example, I chose the Customer Name field for the Base field.
7. In the Base item column, (Next) means compare the current record to the next record in the pivot table. (Previous) means compare the current record

Figure 3.7: Creating the Difference From calculation

to the previous record in the pivot table. You can also pick a specific record, and then all records would be compared to that record, which would then be the baseline. For this example, I chose (Previous).

8. Click the Summarize Values By tab of the Value Field Settings dialog box and click Sum.

9. Click the space next to the Custom Name and type **Difference**.

10. Click OK. You will now see the Difference column in your pivot table, as shown in Figure 3.8.

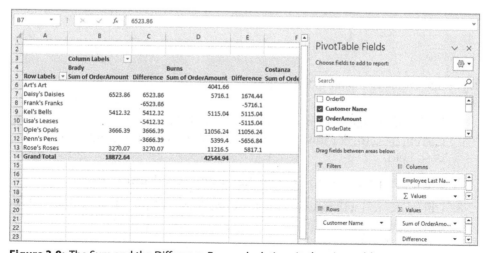

Figure 3.8: The Sum and the Difference From calculations in the pivot table

Displaying the Running Total

Another popular calculation is the running total. This is where the number for a row in the pivot table is added to the numbers in the previous rows within the same column of the pivot table. The % Running Total calculation can be added to the pivot table the same way as the Running Total.

Here's the steps on how to add the Running Total in the pivot table:

1. Click the new field in the Values section of the PivotTable Fields window.

2. Click the Value Field Settings icon. You will now see the Value Field Settings dialog box.

3. Click the Show Values As tab.

4. Click the Show Values As pull-down.

5. Scroll down and select Running Total In. You will now see the dialog box displayed in Figure 3.9.

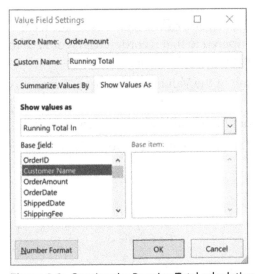

Figure 3.9: Creating the Running Total calculation

6. In the Base field column, you can pick a different field to compare your current field to. For this example, I chose the Customer Name field for the Base field.

7. Click the space next to Custom Name and type **Running Total**.

8. Click OK. You will now see the Running Total column in your pivot table, as shown in Figure 3.10.

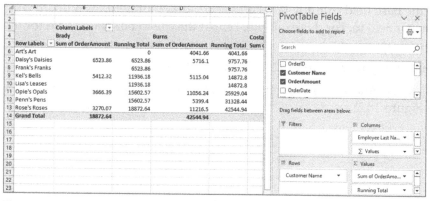

Figure 3.10: The Sum and the Running Total

Displaying the Rank

Another useful calculation that's available is the rank, which can be displayed as either lowest to highest or highest to lowest. The rank will show how the current row compares to the other rows in the pivot table for the field that is being ranked.

Here's the steps on how to show the rank:

1. Click the new field in the Values section of the PivotTable Fields window.
2. Click the Value Field Settings icon. You will now see the Value Field Settings dialog box.
3. Click the Show Values As tab.
4. Click the Show Values As pull-down.
5. Scroll down and click either Rank Smallest to Largest or Rank Largest to Smallest. For this example, I chose the latter. You will now see the dialog box displayed in Figure 3.11.

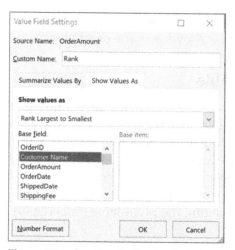

Figure 3.11: Creating the Rank calculation

6. In the Base field column, you can select a different field to compare your current field to. For this example, I chose the Customer Name field for the Base field.

7. Click the space next to Custom Name and type **Rank**.

8. Click OK. You will now see the Rank column in your pivot table, as shown in Figure 3.12.

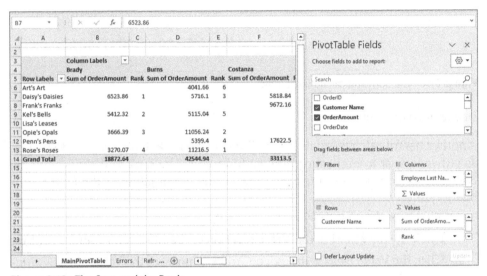

Figure 3.12: The Sum and the Rank

Removing Calculations from the Pivot Table

To remove calculations from a pivot table, you can either drag the fields from the Values section to the field list of the PivotTable Fields window, right-click a field in the Values section and then click Remove Field, or simply uncheck the field on the field list of the PivotTable Fields window.

Remove the rank column from the Values section using one of the three ways just mentioned. Now, just the original sum is showing in the pivot table.

Delaying Calculations in a Pivot Table

If the list of data you are using for the pivot table contains a large amount of data with many rows, many columns, or both, you may experience delays when you add more calculations to the pivot table or as you move your fields within the PivotTable Fields window. This delay can be several seconds or more and can be very frustrating and time-consuming.

There is a feature that will allow you to move your fields around the Pivot-Table Fields window without actually changing the pivot table immediately.

You can decide when the table updates. This is called Defer Layout, and it can really save you time if you are experiencing delays in your pivot table updates.

To enable the Defer Layout feature, check the Defer Layout Update checkbox on the bottom-left corner of the PivotTable Fields window, as shown in Figure 3.13 (1). This will make it so you can move your fields around the PivotTable Fields window, but your changes won't display in the pivot table yet.

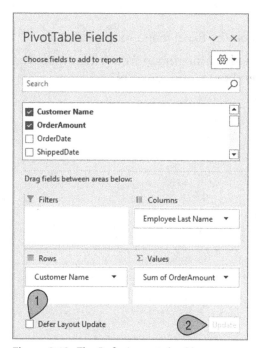

Figure 3.13: The Defer Layout checkbox

When you are ready for the pivot table to show your changes, click the Update button next to the Defer Layout Update checkbox, as also seen in Figure 3.13 (2). You will only experience the delay to update the pivot table when you click the Update button.

Changing the Way Errors Display in the Pivot Table

There will be times that some of the cells in the pivot table will display error values, like #DIV/0!, for example. There are numerous reasons why these errors could occur. The errors could result from having empty cells in the original list of data, from using a non-numeric field in the Values section of the PivotTable Fields window, or for other reasons. You can change the error value or message displayed in the cells.

In the following example, you will change cells that display "#DIV/0!" to a zero.

To change what the pivot table displays when there is an error, follow these steps:

1. Open your spreadsheet containing the error message(s) you want to replace. If you are using the sample data workbook mentioned earlier from the book's download files, then select the Errors sheet. Notice that many of the cells contain the error #DIV/0!, which means division by zero.

2. Click the pivot table to select it.

3. Click the PivotTable Analyze tab on the Excel menu to select it.

4. Click the Options icon on the left side of the ribbon. You will now see the PivotTable Options dialog box, as shown in Figure 3.14.

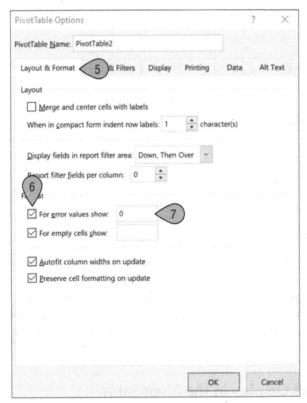

Figure 3.14: The PivotTable Options dialog box

5. Click the Layout & Format tab.

6. Check the For Error Values Show box.

7. Click in the field to the right of the words For Error Values Show and type in what you want displayed when there is an error. I usually just type in a 0, or just leave it blank.

8. Click OK. The pivot table will now display what you typed in step 7, instead of the error, as shown in Figure 3.15.

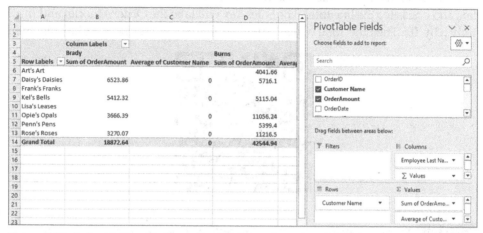

Figure 3.15: A pivot table with the errors showing as 0

Creating Custom Calculations

The calculations contained within the Value Field Settings dialog box are very useful. But there will be times when you want to add your own calculations into the pivot table. The problem is you can't just enter formulas into a cell that is on a pivot table like you can in a cell that is not on a pivot table. If you try clicking a cell within the pivot table and start to type a formula, you will receive the message "We can't change this part of the PivotTable." The good news is that you can add your own formulas to a pivot table by using either Calculated Fields or Calculated Items. Calculated Fields are custom calculations that can include other fields in the formula. Calculated Items are custom calculations that use the different values of one field in the formula.

> **NOTE** Calculated Items and Calculated Fields are not available in pivot tables that use a data model. There is another way to add calculations to the pivot tables that use a data model, and that topic will be covered in Chapter 8, "Improving Your Pivot Table with Power Pivot."

Calculated Fields

A Calculated Field is a formula that you can build for the pivot table that uses the field names in the formula instead of cell references that are used in normal Excel formulas. Otherwise, the math in the formula will work the same as in other Excel formulas.

Calculated Fields can be simple formulas, or they can be more complex. Some Excel functions can be used in a Calculated Field. For this example, we will create two formulas using Calculated Fields within the pivot table. One is for the sales tax, and one is for the line total. The Sales Tax will take the OrderAmount and multiply it by .07. The Line Total will add the OrderAmount and the Sales Tax together.

> **NOTE** For the examples presented in this section of the chapter, you can use the sample file called *Calculated Fields.xlsx* that can be downloaded from the Wiley website at www.wiley.com/go/GGRXL_PivotTables. The steps of each section will tell you which sheet of the sample workbook to use within that section.

Here's how to add a Calculated Field to your pivot table:

1. Click the MainPivotTable sheet of the sample workbook, or on the sheet where your own pivot table is, and click the pivot table to select it.
2. Click the PivotTable Analyze tab to select it.
3. Select the Fields, Items, & Sets icon near the right side of the ribbon, and then click Calculated Field from the menu. You will now see the Insert Calculated Field dialog box, as displayed in Figure 3.16.

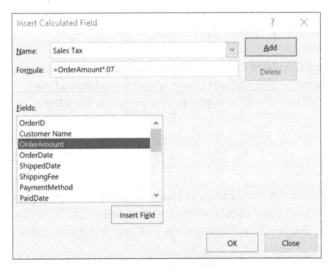

Figure 3.16: The Insert Calculated Field dialog box

4. Click the Name field and give your field a name. For this example, I typed **Sales Tax**.

5. To build your formula, double-click one of the fields you see in the Fields list. This field will show up in your formula. For this example, I used the OrderAmount field.

6. Type in a mathematical operator, like you would in a normal Excel formula. I used the * for multiplication.

7. Type in a number or double-click another field name. I typed **.07**. The Formula should now show **=OrderAmount*.07**.

8. Click OK. You will now see your new formula being used in the Pivot table, as shown in Figure 3.17.

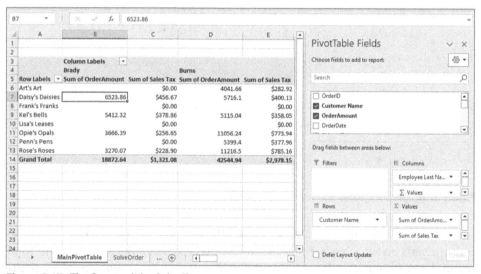

Figure 3.17: The Sum and the Sales Tax

Now, let's add another Calculated Field called Line Total, which will add the OrderAmount and the Sales Tax.

To add Line Total, do the following:

1. Click the pivot table to select it.

2. Click the PivotTable Analyze tab.

3. Click the Fields, Items, & Sets icon near the right side of the ribbon, and then click Calculated Field.

4. Click the Name field and give your field a name. For this example, I entered **Line Total**.

5. To build your formula, double-click one of the fields you see in the Fields list. This field will show up in your formula. For this example, I used the OrderAmount field.

6. Type in a mathematical operator, like you would in a normal Excel formula. I entered the **+** for addition.

7. Type in a number or double-click another field name. I used the Sales Tax column.

8. The Formula should now show **=OrderAmount+'Sales Tax'**.

9. Click OK. You will now see your new formula in the pivot table, as shown in Figure 3.18.

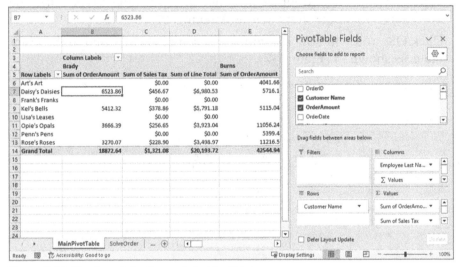

Figure 3.18: The Sum, Sales Tax, and the Line Total

Notice how the Sales Tax and the Line Total are now shown for every column going across on the pivot table. Also notice that the Sales Tax and the Line Total are at the bottom of the list of fields in the PivotTable Fields window. The fields created as Calculated Fields can be moved to and from the Values section of the PivotTable Fields window just like any other field, but they cannot be moved to the other sections of the PivotTable Fields window.

> **NOTE** Notice how the column heading for Sales Tax now says Sum of Sales Tax. To change the column heading, just click it and type something different. If you type in the name of a field that already exists, just type in an extra space at the end of what you typed in, or you will get a message that says "PivotTable field name already exists."

To Change or Delete a Calculated Field

There will be times when you need to change or delete a Calculated Field. Here's how to change or delete a Calculated Field:

1. Click the pivot table to select it.

2. Click the PivotTable Analyze tab.

3. Click the Fields, Items, & Sets icon.

4. Select Calculated Field from the menu that is displayed.

5. Click the pull-down to the right of Name in the Insert Calculated Field dialog box, as shown in Figure 3.19.

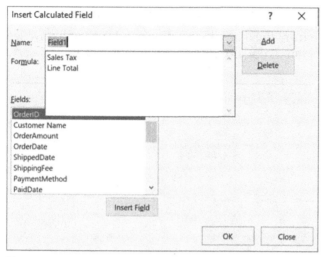

Figure 3.19: Changing or deleting a Calculated Field

6. Choose the field you want to change or delete.

7. Make your changes to the formula for that field or click the Delete button to remove it completely.

8. Click OK to close the dialog box.

Calculated Items

Another way to make your own calculation in a pivot table is to create a Calculated Item. While a Calculated Field appears for every column in the pivot table, the Calculated Item will appear only once. A Calculated Item can make either a new row or a new column in the pivot table. A Calculated Field, on the other hand, will only add more columns to the pivot table. To get to the Calculated Items choice on the Fields, Items, & Sets menu, you have to first click either a column header or a row header of the pivot table. If you click a column header on the pivot table, the Calculated Item will create a new column in the pivot table. If you click a row header of the pivot table, the Calculated Item will create a new row in the pivot table.

A Calculated Item can be a simple formula, or it can be more complex. In the following example, use the CalculatedItem sheet from the downloaded *Calculated Fields.xlsx* file. Within it, you will create a Calculated Item called "Mid Atlantic" that will add the column called "VA" to the column called "PA."

To create the Calculated Item, do the following:

1. Click the CalculatedItem sheet of the sample workbook.

2. Click a column header. For this example, I clicked the cell that contains "VA."

3. Click the PivotTable Analyze tab.

4. Click the Fields, Items, & Sets icon to display the list of options.

5. Select Calculated Item from the menu that is displayed. You will now see the Insert Calculated Item dialog box, as shown in Figure 3.20.

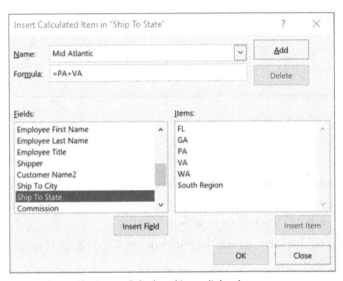

Figure 3.20: The Insert Calculated Item dialog box

6. Click the space next to the Name and enter in a name for your field. For this example, I entered **Mid Atlantic**.

7. Double-click one of the items on the right side of the dialog box to add that value to your formula. I chose PA.

8. Type in a mathematical operator, like you would in a normal Excel formula. I typed the + for addition.

9. Type in a number or double click another item on the right side of the dialog box. I chose **VA**.

10. The Formula should now show **=PA+VA**.

11. Click OK. You will now see the new formula in the pivot table, as shown in Figure 3.21. If you are using the sample data, you may notice that there is already a Calculated Item called "South Region" that sums the values for "FL" and "GA."

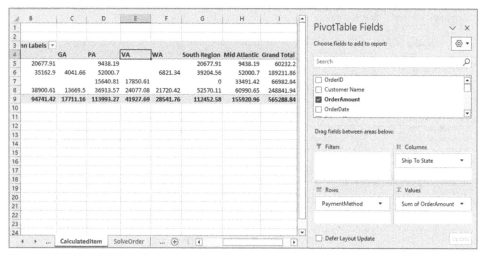

Figure 3.21: The Calculated Item in the pivot table

When a Calculated Item is added to the pivot table, the value in the Calculated Item field will be added to the grand total of the row or the column that the Calculated Item appears in and also to the overall grand total of the pivot table. This could mean the columns or rows that make up the Calculated Item could be counted twice. You might have to filter out the individual rows or columns that comprise the Calculated Item from the pivot table so that the grand total shows the accurate values. Filtering the pivot table will be covered in Chapter 4, "Sorting and Filtering the Pivot Table."

To Change or Delete a Calculated Item

There will be times when you want to change or delete a Calculated Item. To change or delete a Calculated Item, you can do the following:

1. Click a row header or a column header of the pivot table.
2. Click the PivotTable Analyze tab.
3. Click the Fields, Items, & Sets icon.
4. Select Calculated Item from the menu. This will display the Insert Calculated Item dialog box.
5. Click the pull-down to the right of the Name in the Insert Calculated Item dialog box, as shown in Figure 3.22.
6. Choose the field you want to change or delete.
7. Make your changes to the formula for that field or click the Delete button to remove it completely.
8. Click OK to close the dialog box.

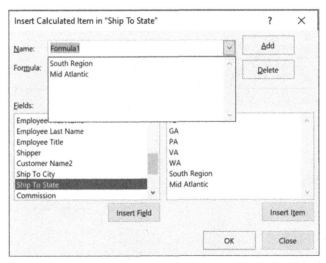

Figure 3.22: Changing or deleting a Calculated Item

Another way to delete a Calculated Item is to use the Solve Order window, as explained in the next section.

The Solve Order

When you have more than one Calculated Item in the pivot table, the order in which the Calculated Items are calculated could make a difference in the numbers that you see on the pivot table. Excel has a way to manage the order in which items are calculated that is called the Solve Order.

To illustrate the Solve Order, we will use the pivot table on the SolveOrder sheet in the *Calculated Fields.xlsx* file mentioned earlier. Our example will show what percent of the sales from the South region are commission sales as compared to the sales that are not commission sales. In the sample data, the commission field has a value of Y if the sale paid commission, and a value of N if the sale did not pay commission. The Calculated Item called Y% is equal to the total of the sales that have Y in the Commission column of the Pivot Table Sales sheet divided by all sales. The Calculated Item called South Region is the sum of the sales from Florida and Georgia. When you click cell G7, the formula is =FL+GA. Notice how the Y% for the South Region is 96%. The number 96% is coming from 53% from FL added to 43% from GA, as shown in Figure 3.23.

It now shows that 96% of the sales for the South Region should pay commission, which is not accurate. To fix this situation, we will change the Solve Order of the Calculated Items.

Here are the steps to change the Solve Order of the Calculated Items:

1. Click the PivotTable Analyze tab.

2. Click the Fields, Items, & Sets icon.

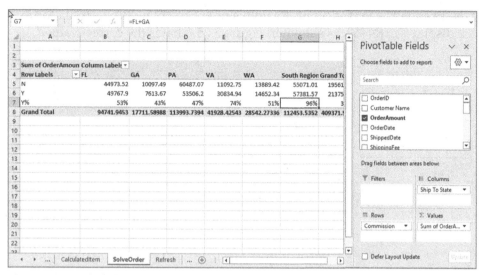

Figure 3.23: Before changing the Solve Order

3. Click Solve Order. You will now see the Calculated Item Solve Order dialog box, as shown in Figure 3.24.

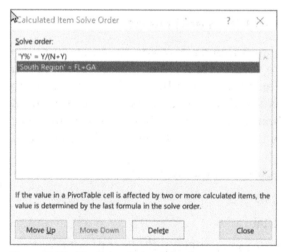

Figure 3.24: The Solve Order dialog box

4. Select the item you want to have calculated earlier. In this case, select South Region = FL + GA.

5. Click the Move Up button. This will place the selected item higher in the order in the Solve order list.

6. Click Close.

Notice the Y% for the South Region is now 51%. Now the formula for that cell displays Y/(N+Y), as shown in Figure 3.25. That is the correct value.

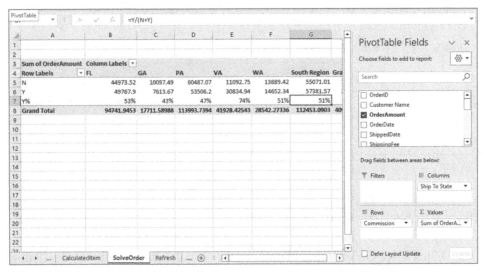

Figure 3.25: After changing the Solve Order

Documenting Your Calculated Items and Fields

Calculated Fields and the Calculated Items allow you to make your own formulas in a pivot table and take your pivot table to the next level. If you have multiple Calculated Fields and Calculated Items, you might want to make a list of the Calculated Items and Calculated Fields that are being used in the pivot table for documentation purposes. Excel has a feature called *List Formulas* that quickly documents the Calculated Items and the Calculated Fields on a separate sheet.

To use the List Formulas feature, follow these steps:

1. Click the pivot table to select it.

2. Click the PivotTable Analyze tab.

3. Click the Fields, Items, & Sets icon near the right side of the ribbon.

4. Select List Formulas from the menu.

5. The Calculated Items and Calculated Fields will display on a new sheet, as shown in Figure 3.26. This shows the Calculated Fields and Calculated Items from all the sheets in the entire workbook.

A1	▾	:	×	✓	fx	Calculated Field				

◢	A	B	C	D	E	F	G	H
1	*Calculated Field*							
2	**Solve Order**	**Field**	**Formula**					
3		1 Sales Tax	=OrderAmount*0.07					
4		2 Line Total	=OrderAmount+'Sales Tax'					
5								
6	*Calculated Item*							
7	**Solve Order**	**Item**	**Formula**					
8		1 'South Region'	=FL+GA					
9		2 'Y%'	=Y/(N+Y)					
10		3 'Mid Atlantic'	=PA+VA					
11								
12								
13	*Note:*		When a cell is updated by more than one formula,					
14			the value is set by the formula with the last solve order.					
15								
16			To change the solve order for multiple calculated items or fields,					
17			on the Options tab, in the Calculations group, click Fields, Items, & Sets, and then click Solve Order.					
18								
19								
20								
21								
22								
23								
24								

◂ ▸ ... | CalculatedItem | **Sheet2** | SolveOrder | Refresh | Pivot Table Sal ... ⊕ : ◂

Figure 3.26: Result of using the List Formulas feature

Limitations of Calculated Fields and Items

While Calculated Fields and Items are helpful, there are some limitations to using them. These limits include the following:

- You will not be able to add a Calculated Item if the same field is used more than once in the Values section of the PivotTable Fields window. For example, if you had a sum and a count on the same field within the Values section, Excel would not allow you to add a Calculated Item. You would get a message that states, "Multiple data fields of the same field are not supported when a PivotTable report has calculated items."

- You will not be able to add a Calculated Item if you have a date field in the Columns section of the PivotTable Fields window. This topic will be discussed in Chapter 6, "Summarizing Your Data by Date and Time."

- You will not be able to add a Calculated Item if the pivot table already contains any of the following calculations from the Summarize Values By tab of the Value Field Settings dialog box. Conversely, you will also not be able to add the following calculations into the pivot table if the pivot table already has a Calculated Item. In either case, you would get a message that states "Averages, standard deviations, and variances are not supported when a PivotTable report has calculated items."

- Average
- StdDev
- StdDevp
- Var
- Varp

While the Calculated Items and Calculated Fields allow you to create your own formulas in a pivot table, there are limits to what you can do with the formulas of the Calculated Items and the Calculated Fields. To access the full power of Excel formulas and functions, you may have to add a formula to the original list of data, which would require you to add a new column to the original list of data and then change the data source of the pivot table. Changing the data source of the pivot table is covered in the next section.

Refreshing Values on the Pivot Table

Realistically, some cells in the list of data on the original sheet, the data source for the pivot table, will probably change from time to time. When the data is changed on the original list of data, the pivot table will have to be refreshed so that it reflects the newest data. There is a way to manually refresh the data and a way to automatically refresh it every time the file is opened. When more rows or more columns are added to the original list of data, you might also have to make the pivot table point to a different range of data. These topics are covered in this section.

NOTE For the examples presented in this section of the chapter, you can use the sample file called *Calculations.xlsx* that is included with this book. You can find the sample files at www.wiley.com/go/GGRXL_PivotTables. This section will use a sheet called SalesByCustomer.

Manual Refresh

If any of the cells on the original list of data change, the pivot table has to be refreshed, or these new changes to the data will not be reflected in the pivot table.

To refresh the pivot table manually, do the following:

1. Select the SalesByCustomer sheet of the sample workbook.

2. Notice how the number for the Art's Art row and the Pierce column of the pivot table is currently 13669.50, as shown in Figure 3.27.

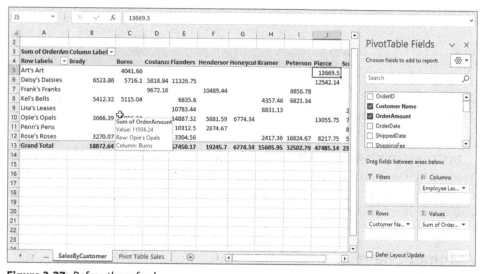

Figure 3.27: Before the refresh

3. Select the Pivot Table Sales sheet at the bottom of the window.

4. Click cell C2. Type **2648.90** and press Enter.

5. Now go back to the SalesByCustomer sheet at the bottom of the window.

6. Notice how the number for the Art's Art row and Pierce still shows 13669.50.

7. Click the pivot table.

8. Click the PivotTable Analyze tab.

9. Click the Refresh icon in the middle of the ribbon, and then click Refresh if the submenu displays. Refresh will refresh the current pivot table. Refresh All will refresh all the pivot tables in the workbook. You can also refresh the current pivot table by right-clicking any cell on the pivot table and then choosing Refresh.

10. Notice how the number for the Art's Art row and Pierce column now displays 13709.50, as shown in Figure 3.28.

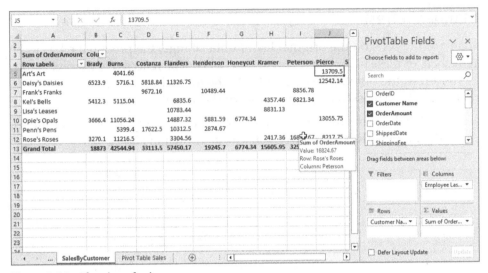

Figure 3.28: After the refresh

In Chapter 9, "Pulling It All Together: Creating a Dashboard from Your Pivot Tables," we will add a clickable button onto the pivot table, which will then refresh the pivot table, so the task of refreshing the data will be more apparent and accessible for the user.

Automatic Refresh

Instead of manually refreshing the pivot table, there is a way to automatically refresh the pivot table each time the workbook is opened. This feature has to be turned on within the PivotTable Options dialog box. You can enable the automatic refresh feature by doing the following:

1. Click a pivot table.

2. Select the PivotTable Analyze tab.

3. Click the Options icon on the left side of the ribbon. This will display the PivotTable Options dialog box.

4. Click the Data tab of the PivotTable Options dialog box, as shown in Figure 3.29.

5. Check the Refresh Data When Opening The File box.

6. Click OK and then click OK on the next window. This will make the pivot table automatically refresh each time the file is open.

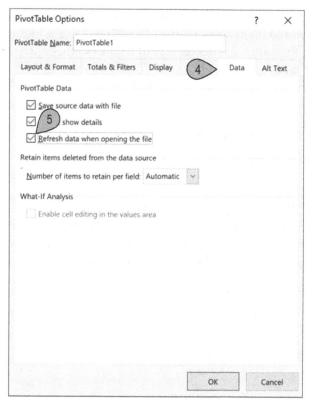

Figure 3.29: The Data tab of the PivotTable Options dialog box

Changing the Data Source

In addition to refreshing the pivot table, sometimes you will need to change the data range that drives the pivot table, or even select a completely different data range for the pivot table. This is called changing the data source, and it could be just as important as refreshing the pivot table. One reason to change the data source would be if more rows or columns are added to the list of data. Another reason is if a whole new list of data is imported into the Excel workbook, as described in Chapter 1, "Preparing the Data for an Excel Pivot Table."

If the pivot table comes from a formatted table, you will not have to change the data source if more data is added to the formatted table. The formatted table will automatically expand when more rows or columns are added. However, you will still have to refresh the pivot table when the data changes on the original data list even for a pivot table that comes from a formatted table.

In the following example, a column is being added to the original table that had not been included in the pivot table. This is a change to the data source for the pivot table. You would use similar steps if you added more rows to the original list of data. In this example I will be using the Main Pivot Table and the Pivot Table Sales sheets from the sample workbook, but of course these steps will work on your own pivot table as well.

To change the data source of the pivot table, do the following:

1. Select the Pivot Table Sales sheet.

2. Notice the Commission Amt in column S.

3. Click the SalesbyCustomer sheet.

4. Click the pivot table.

5. Click the PivotTable Analyze tab.

6. Click the Change Data Source icon in the middle of the ribbon. Click the words *Change Data Source* again if the submenu displays. You will see the Change PivotTable Data Source dialog box, as shown in Figure 3.30.

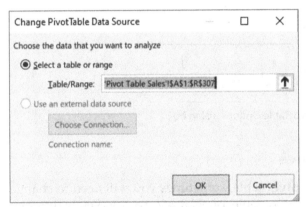

Figure 3.30: The Change PivotTable Data Source dialog box

7. Notice the Table/Range stops at R307. The Commission Amt field is in column S.

8. Highlight the full data range, including the new columns and rows. A quick way to do this is to use the Ctrl+A keyboard shortcut. This will highlight the full range of data. The range will stop at the next completely blank row and the next completely blank column of data.

9. Click OK. You should see the Commission Amt field at the bottom of the fields in the PivotTable Fields window, as shown in Figure 3.31. Any new rows would have updated the pivot table.

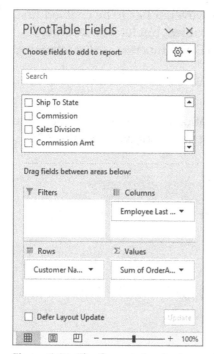

Figure 3.31: The Commission Amt now displays in the PivotTable Fields window

Using Numbers from the Pivot Table in Other Calculations

There will be times when you want a spreadsheet to have access to a value within a pivot table. You might want to use values from the pivot table on the same sheet as the pivot table, on a different sheet in the same workbook, or even on a sheet in a different workbook.

You can use the GETPIVOTDATA function to retrieve a number that is within the pivot data. A formula containing the GETPIVOTDATA function can stand alone, or it can be used as part of any other formula.

The GETPIVOTDATA function can be found in the Lookup & Reference category of Excel functions, but there is a more automatic way to use it.

Enabling the GETPIVOTDATA Function

The easiest way to use the GETPIVOTDATA function is to start a formula in a cell that is anywhere outside of the pivot table and then click the number of the pivot table you are trying to use. This should create the GETPIVOTDATA formula automatically. To use this feature, however, it has to be enabled first. As a default, the feature is probably already enabled, but let's make sure.

To enable the automatic use of the GETPIVOTDATA function, do the following:

1. Click the pivot table.

2. Click the PivotTable Analyze tab.

3. Click the pull-down to the right of the Options icon on the left side of the ribbon. This will display a drop-down menu, as shown in Figure 3.32.

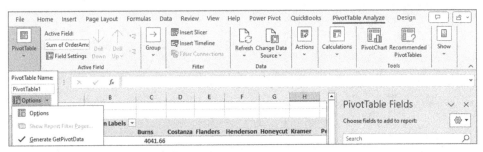

Figure 3.32: Enabling the GETPIVOTDATA function

4. If the Generate GetPivotData menu option is not checked, then click Generate GetPivotData. This will enable the automatic use of the GetPivotData function. If the Generate GetPivotData menu option is already checked, just click any cell to close the submenu.

Using the GETPIVOTDATA Function

To use the GETPIVOTDATA function in a cell, do the following:

1. Click any blank cell outside of the pivot table.

2. Start a formula by typing =.

3. Click a number within the pivot table. You should see the GETPIVOTDATA formula, as shown in Figure 3.33.
   You will get a different variation of the GETPIVOTDATA formula for each different cell you click the pivot table. The first parameter of the GETPIVOTDATA function is always the name of the field you want to use, and the second parameter of the GETPIVOTDATA function is always the location of the first cell of the pivot table that you want to use. The rest of the parameters of the GETPIVOTDATA function are optional, and they would define the data point on the pivot table you are trying to use in the GETPIVOTDATA formula.

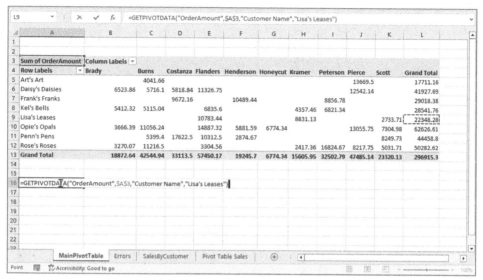

| L9 | ▼ | × | ✓ | ƒx | =GETPIVOTDATA("OrderAmount",$A$3,"Customer Name","Lisa's Leases") | | | | | | |

	A	B	C	D	E	F	G	H	I	J	K	L
1												
2												
3	Sum of OrderAmount	Column Labels ▼										
4	Row Labels ▼	Brady	Burns	Costanza	Flanders	Henderson	Honeycut	Kramer	Peterson	Pierce	Scott	Grand Total
5	Art's Art		4041.66							13669.5		17711.16
6	Daisy's Daisies	6523.86	5716.1	5818.84	11326.75					12542.14		41927.69
7	Frank's Franks			9672.16		10489.44			8856.78			29018.38
8	Kel's Bells	5412.32	5115.04		6835.6			4357.46	6821.34			28541.76
9	Lisa's Leases				10783.44				8831.13		2733.71	22348.28
10	Opie's Opals	3666.39	11056.24		14887.32	5881.59	6774.34			13055.75	7304.98	62626.61
11	Penn's Pens		5399.4	17622.5	10312.5	2874.67					8249.73	44458.8
12	Rose's Roses	3270.07	11216.5		3304.56			2417.36	16824.67	8217.75	5031.71	50282.62
13	Grand Total	18872.64	42544.94	33113.5	57450.17	19245.7	6774.34	15605.95	32502.79	47485.14	23320.13	296915.3
14												
15												
16	=GETPIVOTDATA("OrderAmount",$A$3,"Customer Name","Lisa's Leases")											
17												
18												
19												
20												
21												
22												

| MainPivotTable | Errors | SalesByCustomer | Pivot Table Sales | ⊕ |

Point   Accessibility: Good to go

Figure 3.33: The GETPIVOTDATA formula

4. Press Enter.

5. The number in the cell you just created will change accordingly as the pivot table updates.

Summary

In this chapter, you learned how to change the calculations in your pivot table and how to add new calculations. You discovered the calculations that are built into the pivot table in the Value Field Settings dialog box. You also saw how to add your own calculations using Calculated Fields and Calculated Items as well as how to refresh your pivot tables when the original list of data changes. Finally, you were introduced to the GETPIVOTDATA function, which can be used to capture a value from a pivot table to use outside of the pivot table.

In the next chapter, I will show you many ways to sort and filter the pivot table.

Sorting and Filtering the Pivot Table

You now have a pivot table that is starting to display the results you are looking to achieve from your data. You have learned the skills to create the pivot table, to make the pivot table look better, and to add and change calculations. Now, you want the pivot table to display the data in a certain order, or you might want the pivot table to display only a subset of the data. In this chapter, you will learn many ways to sort the pivot table in the order you want, and you will also learn to filter the pivot table so it displays the exact results you are looking for.

> **NOTE** For the examples presented in this section of the chapter, you can use the sample file called *Sorts and Filters.xlsx* that is included with this book. You can find the sample files at www.wiley.com/go/GGRXL_PivotTables. Each section of this chapter will indicate which sheet to use from this workbook.

Sorting the Pivot Table

The information in the pivot table can be sorted to arrange the data in the order that you want it displayed. You can sort by any column in the pivot table, by any row in the pivot table, or by the rows and columns at the same time. The sort can be in alphabetical order or reverse alphabetical order for words, it can be in ascending or descending order for numbers and dates, or you can create your own order. The rows and columns can be sorted by one field or by multiple fields. You can sort the pivot table by any field that is in either the Rows section, the Columns section, or the Values section of the PivotTable Fields window.

Of course, any list of data that is not a pivot table can also be sorted. But sorting a list of data can sometimes lead to problems. If the steps for the sort are not done correctly, Excel could sort the column that you choose, but not bring the rest of the row of data with the sorted column, which would result in incorrect information being displayed in the list of data. Another situation that could happen is that the column headers could accidentally get sorted into the list, which would make it appear like the column headers are not there anymore. I have seen these issues happen many times. Rest assured that neither of these situations will occur when you sort the pivot table.

> **NOTE** If the pivot table you want to sort or filter still shows the words "Row Labels" and "Column Labels" on the top left of the pivot table, then you might want to show the field names instead. To show the field names in the pivot table, click the Design tab and then select Report Layout ⇨ Show in Tabular Form. Tabular Form makes the pivot table look better in general, and it also displays the real field names on the pivot table. See Chapter 2, "Summarizing and Presenting Data with a Pivot Table," for more ways to improve the appearance of the pivot table.

Sorting by a Column

You can sort a pivot table based on the data within a column. A typical request is to sort the pivot table by the grand totals on the right side of the pivot table so that the highest grand totals will be at the top of the list, going down from there. For this example, you can use the Main Pivot Table sheet from the sample file. Currently, the rows of the pivot table are sorted by the Customer Name in column A, as shown in Figure 4.1.

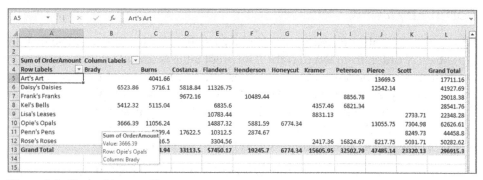

Figure 4.1: Pivot table sorted by customer name

To sort the pivot table by any column, you can do the following:

1. Right-click a number in the Grand Total column, or in any other column that you want to sort.

2. Click Sort.

3. Click Sort Smallest To Largest, or Sort Largest To Smallest. For this example, choose Sort Largest To Smallest. The pivot table will immediately show the results of the sort. Notice how the highest grand totals are at the top of pivot table, going down from there, as shown in Figure 4.2.

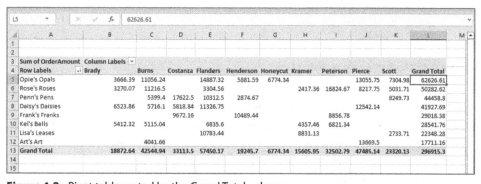

Figure 4.2: Pivot table sorted by the Grand Total column

Just because the Grand Total column is sorted from the highest value to the lowest value does not mean that the other columns are also sorted. In fact, the other columns most likely are not sorted, unless the data just happens to work out that way for another column. You can sort by any column, but you can sort by only one column at a time. A pivot table can also be sorted on any row going across.

Sorting by a Row

Currently, the column headers going across the pivot table are probably in alphabetical order, from left to right. The pivot table is sorted by the header row. A pivot table can be sorted by the values in any row, not just the header row. For this example, we will sort the pivot table on the row for Opie's Opals from left to right so that the columns are in order according to which employee has the best total for Opie's Opals.

To sort the pivot table by any row, follow these steps:

1. Right-click a number on the row that you want to sort. If you are using the sample data, right-click cell B5, which is in the row for Opie's Opals.

2. Click Sort ⇨ More Sort Options. You will now see the Sort By Value dialog box shown in Figure 4.3.

Figure 4.3: The Sort By Value dialog box

3. Choose Largest To Smallest and choose Left To Right.

4. Click OK. The pivot table will immediately show the results of the sort. Notice how the employee with the highest total for Opie's Opals is on the left side of the pivot table, and going across from there the numbers decrease, as shown in Figure 4.4.

Row Labels	Flanders	Pierce	Burns	Scott	Honeycut	Henderson	Brady	Costanza	Kramer	Peterson	Grand Total
Opie's Opals	14887.32	13055.75	11056.24	7304.98	6774.34	5881.59	3666.39				62626.61
Rose's Roses	3304.56	8217.75	11216.5	5031.71			3270.07		2417.36	16824.67	50282.62
Penn's Pens	10312.5		5399.4	8249.73		2874.67		17622.5			44458.8
Daisy's Daisies	11326.75	12542.14	5716.1				6523.86	5818.84			41927.69
Frank's Franks						10489.44		9672.16		8856.78	29018.38
Kel's Bells	6835.6		5115.04				5412.32		4357.46	6821.34	28541.76
Lisa's Leases	10783.44			2733.71				8831.13			22348.28
Art's Art		13669.5	4041.66								17711.16
Grand Total	57450.17	47485.14	42544.94	23320.13	6774.34	19245.7	18872.64	33113.5	15605.95	32502.79	296915.3

Sum of OrderAmount — Column Labels

Figure 4.4: Pivot table sorted across a row

Just because a row is sorted from the highest value to the lowest value from left to right does not mean that the other rows are also sorted. In fact, the other rows most likely are not sorted, unless the data just happens to work out that way for another row. You can sort any row, but you can sort only one row at a time.

Putting the Pivot Table in Ascending Order

Once the pivot table is sorted by a row or a column, you probably will want to return the pivot table to alphabetical order or ascending order at some point. It is easy to put the pivot table back in alphabetical order by the column headers and the row headers.

To sort the rows or columns of the pivot table in alphabetical order, click the drop-down menu next to either Row Labels or Column Labels on the top left of the pivot table, and click Sort A To Z or Sort Z To A. The classic sort icons on the Data tab will also work in the pivot table. The pivot table will immediately show the result of the sort.

Creating Your Own Sort Order

Having the ability to sort any column or any row in alphabetic or numeric order is very useful. You can also put the rows and columns in any order you want. Either you can drag the rows or columns in the order that you want, or you can set up a custom list that can facilitate an alternate sort order.

Creating Your Own Sort Order by Dragging Cells

There are going to be times when you want the pivot table to show the data in an alternative order, other than showing the data in alphabetic or numeric order. Maybe you want to always display a certain value at the top or bottom of the list, or always display a certain value before or after another value, or you want to put the data in whatever order you want.

One way to accomplish this is to drag the rows or columns so they appear in the order you want. The technique of dragging the fields to change the display order can work in either the rows or the columns. As an example, we will change the sample pivot table to display Penn's Pens above Kel's Bells.

To change the sort order of the pivot table by dragging the rows or columns, follow these steps:

1. Click the cell that contains the row header or the column header you want to move. For this example, click cell A11, which contains "Penn's Pens."

2. Move your mouse pointer to the bottom border of the cell so that your mouse pointer changes to the four arrows icon, as shown in Figure 4.5.

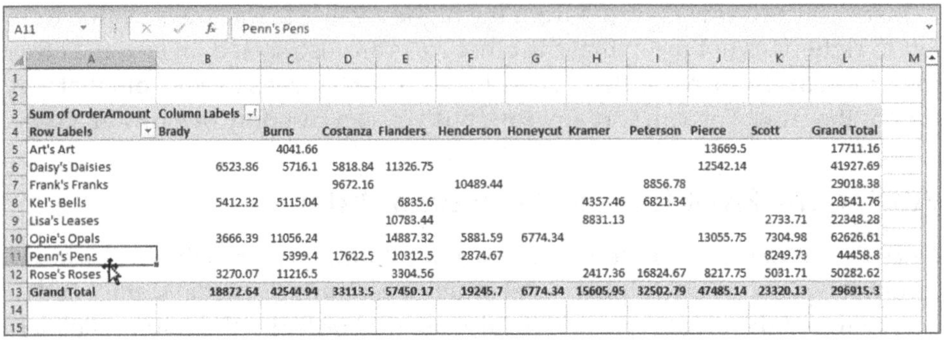

Sum of OrderAmount	Column Labels										
Row Labels	Brady	Burns	Costanza	Flanders	Henderson	Honeycut	Kramer	Peterson	Pierce	Scott	Grand Total
Art's Art		4041.66							13669.5		17711.16
Daisy's Daisies	6523.86	5716.1	5818.84	11326.75					12542.14		41927.69
Frank's Franks			9672.16		10489.44			8856.78			29018.38
Kel's Bells	5412.32	5115.04		6835.6			4357.46	6821.34			28541.76
Lisa's Leases				10783.44			8831.13			2733.71	22348.28
Opie's Opals	3666.39	11056.24		14887.32	5881.59	6774.34			13055.75	7304.98	62626.61
Penn's Pens		5399.4	17622.5	10312.5	2874.67					8249.73	44458.8
Rose's Roses	3270.07	11216.5		3304.56			2417.36	16824.67	8217.75	5031.71	50282.62
Grand Total	18872.64	42544.94	33113.5	57450.17	19245.7	6774.34	15605.95	32502.79	47485.14	23320.13	296915.3

Figure 4.5: Positioning the mouse pointer so you can drag a cell

3. Hold down the left mouse button and drag to the current row above or below another row in the same column, or drag the current column to the right or left of another column. Release the mouse button. The row or column that you wanted to move should be in the new location, as shown in Figure 4.6.

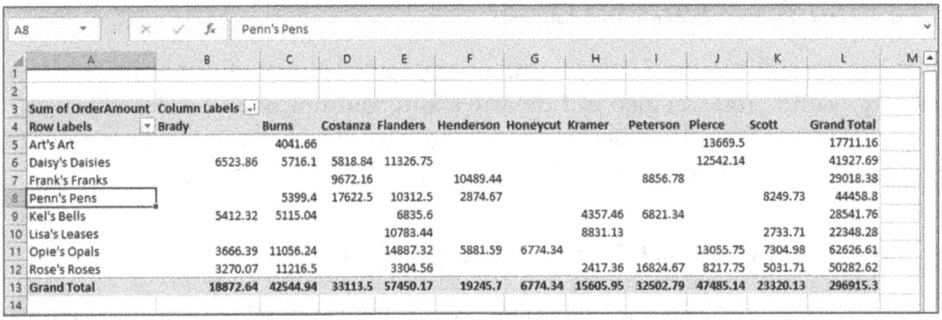

Sum of OrderAmount	Column Labels										
Row Labels	Brady	Burns	Costanza	Flanders	Henderson	Honeycut	Kramer	Peterson	Pierce	Scott	Grand Total
Art's Art		4041.66							13669.5		17711.16
Daisy's Daisies	6523.86	5716.1	5818.84	11326.75					12542.14		41927.69
Frank's Franks			9672.16		10489.44			8856.78			29018.38
Penn's Pens		5399.4	17622.5	10312.5	2874.67					8249.73	44458.8
Kel's Bells	5412.32	5115.04		6835.6			4357.46	6821.34			28541.76
Lisa's Leases				10783.44			8831.13			2733.71	22348.28
Opie's Opals	3666.39	11056.24		14887.32	5881.59	6774.34			13055.75	7304.98	62626.61
Rose's Roses	3270.07	11216.5		3304.56			2417.36	16824.67	8217.75	5031.71	50282.62
Grand Total	18872.64	42544.94	33113.5	57450.17	19245.7	6774.34	15605.95	32502.79	47485.14	23320.13	296915.3

Figure 4.6: Pivot table sorted by dragging a row or column

Dragging the rows and columns to appear in the order you want them is helpful in creating your own sort order, but it can be time-consuming to drag the rows and columns every time you want a different sort order on a pivot table. If there is a custom sort order you use on a regular basis, it will be more efficient to create a custom list, which can be used repeatedly.

Creating Your Own Sort Order by Using a Custom List

A custom list is a list of data that you create that can provide an alternative sort order, rather than just always sorting alphabetically or numerically. You can have as many custom lists as you need. A custom list becomes part of the Excel environment and can be used for sorts in any Excel workbook, not just the current one. When you create a custom list, it can be entered manually, or it can be imported from an existing list from one of your Excel workbooks.

In this example, we will create a custom list that has the desired sort order for company names in the sample file.

Creating a Custom List

It is possible that you already have a list that contains the sort order you want to use. Maybe it is just there to remind you of the desired sort order. For this example, we will use the Custom List sheet that is in the sample workbook.

To create a custom list, follow these steps:

1. Highlight the list of data that you want to use for your custom list if you have one. If you are using the sample data, highlight cells A1 to A8 on the Custom List sheet of the sample workbook.

2. Click the File tab.

3. At the bottom of the File tab menu, click the word *Options*, or click the word *More*, and then click Options. This will open the Excel Options dialog box, as shown in Figure 4.7.

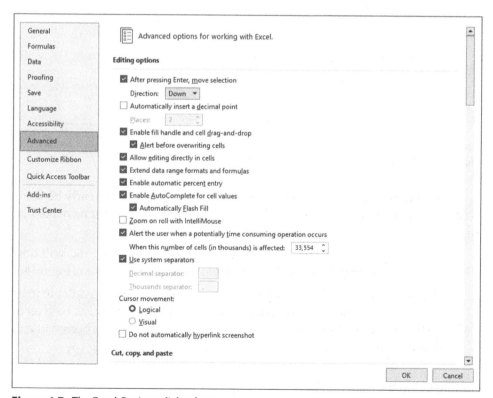

Figure 4.7: The Excel Options dialog box

4. Click the Advanced tab of the Excel Options dialog box.

5. Scroll all the way to bottom of the Advanced tab and click the Edit Custom Lists button found in the General section, as shown in Figure 4.8.

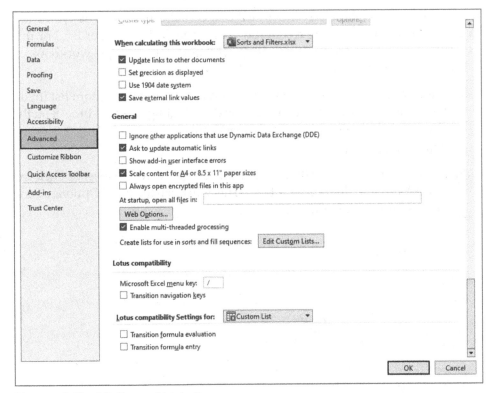

Figure 4.8: The Edit Custom Lists button

You will now see the Custom Lists dialog box. There might already be some custom lists that Excel provides as well as custom lists you might have created previously.

6. Click the Import button on the right side of the dialog box. You will now see the list you highlighted in the section "List entries," as shown in Figure 4.9.

7. Click OK and then click OK again. Your custom list is now available to be used as an alternative sort order in the current workbook, as well as in any other Excel workbook that you use on the computer where you created the custom list.

Sorting Using the Custom List

Now that you have created the custom list, it's time to use that custom list to sort the pivot table. The custom list can be used to sort either the columns or the rows of the pivot table. Any value that is on the pivot table that is not on the custom list will appear alphabetically below the items that are on the custom list. For this example, we will go back to the Main Pivot Table sheet of the sample workbook and sort the rows using the custom list.

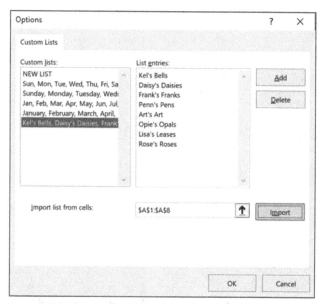

Figure 4.9: The Custom Lists dialog box

To sort the pivot table using a custom list, follow these steps:

1. Click the drop-down menu of the Row Labels or the Column Labels on the pivot table. For this example, I will use the Row Labels.

2. Click More Sort Options. This will show the Sort dialog box, as shown in Figure 4.10.

3. Select the Ascending (A to Z) By option.

Figure 4.10: The Sort dialog box

4. Click More Options. This will show the More Sort Options dialog box, as shown in Figure 4.11.

Figure 4.11: The More Sort Options dialog box

5. Uncheck the Sort Automatically Every Time The Report Is Updated box.

6. Click the drop-down menu below where it says "First key sort order." You will now see the custom lists.

7. Click the custom list you want to use. In this case, it is the list you created in the previous section.

8. Click OK and then click OK again. The pivot table will now be sorted in the order of the custom list, as shown in Figure 4.12.

A8			*fx*	Penn's Pens								
	A	B	C	D	E	F	G	H	I	J	K	L	M
1												
2												
3	Sum of OrderAmount	Column Labels										
4	Row Labels	Brady	Burns	Costanza	Flanders	Henderson	Honeycut	Kramer	Peterson	Pierce	Scott	Grand Total
5	Kel's Bells	5412.32	5115.04		6835.6			4357.46	6821.34			28541.76
6	Daisy's Daisies	6523.86	5716.1	5818.84	11326.75					12542.14		41927.69
7	Frank's Franks			9672.16		10489.44			8856.78			29018.38
8	Penn's Pens		5399.4	17622.5	10312.5	2874.67					8249.73	44458.8
9	Art's Art		4041.66							13669.5		17711.16
10	Opie's Opals	3666.39	11056.24		14887.32	5881.59	6774.34			13055.75	7304.98	62626.61
11	Lisa's Leases				10783.44			8831.13			2733.71	22348.28
12	Rose's Roses	3270.07	11216.5		3304.56			2417.36	16824.67	8217.75	5031.71	50282.62
13	Grand Total	18872.64	42544.94	33113.5	57450.17	19245.7	6774.34	15605.95	32502.79	47485.14	23320.13	296915.3

Figure 4.12: Pivot table sorted using a custom list

Disabling the Use of the Custom List

Once you sort the pivot table using the custom list, you may want to go back to sorting the pivot table in alphabetical order. To do this, you will have to disable the use of the custom list.

To disable the use of the custom list, follow these steps:

1. Click the drop-down menu of the Row Labels or the Column Labels on the pivot table. For this example, I will use the Row Labels.

2. Click More Sort Options.

3. Select the Ascending (A to Z) By option.

4. Click More Options. This will show the More Sort Options dialog box.

5. If necessary, uncheck the Sort Automatically Every Time The Report Is Updated box.

6. Click the drop-down menu below where it says "First key sort order." You will now see the custom lists. Scroll up to the top of the list and click No Calculation.

7. Click OK and then click OK again. The pivot table will now be sorted back in alphabetical order.

Sorting a Pivot Table with Multiple Fields

So far in this chapter, you've seen how to sort the pivot table by one row or one column, which is called a *single-field sort*. When there are multiple fields in the Rows section, Columns section, or Values section of the PivotTable Fields window, each additional field in the Rows, Columns, or Values sections of the PivotTable Fields window could be used to further sort the pivot table. Fields could be sorted within other fields, which is called a *multiple-field sort*. In a multiple-field sort, the fields will be sorted in the top-down order that the fields appear in the Rows, Columns, or Values sections of the PivotTable Fields window. An example would be to sort first by the employee's last name and then by the sales for that employee for each state. The states could potentially display in a different order for each employee. For this example, we will use the Multiple Fields sheet of the sample workbook.

To sort by multiple fields, follow these steps:

1. Right-click the column header or the row header that you want to sort. If you are using the sample data, right-click cell B5 of the Multiple Fields sheet, which should show "FL."

2. Click Sort ➪ More Sort Options. This will display the Sort dialog box, as displayed in Figure 4.13.

Figure 4.13: The Sort dialog box

3. Choose "Descending (Z to A) By and click the drop-down menu below this option.

4. Select Sum Of OrderAmount.

5. Click the More Options button on the bottom of the dialog box. This will display the More Sort Options dialog box, as shown in Figure 4.14.

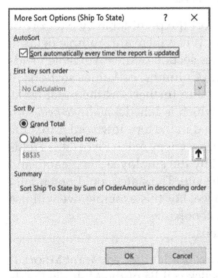

Figure 4.14: The More Sort Options dialog box

6. Select the option for how you want the sort based. The default is to sort based on the Grand Total for the row or column, which you can see is already selected. If you want the sort to be based on a different row or

column, select Values In Selected Row or Values In Selected column, then click the space below that choice, and finally click the row or column you want to use for the sort. Once you've made your selection between the grand total and values in the selected row/column, click OK. For this example, choose Grand Total and click OK.

7. Click OK again. The pivot table should now be sorted the way you want, as shown in Figure 4.15. Notice how the employee names are still sorted alphabetically, but the states for each employee are sorted on the total sales for each state, going left right, from highest to lowest.

B5		× ✓	fx	VA										
	A	B	C	D	E	F	G	H	I	J	K	L	M	
1														
2														
3	Sum of OrderAmount	Column Labels												
4		⊟ Brady				Brady Total	⊟ Burns					Burns Total	⊟ Costanza	
5	Row Labels	VA	WA	PA	FL		FL	PA	VA	WA	GA		FL	PA
6	⊟ Art's Art										4041.66	4041.66		
7	Check										4041.66	4041.66		
8	(blank)													
9	⊟ Daisy's Daisies	6523.86				6523.86			5716.1			5716.1		
10	Credit Card	6523.86				6523.86								
11	(blank)								5716.1			5716.1		
12	⊟ Frank's Franks													967

Figure 4.15: Pivot table sorted by employee last name and by value of each state

You have learned many ways to sort the pivot table in this chapter. Now that you know how to sort the pivot table in the order you want, the next section will show you how to make the pivot table display only certain rows or columns based on criteria that you select. This is called a *filter*, and the pivot table can be filtered in even more ways than it can be sorted.

Filtering the Pivot Table

The pivot tables we have used so far as examples in the book have summarized all the data from the original list, including all columns and all rows. Of course, in the real world, there will be many times you want to display only certain data based on various criteria. Maybe you just want to see data for a certain city, for several cities, for one or two departments, or for whatever combination of the data you want.

A filter enables you to make the pivot table display only the information you want based on the criteria you choose. A pivot table can be filtered by as many fields as you want, so you can show the exact results you are looking for. A pivot table can be filtered by any field on the field list in the PivotTable Fields window, whether the field is being used in one of the other sections of the PivotTable Fields window or not. First, I will show how to filter the pivot table by the fields that are displayed on the pivot table, and then, later in this chapter, I will show you how to filter the pivot table by any field in the fields list by using slicers and timelines.

Filter by Selection

A quick way to filter the pivot table is to start by selecting the items you want to filter. For this example, you can use the Main Pivot Table sheet of the sample workbook. Instead of showing every employee, you want the pivot table to display the columns only for Burns, Costanza, and Henderson. Selecting the data to create a filter will work the same way for rows or columns.

To filter the pivot table by selecting the data, follow these steps:

1. Click a column header or row header that you want to use in the filter. If you are using the sample data, click cell C4, which contains "Burns."

2. Select the other fields you want to use in the filter. Do this by holding down the Ctrl key and clicking the other row headers or column headers you want to use in the filter.

3. In the sample data, click cells D4 and F4. The cells should all be selected.

4. Release the Ctrl key after selecting all the desired rows or columns.

5. Right-click one of the selected cells. This will display a menu of options.

6. Choose Filter to display the filter options on a submenu. You will now see the options shown in Figure 4.16. Notice how you can not only keep the selected items but could also hide the selected items.

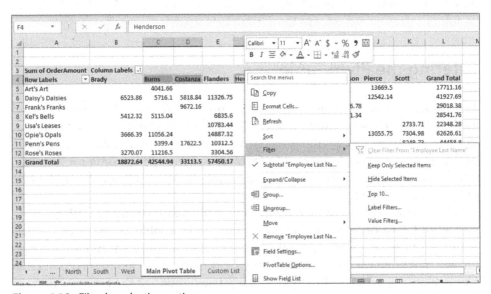

Figure 4.16: Filter by selection options

7. Select Keep Only Selected Items. The pivot table is now filtered to display only the items you selected, as shown in Figure 4.17.

E10	▾	:	×	✓	*f*x	25896.57		
◢	A		B		C	D	E	F
1								
2								
3	Sum of OrderAmount	Column Labels ⊤						
4	Row Labels	▾	Burns		Costanza	Henderson	Grand Total	
5	Art's Art		4041.66				4041.66	
6	Daisy's Daisies		5716.1		5818.84		11534.94	
7	Frank's Franks				9672.16	10489.44	20161.6	
8	Kel's Bells		5115.04				5115.04	
9	Opie's Opals		11056.24			5881.59	16937.83	
10	Penn's Pens		5399.4		17622.5	2874.67	25896.57	
11	Rose's Roses		11216.5				11216.5	
12	Grand Total		42544.94		33113.5	19245.7	94904.14	
13								

Figure 4.17: Pivot table filtered by selection

Notice how the row totals and the column totals show just the totals for the rows and columns that are being displayed. You just created a filter. But now that you have created a filter, you might be wondering if you can get those filtered columns or rows back. Don't worry. The rows or columns that are not display-ing have not been permanently deleted. They are just hidden temporarily. It is just as easy to get the hidden rows or columns back again.

Clearing the Filter

The filters on the pivot table can always be easily cleared. When the workbook gets saved, the sorts and filters get saved with it. The pivot table will still be sorted and filtered the next time the workbook is opened, but the filters can still be cleared.

To clear the filter, you can either click the drop-down menu of the row header or the column header on the pivot table and select Clear Filter, or you can click the PivotTable Analyze tab and select Clear ⟴ Clear Filters. In the sample data, click the drop-down menu in cell B3 and select Clear Filter from Employee Last Name. The pivot table will then show all the data again.

Using AutoFilters

Filtering the data by selecting the data is quick and easy, but there are other ways to filter the pivot table. Notice the drop-down menus to the right of the row and column headings on the top left of the pivot table. These drop-down menus are called AutoFilters, which will give you many more ways to filter the pivot table. AutoFilters work the same way for the columns as they do for the rows. For this example, we will use the Main Pivot Table sheet of the sample workbook. We want to show only Art's Art and Kel's Bells.

To filter the pivot table using an AutoFilter, follow these steps:

1. Click the drop-down menu next to the Row Labels or the Column Labels. For this example, click the drop-down menu for the Row Labels. You will see the classic sort and filter menu, as shown in Figure 4.18. On this menu, you can pick and choose as many items as you want to display.

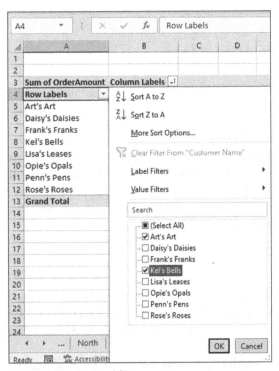

Figure 4.18: Sort and filter menu

2. Uncheck (Select All). This will unselect all the rows. Note that if you click it again, it will select (check) all of the rows. Leave it unchecked.

3. In the sample data, choose Art's Art and Kel's Bells.

4. Click OK. The pivot table will immediately show the results, as shown in Figure 4.19. The totals for the rows and columns will adjust accordingly to reflect the filtered data.

Clear the filter by clicking on the drop-down menu next to Row Labels and then clicking Clear Filter.

	A	B	C	D	E	F	G	H
1								
2								
3	Sum of OrderAmount	Column Labels						
4	Row Labels	Brady	Burns	Flanders	Kramer	Peterson	Pierce	Grand Total
5	Art's Art		4041.66				13669.5	17711.16
6	Kel's Bells	5412.32	5115.04	6835.6	4357.46	6821.34		28541.76
7	Grand Total	5412.32	9156.7	6835.6	4357.46	6821.34	13669.5	46252.92
8								

Figure 4.19: Pivot table filtered using an AutoFilter

Checking or unchecking the items you want on the AutoFilters menu is a useful and popular feature. But sometimes there will be a need to filter the pivot table beyond just checking or unchecking the items you want. The AutoFilters drop-down menu also contains features called Label Filters, Value Filters, and Date Filters, which all will give you even more flexibility in filtering the pivot table. The Date Filters option will appear in the AutoFilter drop-down menu only with date fields.

Label Filters

Above the list of items in the AutoFilter drop-down menu, you will see a Label Filters choice, which gives you more flexibility in filtering the pivot table. Label Filters allow you to search the beginning of a field, the end of a field, or any-where in the middle of a field for what you are looking for. Label Filters allow wildcards in the text you are trying to match. The wildcard characters are ? and *. The ? represents a single character within the text. The * represents any number of characters within the text, including a single character, multiple characters, or even no characters at all. The search strings that you use for Label Filters are not case-sensitive and can be made up of one or more characters. Table 4.1 shows some examples of using wildcards in Label Filters.

Table 4.1: Examples of wildcards in label filters

SEARCH STRING	MEANING	EXAMPLES OF MATCHES
?a*	The letter *a* has to be the second character of the text string, and then it doesn't matter what comes after the *a*.	Candy, car, LA, many, rank
A*	The letter *a* has to be the first character of the text string, and then it doesn't matter what comes after the *a*.	A, Apple, Art
a	The letter *a* could be anywhere in the text string.	A, any, Apple, Art, Candy, Car, crash, flat, LA, many, pizza, rank, tea

Continues

Table 4.1 (*continued*)

SEARCH STRING	MEANING	EXAMPLES OF MATCHES
*a	The letter *a* has to be the last character in the text string, and it doesn't matter what comes before the *a*.	A, LA, pizza
??a*	The letter *a* has to be the third character of the text string, and then it doesn't matter what comes after the *a*.	Crash, flat, tea
*a??	Anything could be before the letter *a*, but there has to be two characters after the letter *a*.	Any, many, rank, crash

For this example, I want to see the employees whose last name ends with the letters *son*.

Follow these steps:

1. Click the drop-down menu for the Row Labels or the Column Labels. For this example, click the drop-down menu for the Column Labels.

2. Click Label Filters. You will see the menu shown in Figure 4.20.

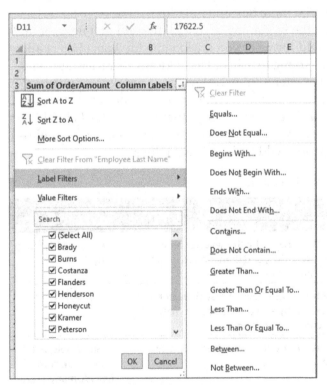

Figure 4.20: The Label Filters menu

3. Click Ends With. You will see the Label Filter dialog box, as shown in Figure 4.21.

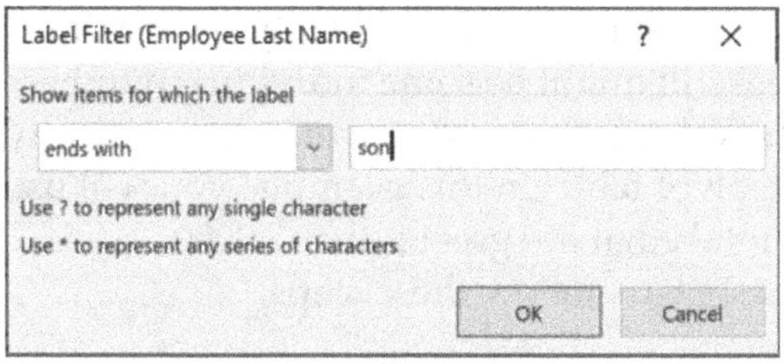

Figure 4.21: The Label Filter dialog box

4. Type **son** into the textbox on the right and click OK. As shown in Figure 4.22, the pivot table will now show the records for customers with a name ending in *son*, which is what you are looking for.

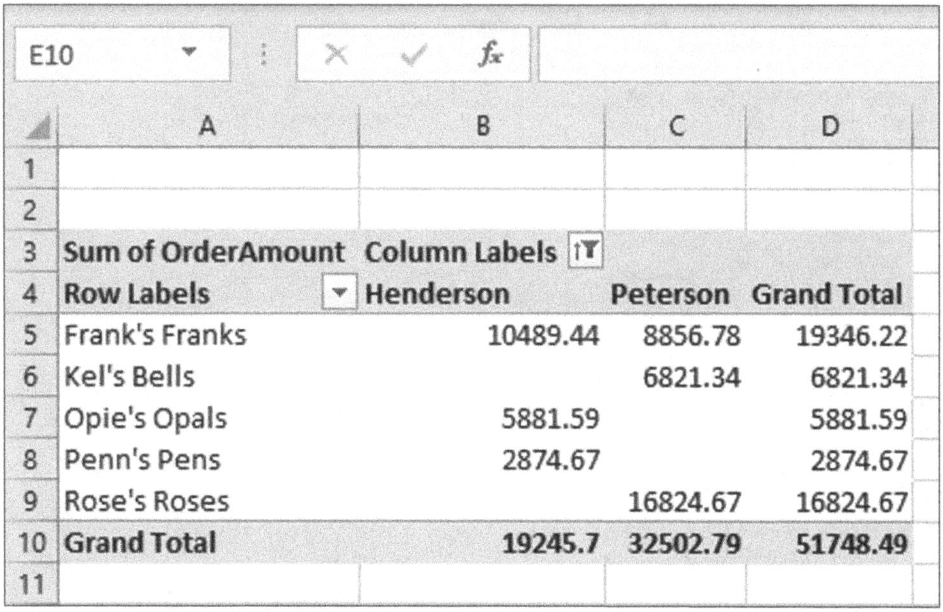

	A	B	C	D
1				
2				
3	**Sum of OrderAmount**	**Column Labels**		
4	**Row Labels**	**Henderson**	**Peterson**	**Grand Total**
5	Frank's Franks	10489.44	8856.78	19346.22
6	Kel's Bells		6821.34	6821.34
7	Opie's Opals	5881.59		5881.59
8	Penn's Pens	2874.67		2874.67
9	Rose's Roses		16824.67	16824.67
10	**Grand Total**	**19245.7**	**32502.79**	**51748.49**
11				

Figure 4.22: Pivot table filtered using Label Filters

You can again clear the filter by clicking the drop-down menu next to Column Labels and choose Clear Filter.

Value Filters

So far, the filters in this chapter have been on the row headers and the column headers of the pivot table. You can also filter on the values of the totals on the right side or at the bottom of the pivot table by using Value Filters.

The Value Filters section of the AutoFilter drop-down menu allows you to filter by the totals on the right side of each row and at the bottom of each column. For example, if you click Value Filters of the field header for the rows and used "greater than 5000" as the filter, the pivot table would show the rows that have a row total greater than 5000, but there still might be some individual numbers in that row that are less than 5000. The Value Filters option works the same way on the rows or on the columns of the pivot table. In this example, you will use Value Filters to show the rows with totals that are greater than 50000.

To filter the pivot table using Value Filters, follow these steps:

1. Click the drop-down menu for the Row Labels or the Column Labels. In this example, click the drop-down menu for the Row Labels.

2. Choose Value Filters. You will see the Value Filters menu, as shown in Figure 4.23.

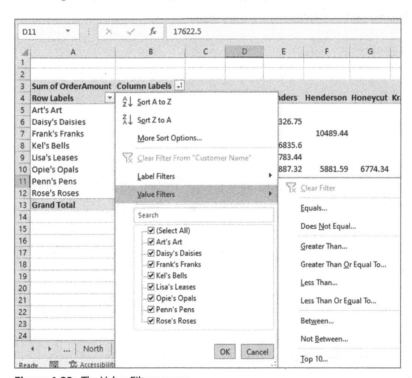

Figure 4.23: The Value Filters menu

3. Choose Greater Than. You will see the Value Filter dialog box, as shown in Figure 4.24.

4. Type **50000**, or the value you want.

5. Click OK. In the example, the pivot table will show only the rows where the row total is greater than 50000, as shown in Figure 4.25.

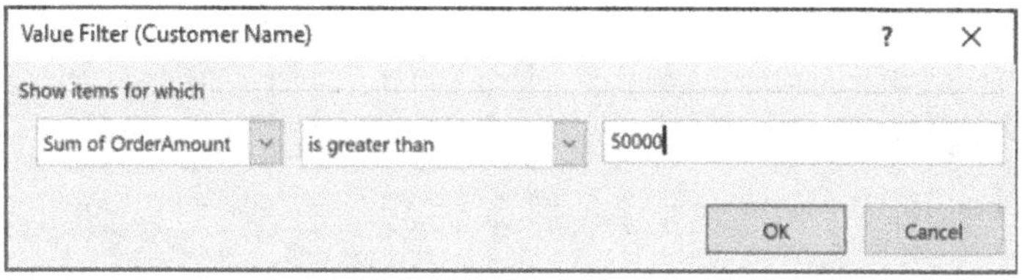

Figure 4.24: The Value Filter dialog box

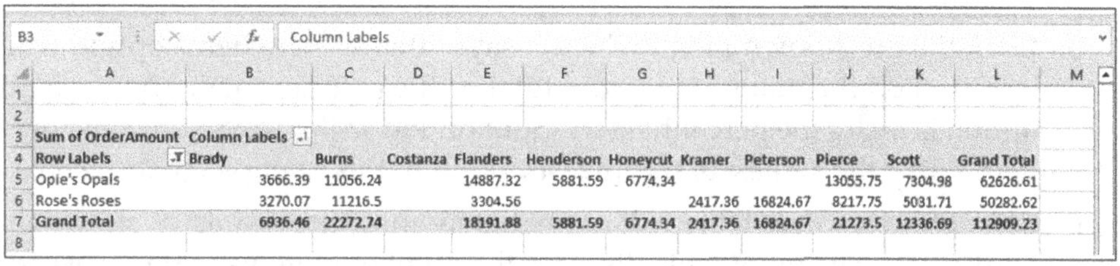

Figure 4.25: Pivot table filtered using Value Filters

You can again clear the filter by clicking the drop-down menu next to Row Labels and choose Clear Filter.

Top 10 Filters

The Value Filters provide numerous ways to filter the totals on the pivot table. An interesting choice on the Value Filters menu is Top 10, which allows you to choose how many rows or columns you want to see.

There will be times when you want the pivot table to show a specific number of results. For example, maybe you want to see the top three salespeople or the five least selling products or something similar. The Top 10 choice lets you pick the number of items that you want to display in the pivot table. Even though the option is called "Top 10," you will be able to pick either the lowest numbers or the highest numbers, and you will also be able to choose the number of rows or columns you want the pivot table to display. In this example, you want the pivot table to show the top three customers by the total sales on the right side of the pivot table.

To filter the pivot table using Top 10, follow these steps:

1. Right-click a column header or a row header in the pivot table. For this example, right-click cell A7.

2. Select Filter ⇨ Top 10. This will display the Top 10 Filter dialog box, as shown in Figure 4.26.

3. If you click the drop-down menu where it says "Top," you can choose Top or Bottom. For this example, choose Top.

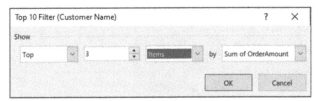

Figure 4.26: The Top 10 Filter dialog box

4. Use the spin button to choose the number of items you want to see. Choose 3.

5. Click the drop-down menu where it says "Items." The Items option will be based on the value in the row total or the column total. The Percent option is really the percentile. The Sum option will always show just one item, either the highest or the lowest value. For this example, choose Items.

6. Click OK. The pivot table will immediately show the results, as shown in Figure 4.27. The pivot table displays the number of items that you asked for, but the rows are probably not sorted. The filter and the sort are two different steps. Just sort the pivot table as needed, as demonstrated earlier in this chapter.

B3				✕ ✓ *fx*	Column Labels									
◢	A		B	C	D	E	F	G	H	I	J	K	L	M
1														
2														
3	Sum of OrderAmount	Column Labels ↴												
4	Row Labels	↴ Brady		Burns	Costanza	Flanders	Henderson	Honeycut	Kramer	Peterson	Pierce	Scott	Grand Total	
5	Opie's Opals		3666.39	11056.24		14887.32	5881.59	6774.34			13055.75	7304.98	62626.61	
6	Penn's Pens			5399.4	17622.5	10312.5	2874.67					8249.73	44458.8	
7	Rose's Roses		3270.07	11216.5		3304.56			2417.36	16824.67	8217.75	5031.71	50282.62	
8	Grand Total		6936.46	27672.14	17622.5	28504.38	8756.26	6774.34	2417.36	16824.67	21273.5	20586.42	157368.03	
9														

Figure 4.27: Pivot table filtered using a Top 10 filter

You can again clear the filter by clicking the drop-down menu next to Row Labels and choose Clear Filter.

The Value Filters are based on the row totals or the column totals, not on each individual number in the pivot table. There is an interesting way to filter on each individual number. Look at the "Filter on 1 number" sheet in the sample workbook. You could make a change to only include the items where the individual number shown on the pivot table is greater than 5000. On this sheet, you can make a Calculated Field with the following formula:

```
"If(OrderAmount<5000,0,OrderAmount)
```

This formula will show a zero if the number is less than 5000. Then, you can remove the original sum from the Values section of the PivotTable Fields window so the pivot table shows only the calculated field. It is showing only the numbers that are greater than or equal to 5000.

The interesting thing is that the row totals and column totals do not change. The row and column totals that the pivot table displays are the same for either the Calculated Field or the original sum. So, you can remove the Grand Totals using the Design tab and then just insert normal formulas for the row totals and column totals. If you look closely, the row totals and the column totals are outside of the pivot table. The sample sheet called "Filter on 1 number" shows the final results of these steps, and it includes the Calculated Field. This example comes from my years of IT experience—sometimes you have to get creative to show the results you want!

Date Filters

So far, I showed you how to filter the pivot table by the row or column headers and by the totals on the right side and the bottom of the pivot table. A pivot table can also be filtered by a date range if there is a date field in either the Rows section or the Columns section of the PivotTable Fields window by using Date Filters.

Obviously, the pivot table can be sorted and filtered in many ways. Another powerful feature of the pivot table is that the pivot table can summarize your data by second, minute, hours, date, month, quarter, year, or any combination of these time periods. Managing dates in the pivot table will be covered in Chapter 6, "Summarizing the Data by Date and Time." For the purposes of this chapter, when there is a date field in the Rows section or the Columns section of the PivotTable Fields window, you will also be able to filter the data on various date ranges using Date Filters. For this example, you can use the "Pivot Table with a date" sheet from the sample workbook. Let's make the pivot table show the data from January 1, 2023, to March 31, 2023, based on the OrderDate field.

To filter on a date field using Date Filters, follow these steps:

1. Click the drop-down menu next to the date field on the pivot table. For the sample data, click the drop-down menu next to the OrderDate field in cell B3 of the "Pivot Table with a date" sheet in the sample workbook.

2. Click Date Filters. You will see the menu shown in Figure 4.28. Notice the many different date ranges that are available. You will see even more choices if you hover your mouse on All Dates in the Period.

3. Select Between. You will see the Date Filter dialog box, as shown in Figure 4.29.

4. Click the first text box and type **1/1/2023**. You can also choose a date by clicking the calendar icon.

5. Enter **3/31/2023** into the second text box. You can also choose a date by clicking the calendar icon.

6. Click OK. The pivot table will now display only the data that has an OrderDate between the two dates you typed and including the two dates you typed, as shown in Figure 4.30.

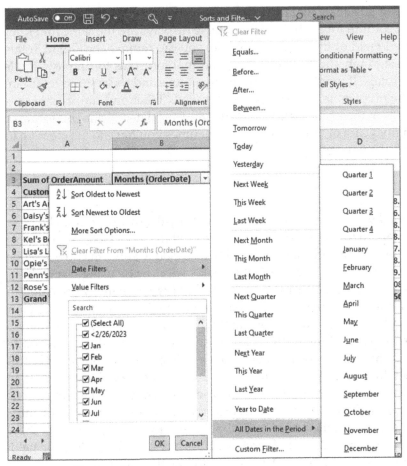

Figure 4.28: The Date Filters menu

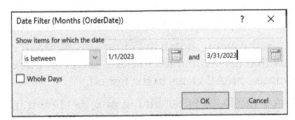

Figure 4.29: The Date Filter dialog box

Showing Items with No Data

If you used the sample data for the previous example, you will notice that January is not showing on the pivot table, even though the date range is between 1/1/2023 and 3/31/2023. That is because there are no records for January in the actual data. Sometimes you will want to display a column or a row in a pivot table even if it has no data. For this example, simply use the same sheet that you used in the previous example, either from the sample data or from your own sheet.

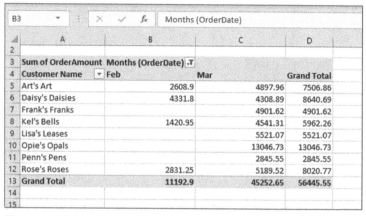

B3	▾	× ✓ *fx*	Months (OrderDate)	

▲	A	B	C	D
2				
3	Sum of OrderAmount	Months (OrderDate) .▼		
4	Customer Name ▾	Feb	Mar	Grand Total
5	Art's Art	2608.9	4897.96	7506.86
6	Daisy's Daisies	4331.8	4308.89	8640.69
7	Frank's Franks		4901.62	4901.62
8	Kel's Bells	1420.95	4541.31	5962.26
9	Lisa's Leases		5521.07	5521.07
10	Opie's Opals		13046.73	13046.73
11	Penn's Pens		2845.55	2845.55
12	Rose's Roses	2831.25	5189.52	8020.77
13	Grand Total	11192.9	45252.65	56445.55
14				
15				

Figure 4.30: Pivot table filtered using a Date Filter

To show items with no data, follow these steps:

1. Right-click a field name on the pivot table. If you are using the sample date, right-click cell b3, which should contain "Months (OrderDate)."

2. Choose Field Settings, which will display the Field Settings dialog box.

3. Click the Layout & Print tab, as shown in Figure 4.31.

Figure 4.31: Layout & Print tab of the Field Settings dialog box

4. Check Show Items With No Data and click Ok.

5. The pivot table will now show additional columns or rows, as shown in Figure 4.32.

B3		✕ ✓ ƒx	Months (OrderDate)					
	A	B	C	D	E	F		
3	Sum of OrderAmount	Months (OrderDate) .T						
4	Customer Name	<2/26/2023	Jan	Feb	Mar	Apr	May	
5	Art's Art				2608.9	4897.96		
6	Daisy's Daisies				4331.8	4308.89		
7	Frank's Franks					4901.62		
8	Kel's Bells				1420.95	4541.31		
9	Lisa's Leases					5521.07		
10	Opie's Opals					13046.73		
11	Penn's Pens					2845.55		
12	Rose's Roses				2831.25	5189.52		
13	Grand Total				11192.9	45252.65		

Figure 4.32: Pivot table showing items with no data

6. Use the AutoFilter to eliminate any rows or columns that you don't want to see.

Using the Filters Section

You have learned many ways to filter the rows and columns of the pivot table. Next, you'll see how to filter the overall pivot table using the Filters section of the PivotTable Fields window.

The examples that we've used in the book so far have explored the Rows section, the Columns section, and the Values section of the PivotTable Fields window. But we haven't used the Filters section of the PivotTable Fields window yet. The Filters section of the PivotTable Fields window provides another way to filter the pivot table, but at a higher level. Think about the larger grouping field used at your company or organization, such as product line, state, or country, for example. That's the type of field you would move into the Filters section of the PivotTable Fields window. For this example, we will use the Main Pivot Table sheet of the sample workbook. Let's say we wanted to use the Sales Division field in the Filters section and display the items from the East division.

To filter the pivot table using the Filters section of the PivotTable Fields window, follow these steps:

1. Drag the field you want to use for a filter to the Filters section. In this case, drag the Sales Division field into the Filters section of the PivotTable Fields window, as shown in Figure 4.33. Notice that after dragging the field to the Filters area, cell A1 in the pivot table contains "Sales Division," and cell B1 contains a drop-down menu.

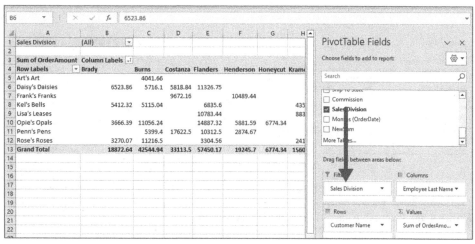

Figure 4.33: Moving a field into the Filters section

2. Click the drop-down menu for Sales Division in cell B1. You will see the options shown in Figure 4.34. On this menu, you can choose one value from the list, or you can click where it says "Select Multiple Items" so you can pick more than one to get different combinations of data.

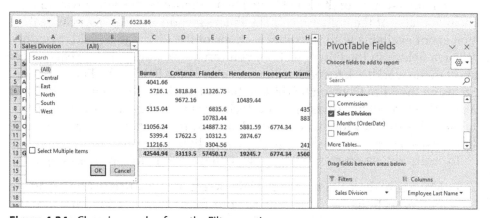

Figure 4.34: Choosing a value from the Filters section

3. Choose East and click OK. The pivot table now will show the records from the East division, as shown in Figure 4.35.

You can clear the filter by clicking the drop-down menu in cell B1 and clicking All followed by OK.

The Filters section can be used in conjunction with the other filters on the pivot table. The values of the field in the Filters section do not display on the pivot table, but the pivot table is still being filtered by that field.

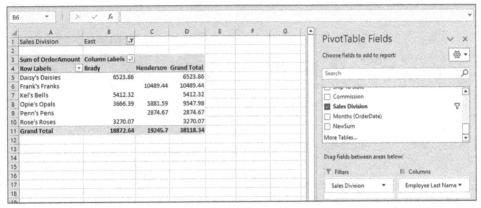

Figure 4.35: Pivot table filtered using the Filters section

Creating New Sheets from the Field in the Filters Section

From the previous example, the managers of each division want to see a report showing just their division. You could create each one individually using the drop-down menu in cell B1. But a more efficient way would be to make a separate sheet from the values of the fields in the Filters section.

The Filters section of the PivotTable Fields window gives you a way to filter the pivot table at the higher level. The Filters section also has a special feature that is not available with the other sections of the PivotTable Fields window. When a field is in the Filters section, you can quickly and easily create a new sheet in the workbook for each different value of the field in the Filters section. So, using the Sales Division field from the sample data, you could easily make a new sheet for all five divisions, and each sheet would have a pivot table containing only the data for that division. This feature can save you a great deal of time, instead of having to create each filter individually.

To create a sheet for each value in the Filters section, follow these steps:

1. Make sure there is a field in the Filters section. If there is not a field in the Filters section, then drag one of your fields from the field list into the Filters section of the PivotTable Fields window. For this example, the Sales Division field should be in the Filters section.

2. Select the PivotTable Analyze tab.

3. Click the drop-down menu to the right of the word *Options* on the left side of the ribbon and select Show Report Filter Pages. This will display the Show Report Filter Pages dialog box, as shown in Figure 4.36. If you had multiple fields listed, you would need to select the field you want to use to create the pages. In this case, there is only one field, Sales Division, which is already highlighted.

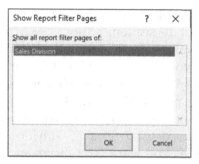

Figure 4.36: The Show Report Filter Pages dialog box

4. Click OK. You now see new sheets on the bottom of the screen, as shown in Figure 4.37. There is a new sheet for each different value of the field in the Filters section, and each sheet is a pivot table that shows only the data for that value.

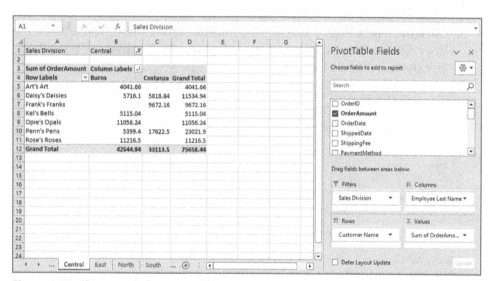

Figure 4.37: Sheets made from using Show Report Filter Pages

5. Click the Main Pivot Table sheet.

Using Slicers and Timelines

You've already been shown many ways to filter the pivot table. The filters in this chapter are all based on the fields in the different sections of the PivotTable Fields window. There will be situations when you want to filter the pivot table on fields that are not in any of the sections of the PivotTable Fields window.

Slicers and timelines will give you the flexibility to filter the pivot table on any field in the field list, whether the field is in one of the sections or not.

A slicer is a window that shows the different values of a field from the list of data that drives the pivot table. A slicer allows you to filter the pivot table on the field it displays, and it can come from any field from the list of fields on the PivotTable Fields window. A slicer also makes the pivot table more visual, more interactive, and more user-friendly. A timeline is a special type of slicer that works only with date fields, so the user can choose a date range using a timeline.

You can have as many slicers and timelines as you want. The slicers and timelines work in conjunction with the other filters already on the pivot table. For this example, use the Main Pivot Table sheet in the sample workbook. Let's add a slicer based on the Shipper field.

To add a slicer to the pivot table, follow these steps:

1. Click the pivot table.
2. Click the PivotTable Analyze tab.
3. Click the Insert Slicer icon near the middle of the ribbon. You will see the Insert Slicers dialog box, as shown in Figure 4.38. The Insert Slicers dialog box shows all fields in the field list.

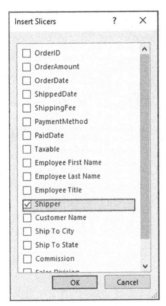

Figure 4.38: The Insert Slicers dialog box

4. Choose as many fields as you want. Choosing multiple fields for slicers allows you to filter on more combinations of your data. For this example, choose Shipper.
5. Click OK. This will display the slicer window for Shipper, as shown in Figure 4.39. You can move the slicer windows anywhere you want.

Figure 4.39: Slicer window for the Shipper field

6. Select an item on the slicer window to be used for a filter. The pivot table will immediately filter the data based on your selection from the slicer window.

If you want to pick more than one item from a slicer window, you can either click the check marks icon ( ) at the top of the slicer window or hold down the Ctrl key as you pick multiple items. The check marks icon toggles between being able to choose one item or multiple items from the slicer.

To clear the filter from the slicer, click the X icon ( ) in the top-right corner of the slicer window.

The appearance and functionality of the slicer can be managed in several ways. When you click a slicer window, the Slicer contextual tab will display on the right side of the tabs. If you right-click the slicer window and then click Slicer Settings, you will see the Slicer Settings dialog box shown in Figure 4.40.

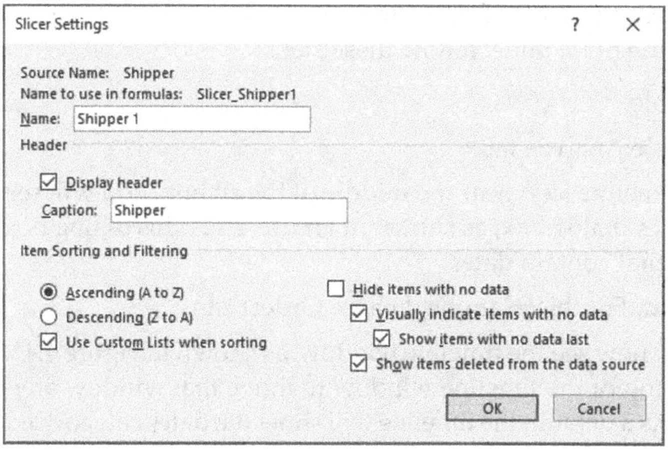

Figure 4.40: The Slicer Settings dialog box

You can find additional settings for the slicer by right-clicking the slicer and choosing Size and Properties, which will display the Format Slicer window shown in Figure 4.41.

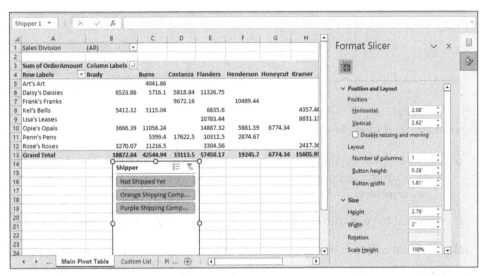

Figure 4.41: The Format Slicer window

Creating a Timeline

Slicers provide a very visual and interactive way to filter the pivot table. Slicers work with text fields, number fields, and date fields. Timelines, on the other hand, work only with date fields. You can use a timeline to display the data from specific years, months, quarters, or days, based on a date field. Using date fields in the pivot table will be discussed in detail in Chapter 6. Let's add a timeline that will allow you to display a specific month from the data. For this example, we will add a timeline based on the OrderDate field.

To add a timeline to the pivot table, follow these steps:

1. Click the pivot table.

2. Click the PivotTable Analyze tab.

3. Click the Insert Timeline icon near the middle of the ribbon. You will see the Insert Timelines dialog box, as shown in Figure 4.42. This dialog box lists all the fields that contain dates.

4. Choose a date field. For this example, I chose OrderDate.

5. Click OK. You will now see the timeline window, as shown in Figure 4.43. You can drag the top of the timeline window to move that window anywhere you want. As a default, the timeline will show the dates categorized

by month. You can scroll back and forth to see the full range of months reflected in the data.

Figure 4.42: The Insert Timelines dialog box

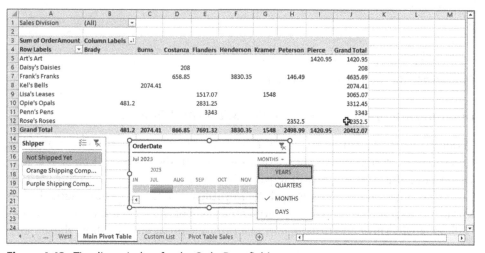

Figure 4.43: Timeline window for the OrderDate field

6. Click the drop-down menu to the right of the word *Months* on the right side of the timeline window. You can then make the timeline separate the dates by years, quarters, months, or days. Choose Months.

7. Click the space below the year, quarter, month, or day you want to see. The pivot table will immediately show the results of your choice. Note that the date range can be extended by dragging the sizing handles to the right or the left of the section you selected.

8. To clear the filter from the timeline, click the X icon () in the top-right corner of the timeline window.

The appearance and functionality of the timeline can be easily managed. When you click a timeline window, the Timeline contextual tab will be available. If you right-click the timeline window and then click Size and Properties, you will see the Format Timeline window shown in Figure 4.44.

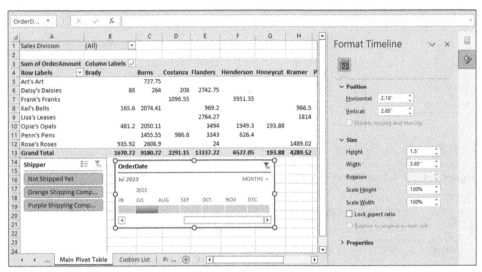

Figure 4.44: The Format Timeline window

Updating Multiple Pivot Tables Using Slicers and Timelines

When a slicer or a timeline is first added to a pivot table, the slicer and the timeline will change only one pivot table. In real life, there will be sheets and workbooks that contain multiple pivot tables. There is a quick technique that can make slicers and timelines update multiple pivot tables simultaneously. For this example, use the "Multiple Pivot Tables" sheet from the sample workbook.

To make the slicer and timeline update multiple pivot tables, follow these steps:

1. Right-click the slicer or the timeline window.

2. Click Report Connections. This will display the Report Connections dialog box, as shown in Figure 4.45. This dialog box displays the pivot tables on the sheets of the entire workbook. You can choose as many pivot tables as you want. For this example, I selected the two pivot tables on the "Multiple Pivot Tables" sheet from the sample workbook.

3. Click OK.

4. Repeat these steps for each slicer or timeline that you want to update multiple pivot tables.

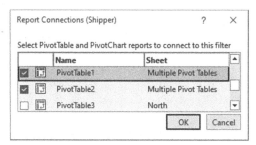

Figure 4.45: Report Connections dialog box

Now when you choose an item from the slicer or timeline, it will update the pivot tables you chose in the previous steps. Slicers and timelines will be discussed further in Chapter 6 and in Chapter 9, "Pulling It All Together - Creating a Dashboard from Your Pivot Tables."

Removing a Slicer or a Timeline Window

To remove a slicer or timeline window completely, click the top of the slicer window or the top of the timeline window so the window is selected, and press the Delete key on your keyboard. The slicer or the timeline window will no longer be on the screen, and the pivot table will no longer reflect the filter from the slicer or timeline that was closed.

Summary

In this chapter, you learned many ways to sort and filter the pivot table, so the pivot table displays the exact data you want to see, in the way you want to see it. You also learned how to add slicers and timelines to the pivot table to make the pivot table more interactive. In the next chapter, you will learn how to visualize the pivot table with charts.

Making the Pivot Table More Visual with Charts

At the end of Chapter 4, "Sorting and Filtering the Pivot Table," we added slicers and timelines to a pivot table to make it more visual and interactive. Another great way to help visualize the pivot table is by representing the pivot table with a chart. One of Excel's great features is the ability to create a chart from a range of data. A chart can also come from a pivot table.

There's the old saying, "A picture is worth a thousand words." In Excel, a chart can tell the story of the data much quicker than analyzing the data itself. In this chapter, you will learn how to create a chart from a pivot table, how to manage the chart, and how to make the chart look better. It will also cover other popular topics about charts. A chart that comes from a pivot table is also called a PivotChart, so the terms *chart* and *PivotChart* will be used interchangeably in this chapter.

When a chart comes from a pivot table, the pivot table is the data source for the chart. If the pivot table changes, the chart will change, and if the chart changes, the pivot table will change. They are linked to each other. A pivot table can have as many charts as you need. Even if you move a chart for a pivot table to a different sheet, the pivot table and the chart are still linked to each other; if one changes, the other also changes.

In this chapter, you will learn how to create a column chart, a pie chart, and a combo chart, all with a pivot table as the source. The other Excel chart types that are not specifically discussed in this chapter work in similar ways.

Creating a Chart from a Pivot Table

Creating a chart from a pivot table is like creating a chart with a range of data, but there are some differences. For example, the following chart types are not available when you create the chart from a pivot table: X Y (Scatter), Map, Stock, Funnel, Treemap, Sunburst, Histogram, Box & Whisker, and Waterfall. Another difference is that once the chart is created from a pivot table, you will not be able to change the data source of the chart like you can with a chart that was created from data that is not within a pivot table. In this example, we will create a column chart.

NOTE For the examples presented in this section of the chapter, you can use the sample file called *Charts.xlsx* that is included with this book. You can find the sample files at www.wiley.com/go/GGRXL_PivotTables. Most sections of this part of the chapter will use the Main Pivot Table sheet. If other sheets are needed, it will be noted in the steps for each section of the chapter.

To create a column chart from a pivot table, follow these steps:

1. Click a pivot table. If you are using the sample data, click the pivot table on the Main Pivot Table sheet of the sample workbook.

2. Select the PivotTable Analyze tab.

3. Click the PivotChart icon on the right side of the ribbon. You will see the Insert Chart dialog box, as shown in Figure 5.1. When you choose a chart type on the left side of the dialog box, you will see different variations of that chart type at the top of the dialog box, if that chart type is available for charts that come from pivot tables.

4. Choose the chart type and the variation that you want, and click OK. For this example, choose the Column category on the left and the first variation at the top. You will now see the chart shown in Figure 5.2.

5. Move or resize the chart window as necessary.

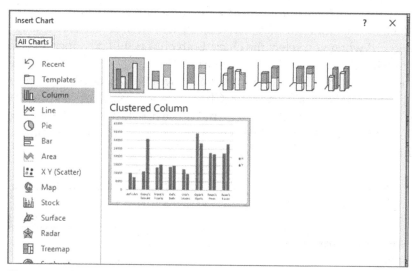

Figure 5.1: The Insert Chart dialog box

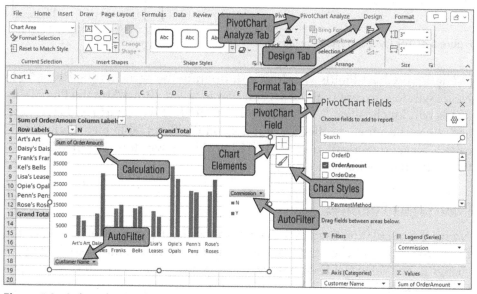

Figure 5.2: A chart that is selected

As shown in Figure 5.2, when the chart is selected, you will see the Design tab and the Format tab on the right side of the ribbon. You will also see two icons, a plus sign and a paintbrush, on either the left or the right of the chart. The plus sign icon is called Chart Elements, and the paintbrush icon is called

Chart Styles. Additionally, when the chart is selected, the tab that is usually named PivotTable Analyze will now be named PivotChart Analyze, and the window on the right that is usually called PivotTable Fields will now be called PivotChart Fields. The names of these two objects will change when you select the pivot table and when you select the chart. Both objects will disappear if you select a cell outside the pivot table or the chart.

Most of the icons on the PivotTable Analyze tab will be identical to the icons on the PivotChart Analyze tab. The PivotChart Analyze tab does include the Move Chart icon and the Field Buttons icon. Figure 5.3 shows the PivotTable Analyze tab, and Figure 5.4 shows the PivotChart Analyze tab. The differences are highlighted.

Figure 5.3: The PivotTable Analyze tab

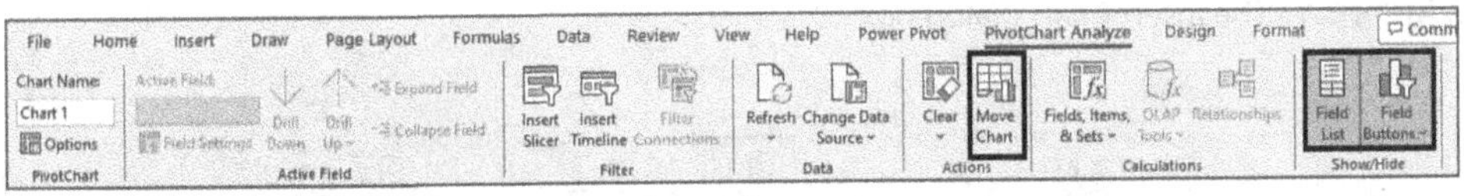

Figure 5.4: The PivotChart Analyze tab

The PivotChart Fields window will operate the same as the PivotTable Fields window, except that the section that is called "Rows" on the PivotTable Fields window is called "Axis (Categories)" on the PivotChart Fields window, and the section that is called "Columns" on the PivotTable Fields window is called "Legend (Series)" on the PivotChart Fields window. Figure 5.5 shows the PivotChart Fields window.

PivotChart Features

Notice the calculation used in the chart is shown in the upper-left corner of the chart. You can right-click this calculation and then click Value Field Settings to change it. The Value Field Settings are discussed in Chapter 3, "Using Calculations in Pivot Tables."

You can sort and filter the chart by using the AutoFilter drop-down menus that appear on the chart. Figure 5.6 displays the menu for the Customer Name filter in the example.

If you sort or filter the chart, the pivot table will also be sorted and filtered, and if you sort or filter the pivot table, the chart will also be sorted and filtered. You can read more about sorts and filters in Chapter 4, "Sorting and Filtering the

Pivot Table." Slicers and timelines also work with a chart, and you will learn how to coordinate slicers, timelines, charts, and other objects in Chapter 9, "Pulling It All Together - Creating a Dashboard from Your Pivot Tables."

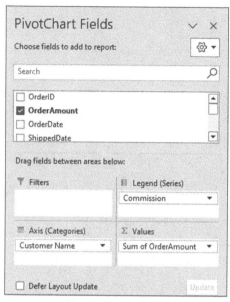

Figure 5.5: The PivotChart Fields window

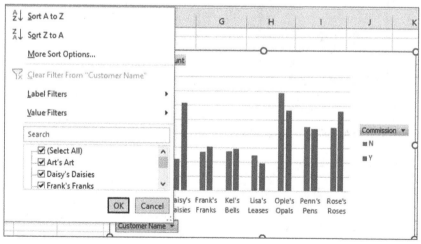

Figure 5.6: Using AutoFilters to sort and filter the chart

One important icon that appears on the right side of the PivotChart Analyze tab is Field Buttons. This icon allows you to turn on or turn off the filters and the values on the chart. If you click the Field Buttons icon, it will toggle

all of the filters either on or off. Figure 5.7 shows a chart with all filters on, and Figure 5.8 shows a chart with all filters off. You can also turn the filters on and off individually by clicking the drop-down menu on the Field Buttons icon of the PivotChart Analyze tab, as shown in Figure 5.9.

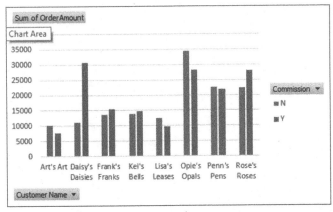

Figure 5.7: A chart with AutoFilters turned on

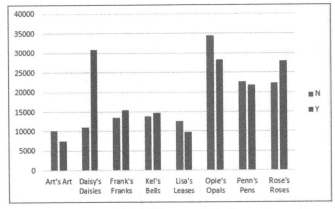

Figure 5.8: A chart with AutoFilters turned off

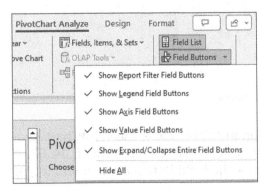

Figure 5.9: The menu for the Field Buttons icon on the PivotChart Analyze tab

The Design Tab and the Format Tab for a Chart

The Design tab that appears when you click the chart is the same as the Chart Design tab that you would see when you select a chart that does not come from a pivot table. The Design tab is used to add components to the chart, to manage the chart, and to change the appearance of the overall chart. The Add Chart Element icon on the left side of the Design tab is where you add, change, or delete chart components. You can find the same choices by clicking the Chart Elements icon that is to the left or the right of the chart. You will learn to manage the chart elements later in this chapter.

The Quick Layout icon displays preset combinations of different chart elements, as shown in Figure 5.10. If you select the Quick Layout icon and move your mouse to the different layouts, the chart will preview your choice. Select an option to apply a layout to the chart.

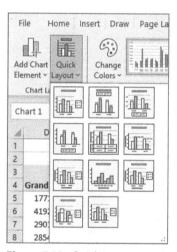

Figure 5.10: Quick Layouts on the Design tab

The Change Colors icon allows you to quickly change the color scheme of the chart. If you select the Change Colors icon and move your mouse to the different colors, the chart will preview your choice. Select an option to apply the color scheme to the chart.

The Chart Styles group in the middle of the Design tab shows preset formats for the chart. These can also be found when you click the Chart Styles icon to the left or the right of the chart. When you hover the mouse over one of the chart styles, you will be able to see what that style looks like on your chart. Click one of the chart styles to apply it to the chart.

The Switch Row/Column icon toggles between two different views of the data. It changes the chart so that the data that is currently displayed in the x-axis displays on the legend, and what is displayed in the legend displays as the x-axis. In addition, this will transpose the pivot table so that what used to be in the Rows section of the PivotTable Fields window will show up in the Columns section, and vice versa. Figure 5.11 shows the chart and pivot table before you click the Switch Row/Column icon, and Figure 5.12 shows the chart and pivot table after you click the Switch Row/Column icon.

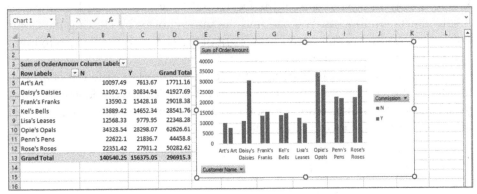

Figure 5.11: A chart before using Switch Row/Column

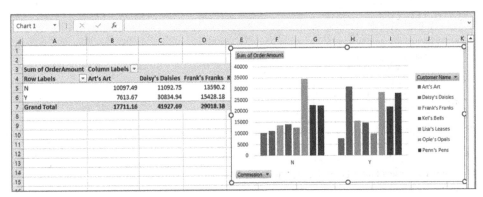

Figure 5.12: A chart after using Switch Row/Column

The Select Data icon would usually allow you to select a different data range for a chart. But since a chart that comes from a pivot table does not allow you to choose a different range, this icon is mostly ineffective.

The Change Chart Type icon allows you to quickly change the chart type. This presents the same dialog box you saw earlier in Figure 5.1.

The Move Chart icon allows you to move the chart to an existing sheet or to a new sheet. Even if the chart gets moved to a different sheet, it will still change as the pivot table changes, and vice versa.

The Format tab that appears when you click the chart has the same options as the Format tab that you would see when you select a chart that does not come from a pivot table. The Format tab is used to change the appearance of each individual component of the chart. Figure 5.13 shows the Format tab.

If you double-click any part of the chart, you will get the Format window on the right side of the screen, as shown in Figure 5.14. The Format window will provide even more formatting options than the Format tab. The Format window will vary depending on where you double-clicked the chart. Close the Format window for now. Some specific examples of using the Format window will be shown later in this chapter.

Figure 5.13: The Format tab for charts

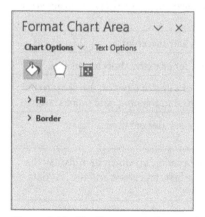

Figure 5.14: The Format window on the right

You've already been introduced to some possibilities of changing the chart by using the PivotChart Analyze tab, the Design tab, the Format tab, the AutoFilters on the chart, the Chart Elements icon, the Chart Styles icon, the PivotChart Fields window, and the Format window that appears when you double-click the chart. Next, we will explore some specific ways to manage and change the chart.

Managing and Modifying Chart Elements

As you share pivot tables and charts with other people, you may have to change the appearance of the chart. The charts are very flexible and can be customized in many ways. You may want to change the number formats, add more chart elements, or change just about anything on the chart.

Chart elements can be added to the chart, removed from the chart, or modified. Table 5.1 lists the chart elements.

Table 5.1: Chart elements

CHART ELEMENT	DESCRIPTION
Axes	Makes the y-axis on the left and x-axis on the bottom of the chart appear or disappear.
Axis Titles	The horizontal title will be at the bottom of the chart, and the vertical title will be on the left of the chart.
Chart Title	The title at the top of the chart.
Data Labels	The numbers on each bar or series on the chart.
Data Table	The numbers below the chart.
Error Bars	Can show the standard error amount, a percentage, or a standard deviation, or you can set your own values to display the exact error amounts you want.
Gridlines	The horizontal and vertical lines within a chart.
Legend	Color coded to show what each series in the chart represents.
Lines	Drop lines extend from the top of a line or a bar on the chart to help clarify where one data point ends and the next data point starts.
Trendline	A trendline shows that values for a series are increasing or decreasing at a certain rate.
Up/Down Bars	Used in charts with multiple data series, up-down bars display the difference between values in the first data series and the last data series.

Most of the chart elements are labeled in Figure 5.15, which is derived from the ChartElements sheet in the sample workbook. Not every chart element will be available for every chart type.

Let's add some of the most popular chart elements to the chart. Remember, you can find the Chart Elements either by clicking the Design tab and choosing the Add Chart Element icon on the left side of the ribbon or by clicking the Chart Elements icon to the left or the right of the chart.

The Chart Title

The chart title will usually appear at the top of the chart. If your chart already has a chart title, you can just click it, and type over it to change the chart title. If your chart does not have a chart title, it is easy to add a chart title to a chart.

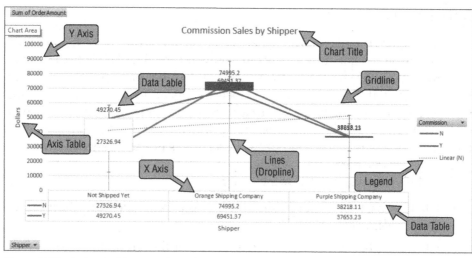

Figure 5.15: A chart with some chart elements

To add a chart title, follow these steps:

1. Select the chart.
2. Click the Chart Elements icon to the right or left of the chart.
3. Check Chart Title.
4. Click the Chart Elements icon or click away from the chart to close the Chart Elements menu.
5. Select on the Chart Title, type what you want for the title, and press Enter to change the chart title, as shown in Figure 5.16. In this case, the title has been changed to "Commission Sales By Customer."

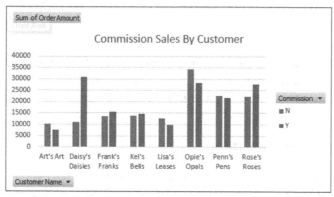

Figure 5.16: A chart with a chart title

Data Labels

One of the more popular chart elements is data labels, which are the numbers that appear on the bars of the chart. If you want the data labels to appear on all of the bars of the chart, click the background of the chart so that none of the bars is selected. If you want the data labels to appear on just one series within the chart, click a single bar. The other bars of the same color should also be selected. If you want the data labels to appear on just one singular bar, click the bar you want, wait a second or two, click that same bar a second time, and then only that one bar will be selected.

To add the data labels, follow these steps:

1. Click a chart. If you are using the sample data, click the chart on the DataLabels sheet.

2. Click the Chart Elements icon to the right or the left of the chart.

3. Check Data Labels. Move your mouse to the right of Data Labels and click the arrow to see other options, as shown in Figure 5.17. If you hover your mouse on each choice, the chart will preview that choice. Choose the option you want. For this example, choose Outside End.

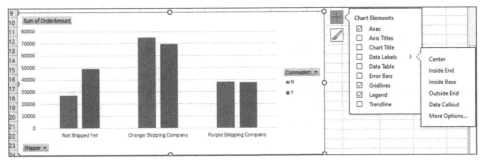

Figure 5.17: Data Label options

4. Click the Charts Elements icon or click away from the chart to close the Chart Elements menu. You will now see the data labels on some or all of the bars or sections of the chart, as shown in Figure 5.18.

Changing the Number Format of the Data Labels

As a default, the data labels will have the same number format as the corresponding numbers from the pivot table. The appearance of the data labels can be changed in many ways. You may want to change the number format of the data labels or the number of decimal places that display with the data labels. In this example, let's make the numbers show as currency format with zero decimal places.

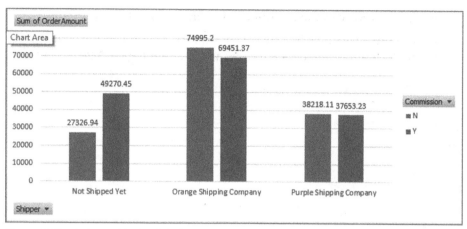

Figure 5.18: A chart with data labels

To change the number format of the data labels, follow these steps:

1. Click away from the chart.

2. Double-click one of the numbers of the data labels. You will now see the Format Data Labels window, as shown in Figure 5.19.

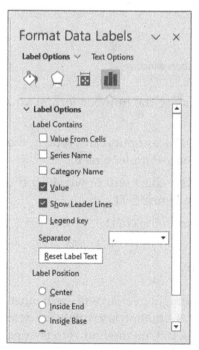

Figure 5.19: The Format Data Labels window

3. Scroll all the way to the bottom of the Format Data Labels window.

4. Click the arrow to the left of the word *Number* and scroll down even further on the Format Data Labels window, as shown in Figure 5.20.

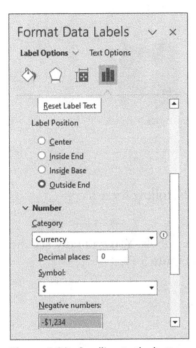

Figure 5.20: Scrolling to the bottom of the Format Data Labels window

5. Click the Category drop-down menu. Choose the number format you want. For this example, choose Currency.

6. Click the space to the right of the Decimal Places option and type in the number of decimal places you want. For this example, type **0**.

7. Close the Format Data Labels window. The chart will now reflect the number format that you chose as shown in Figure 5.21.

8. Repeat steps 1 through 7 for the other series in the chart.

Changing the Data Labels to Display Vertically

If there are many bars on the chart, the data labels might overlap with each other, making the chart look messy. A good way to fix this situation is to rotate the data labels. There are two ways to rotate the data labels. One method is to change the chart style, and another is to change the text direction of the data labels.

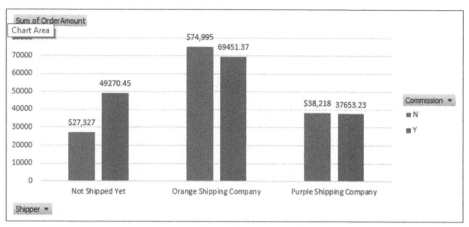

Figure 5.21: A chart with currency data labels

To make the data labels vertical by changing the chart style, click the Chart Styles icon to the right or the left of the chart, and choose the second style from the top, as shown in Figure 5.22. Click away from the chart to close the Chart Styles menu.

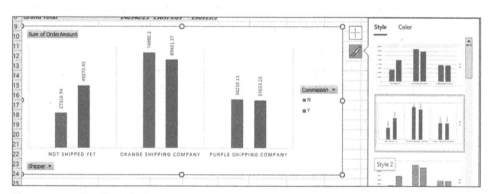

Figure 5.22: The Chart Styles menu

The data labels should now be vertical, as shown in Figure 5.23.

When you change the chart style, other changes might have happened to the chart at the same time. Notice that the data labels are no longer in currency format, for example. The chart styles are preset formats. Click the Chart Styles icon and choose the first chart style to put the chart back the way it was. You can also use the Undo command to go back to the way it was before. Instead of changing the chart style, you may prefer to change the text direction of the data label without changing anything else about the chart.

Figure 5.23: The chart displaying the second chart style

To change the text direction of the data labels, follow these steps:

1. Click away from the chart.

2. Double-click one of the numbers of the data labels. You should now see the Format Data Labels window on the right side of the screen.

3. Click the Size & Properties icon near the top of the Format Data Labels window. This should be the third icon from the left.

4. Expand the Alignment option.

5. Click the drop-down menu next to Text direction. You will see the menu shown in Figure 5.24.

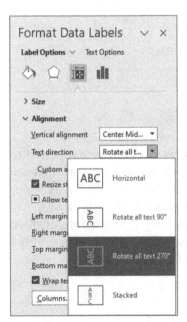

Figure 5.24: Changing the text direction

6. Choose the option you want. For this example, choose Rotate All Text 270°. The chart will immediately reflect your choice, as shown in Figure 5.25.

7. Close the Format Data Labels window.

8. Repeat steps 1 through 7 for the other series in the chart.

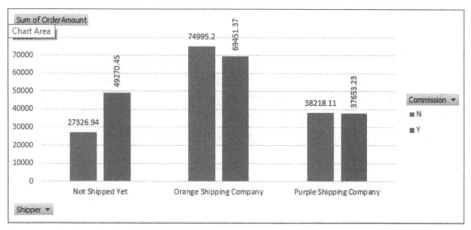

Figure 5.25: The chart showing rotated data labels

Trendlines

Another popular chart element is the trendline. A trendline will show whether chart values are going up, down, or remaining relatively consistent. An existing trendline can also be extended to show where the data might go in the future, based on the existing values. A trendline is not available on the following chart types: Pie, Area, Surface, and Radar. The trendline will be relatively vertical for Bar charts, and relatively horizontal for Column, Line, and Combo charts.

Adding a Trendline to a Chart

For this example, you can use the chart on the Trendline sheet of the sample workbook or any chart in your own workbooks. Notice how each row in the pivot table on the Trendline sheet shows a different month. This topic will be discussed in Chapter 6, "Summarizing the Data by Date and Time."

To add a trendline, follow these steps:

1. Click a chart. If you are using the sample data, click the chart on the Trendline sheet.

2. Click the Chart Elements icon to the right or the left of the chart to open the Chart Elements menu.

3. Check the Trendline option. You will see the Add Trendline dialog box, as shown in Figure 5.26.

Figure 5.26: The Add Trendline dialog box

4. Choose the series that you want. Each series can have its own trendline to be added separately using these steps. If you are using the sample data, choose Orange Shipping Company.

5. Click OK. The chart will now show the trendline, as shown in Figure 5.27.

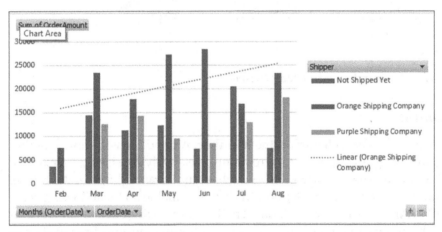

Figure 5.27: A chart with a trendline

6. If you move your mouse to the right of the Trendline option on the Chart Elements menu and click the arrow, you will see a list of different trendline types, as shown in Figure 5.28.

7. If you hover your mouse on each different trendline type, the chart will preview your choice. Choose the one you want.

8. Close the Chart Elements menu by clicking away from the chart.

Creating a Forecast from a Trendline

A trendline can show a forecast into the future. The forecast is based on the current values of the chart and provides only a general idea of where the data might be headed. Of course, in real life, anything can happen that could affect the actual future values of the data.

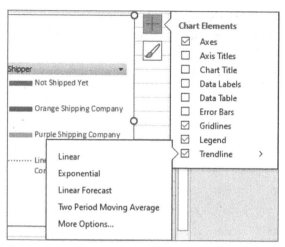

Figure 5.28: Trendline types

To show a forecast for the trendline, follow these steps:

1. Click away from the chart.

2. Double-click a trendline. The Format Trendline window will appear on the right side of the screen, as shown in Figure 5.29.

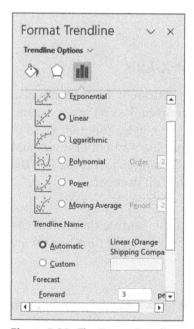

Figure 5.29: The Format Trendline window

3. Scroll down in the Format Trendline window.

4. Change the number to the right of Forward. This is the number of periods that you want to forecast. If you are using the sample data, type **3**.

5. Close the Format Trendline window. The trendline on the chart will now display the forecast, as shown in Figure 5.30.

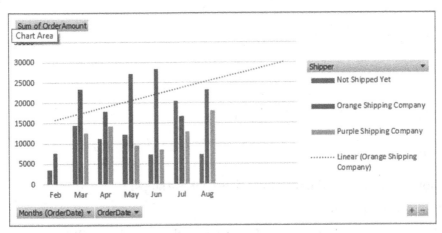

Figure 5.30: A chart with a trendline with a forecast

To remove the trendline, simply click the trendline and press the Delete key on the keyboard.

Formatting the Numbers of the Y-Axis or X-Axis

The numbers on the left side of the chart or on the bottom of the chart can also be formatted. The numbers on the left side of the chart make up the y-axis, and the numbers at the bottom of the chart make up the x-axis. You may want to reduce the number of decimal places or even reduce the number of digits that display for larger numbers. In this example, we will change the numbers on the y-axis to show as thousands instead of showing the full number.

To format the numbers on the y-axis, follow these steps:

1. Click a sheet with a chart. If you are using the sample data, click the ByShipper sheet of the sample workbook. Notice how the numbers on the left side of the chart show the full numbers.

2. Click away from the chart.

3. Double-click one of the numbers on the left of the chart. This will open the Format Axis window on the right side of the screen.

4. Click the drop-down menu next to Display Units, as shown in Figure 5.31.

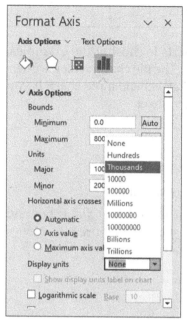

Figure 5.31: Changing the display units

5. Choose the option you want. For this example, choose Thousands. The chart will immediately show the results, as shown in Figure 5.32. Notice how the data labels changed as well.

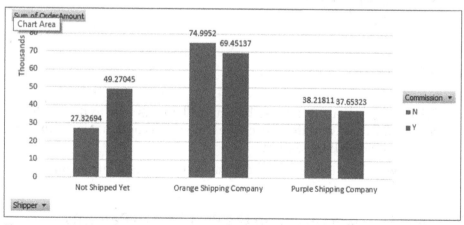

Figure 5.32: A chart showing thousands in the y-axis

6. Close the Format Axis window.

Creating and Managing a Pie Chart

So far in this chapter, you have seen column charts in most of the examples. Another popular chart type is the classic pie chart. The pie chart has some interesting features that are unique to the pie chart. Let's create a pie chart. If you are using the sample data, you can use the ByState sheet.

To create a pie chart, follow these steps:

1. Click the pivot table.
2. Click the PivotTable Analyze tab.
3. Select the PivotChart icon on the right side of the ribbon.
4. Choose the Pie category on the left side of the Insert Chart dialog box and click OK. You will now see the pie chart, as shown in Figure 5.33. Notice how the data labels are not on the pie chart.

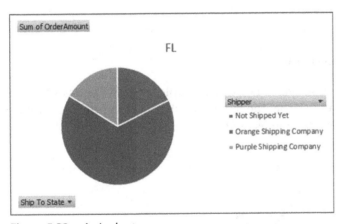

Figure 5.33:   A pie chart

5. Select the pie chart and click the Chart Elements icon to the left or the right of the chart, and then check the Data Labels option. Notice the data labels display in the pie chart.
6. Click away from the pie chart to close the Chart Elements menu.

Changing the Data Labels on the Pie Chart to Percents

Notice how the data labels on the pie chart show the actual numbers from the pivot table. Many people prefer to show percents on a pie chart, instead of the actual numbers. Let's change the numbers on the pie chart to show as percents.

To show the data labels as percents, follow these steps:

1. Click away from the chart.

2. Double-click a number on the pie chart. This will display the Format Data Labels window on the right side of the screen, as shown in Figure 5.34.

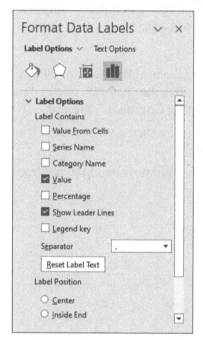

Figure 5.34: The Format Data Labels window

3. Uncheck Value, and check Percentage.

4. Close the Format Data Labels window. You will now see the data labels display as percents, as shown in Figure 5.35.

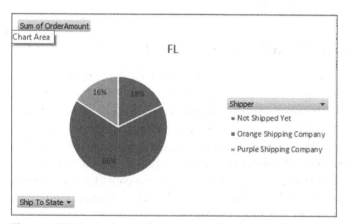

Figure 5.35: A pie chart with percents as data labels

Separating a Section from a Pie Chart

There will be times when you want to draw attention to one particular section of the pie chart. Each section of the pie chart is called a *slice*, like a real pie. Any slice can be separated from the other slices. If you are using the sample data, we will separate the slice representing the "Purple Shipping Company" shipper.

To separate a slice from a pie chart, follow these steps:

1. Click away from the chart.

2. Click a slice of the pie chart without selecting the numbers within the slice. If you are using the sample data, click the slice that has 16% as the data label. This is the slice for the "Purple Shipping Company" shipper.

3. Pause a second or two, and then click the same slice a second time. The slice should now be the only slice that is selected.

4. Drag the slice away from the pie. The slice should now be separated from the pie, as shown in Figure 5.36.

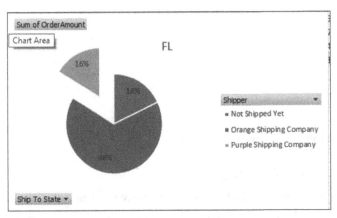

Figure 5.36: A pie chart with a separated slice

Changing the Pie Chart to a Doughnut Chart

Notice how the pie chart displays only the first column of data from the pivot table. The pie chart in the sample data shows only the data for "FL," for example. If the pivot table contains more than one column of data, you can move the columns so that the column that you want the pie chart to display is the first column of values in the pivot table. To move the columns, see Chapter 4, "Sorting and Filtering the Pivot Table." If you really want to display all columns from the pivot table at the same time, you can change the pie chart to a doughnut chart or just create a doughnut chart instead of a pie chart. A doughnut chart can display data from multiple columns of a pivot table.

To change the pie chart to a doughnut chart, follow these steps:

1. Select the pie chart.
2. Click the Design tab.
3. Select the Change Chart Type icon on the right side of the ribbon.
4. Select the Pie category on the left and click the Doughnut chart variation on the top right of the dialog box. Click OK. You will now see the doughnut chart, as shown in Figure 5.37.

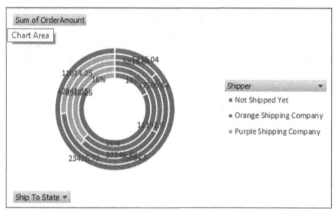

Figure 5.37: A doughnut chart

The doughnut chart displays data from multiple columns of the pivot table. The innermost ring of the doughnut chart represents the leftmost column of values from the pivot table, and the outermost ring represents the rightmost column of data from the pivot table. While the doughnut chart does show all the columns of data from the pivot table, obviously you will have to spend some time formatting the doughnut chart so that it looks better. Ideally, this chapter gave you some ideas on how to format the chart.

Creating a Combo Chart

Another popular chart type is the combo chart. A combo chart can show multiple chart types within the same chart. A good example of a combo chart would be a chart that shows a column chart and a line chart in the same chart, but other combinations of chart types can be displayed in a combo chart as well. The second chart type of the column chart will usually display on a second y-axis, which would display on the right side of the chart. A combo chart can be used to represent two ranges of values from the pivot table. In this example, you can use your own pivot table, or you can use the sheet named Combo from the sample workbook.

NOTE   A combo chart used to be called a "2-Axis" chart in previous versions of Excel.

To create a combo chart, follow these steps:

1. Select a pivot table. If you are using the sample data, select the pivot table on the Combo sheet.

2. Click the PivotTable Analyze tab.

3. Select the PivotChart icon on the right side of the ribbon.

4. Choose the Combo icon on the bottom left of the Insert Chart dialog box. The Insert Chart dialog box will now change, as shown in Figure 5.38.

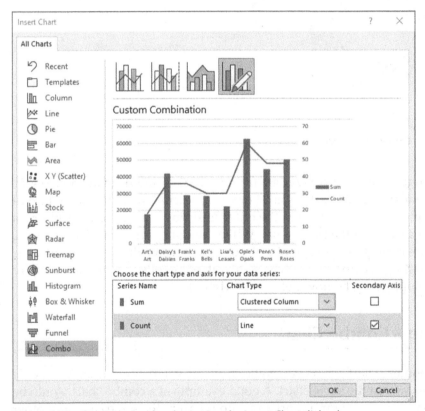

Figure 5.38: Creating a combo chart using the Insert Chart dialog box

5. Click the drop-down menu for the first series, and choose the first chart in the Column category, which is the Clustered Column chart.

6. Click the drop-down menu for the second series, and choose the first chart in the Line category, which is the Line chart.

7. Check the Secondary Axis box to the right of the second series. This will display the second series on the second y-axis on the right of the chart.

8. Click OK. You will now see the combo chart, as shown in Figure 5.39. Notice how the line is actually on the second y-axis on the right of the chart.

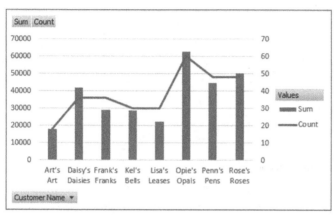

Figure 5.39: A combo chart

Creating and Using Chart Templates

As you continue to create charts, you could be creating charts that are similar to charts that you have created in the past for other pivot tables. Instead of creating charts from scratch each time, you can create chart templates for the charts that you use repeatedly. The chart templates will allow you to make similar charts in the future without having to reinvent the wheel each time. Creating and using chart templates can save you time when you make similar charts from pivot tables going forward. In this example, the combo chart will be used to create a chart template. If you are using the sample data, select the CustomerSumandCount sheet, which has a combo chart with many of the formatting features that were discussed in this chapter.

To create a chart template, follow these steps:

1. Right-click a chart. If you are using the sample data, right-click the chart on the CustomerSumandCount sheet.

2. Click Save As Template. You will now see the Save Chart Template dialog box, as shown in Figure 5.40. Your window will show different chart templates or might show no templates at all.

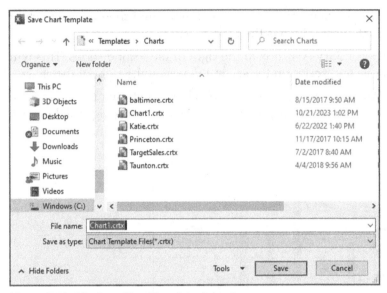

Figure 5.40: The Save Chart Template dialog box

3. In the Save Chart Template dialog box, **do not** change the folder name at the top of the dialog box. This is where Excel will search for the templates when you want to reuse them.

4. Give the template a specific file name and click Save. You can have as many chart templates as you need. The chart templates can be used for any chart you create on any workbook from that point forward, even for charts that do not come from a pivot table.

To create a chart using a chart template, follow these steps:

1. Select a pivot table. If you are using the sample data, select the pivot table on the EmployeeSumandCount sheet.

2. Click the PivotTable Analyze tab.

3. Select the PivotChart icon on the right side of the window.

4. Click the Templates icon on the top left of the Insert Chart dialog box. You will now see the available templates, as shown in Figure 5.41. The available templates that you see will differ from what is shown here.

5. Choose the template you want, and click OK. You will now see the chart, and it will have the same format and the same chart elements of the template you chose, as shown in Figure 5.42. The template gave you a great head start in creating a chart.

6. Modify the chart as needed.

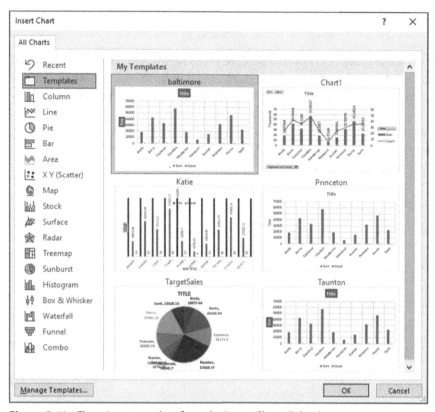

Figure 5.41: Choosing a template from the Insert Chart dialog box

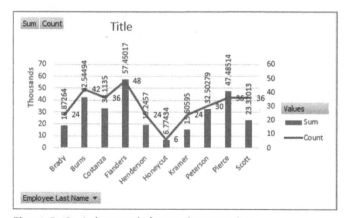

Figure 5.42: A chart made from a chart template

Summary

In this chapter, you learned how to visualize pivot tables with charts. You learned how to create a column chart, a pie chart, and a combo chart; how to change the format of the chart; how to add, change, or delete chart elements; and how to create and use chart templates.

In the next chapter, you will learn how to summarize the pivot table by second, minute, hour, date, month, quarter, and year, and you will learn other ways to show date ranges in the pivot table.

CHAPTER

6

Summarizing Data by Date and Time

So far, the pivot tables in this book have summarized the data by one or two columns, maybe by employee, employee by department, or something similar. One of the great uses of a pivot table is to be able to summarize the data by second, minute, hour, date, month, quarter, or year, or any combination of these. Maybe you'd like to summarize your employee data by month, your state data by year, or any of your data by any other time period. This chapter will show you how you can summarize your data using date and time fields.

Obviously, to sort by date and time, at least one of the fields in your data must be a date/time data type. If necessary, see Chapter 1, "Preparing the Data for an Excel Pivot Table," to convert a column to a date/time data type, if necessary.

Some date/time fields contain only a date, some contain only a time, and some contain both the date and the time. The examples in this chapter using date periods will work with date/time fields that contain only dates and with date/time fields that contain both the date and time. The examples in this chapter using time periods will work with date/time fields that contain only the time and with date/time fields that contain both the date and time. You will be able to use these techniques on your own date/time fields.

Summarizing a Pivot Table by the Built-In Date Periods

One of the great features of a pivot table is to be able to summarize the data by day, month, quarter, and year. This is accomplished by moving a date/time field to either the Rows section or the Columns section of the PivotTable Fields window. Then the data can be grouped by individual date, month, quarter, or year, or by any combination of these time periods. If the column you are using contains both the date and the time, you would also be able to summarize it by second, minute, or hour. All of these time periods are based on a calendar year. Managing fiscal periods will be covered later in this chapter.

The examples in this section show how to summarize the pivot table specifically by month and year. You can use the exact steps to summarize the pivot table by other time periods including day, month, quarter, year, or any combination, as well as second, minute, hour, or any combination. If a date/time field contains both the date and time, you can mix and match all the available time periods.

NOTE   For the examples presented in this section of the chapter, you can use the sample file called *DatesAndTimes.xlsx* that is included with this book. You can find the sample files at www.wiley.com/go/GGRXL_PivotTables. Each subsection of this chapter will indicate which sheet to use from this workbook.

Summarizing a Pivot Table by a Single Period of Time

A popular request is to summarize the data by month, where each column in the pivot table would represent a different month. For example, you could show a summary for each employee by month.

To summarize data by month, do the following:

1. Select the pivot table that you want to summarize by month. If you are using the sample data, select the pivot table on the ByEmployee sheet of the sample workbook. In the sample sheet, notice how the pivot table is summarized by employee last name, as shown in Figure 6.1.

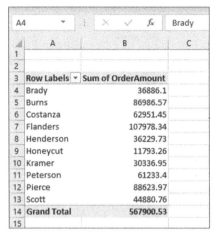

Row Labels ▼	Sum of OrderAmount
Brady	36886.1
Burns	86986.57
Costanza	62951.45
Flanders	107978.34
Henderson	36229.73
Honeycut	11793.26
Kramer	30336.95
Peterson	61233.4
Pierce	88623.97
Scott	44880.76
Grand Total	567900.53

Figure 6.1: Pivot table summarized by employee last name

2. Drag a date/time field from the fields list into the Columns section of the PivotTable Fields window. If you are using the sample data, drag the OrderDate field into the Columns section of the PivotTable Fields window. The pivot table will immediately summarize the data by either date, month, quarter, or year, as shown in Figure 6.2.

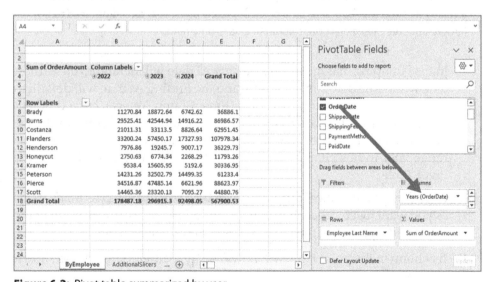

Figure 6.2: Pivot table summarized by year

3. Right-click one of the column headers in the pivot table that displays either the date, month, quarter, or year. If you are using the sample data, right-click cell B4.

4. Select Group. You will see the Grouping dialog box, as shown in Figure 6.3.

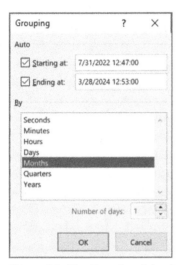

Figure 6.3: The Grouping dialog box

NOTE   If you get a dialog box that says "Cannot group that selection," Excel is not seeing the column that you are trying to use as a date/time field. You will need to look at the column in your pivot table that you are trying to use as a date to see if any of the values are not actually dates. Every single item in the column must contain either a value that Excel sees as a date/time or a completely blank cell. You might need to go back to Chapter 1 to convert the column to a date/time field.

5. In the Grouping dialog box, the Starting At date will default to the earliest date within the date/time column, and the Ending At date will default to the most recent date within the date/time column. You can enter different dates to change the date range of the pivot table. For this example, we don't need to change the dates. You can find more ways to filter on a date range later in this chapter and in Chapter 4, "Sorting and Filtering the Pivot Table."

6. In the By section of the Grouping dialog box, you can select as many items as you want just by checking an item. For this example, uncheck all of the boxes and check only the word Months, and then click OK.

Each column in the pivot table will now display a different month, as shown in Figure 6.4.

Notice how there is not a column for December. That is because there is no data for this month. If you would like to show all months, even if they do not have data, then Right-click one of the month names on the pivot table, choose Field Settings, click the Layout & Print tab, select Show Items With No Data, and click OK.

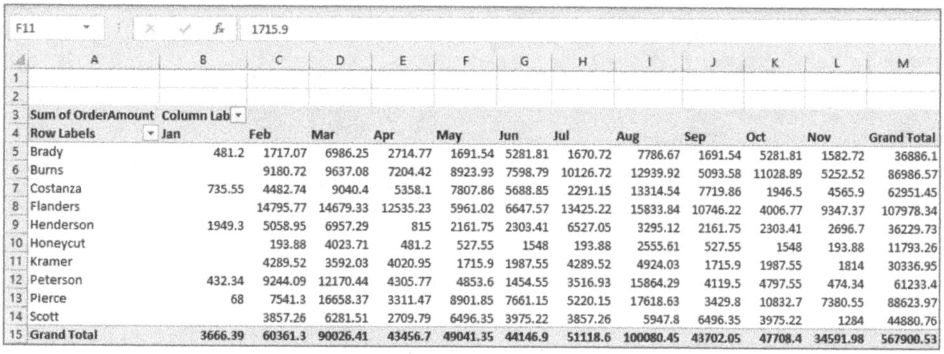

	F11	▾	⋮	×	✓	*fx*	1715.9						

⊿	A	B	C	D	E	F	G	H	I	J	K	L	M
1													
2													
3	Sum of OrderAmount	Column Lab ▾											
4	Row Labels ▾	Jan	Feb	Mar	Apr	May	Jun	Jul	Aug	Sep	Oct	Nov	Grand Total
5	Brady	481.2	1717.07	6986.25	2714.77	1691.54	5281.81	1670.72	7786.67	1691.54	5281.81	1582.72	36886.1
6	Burns		9180.72	9637.08	7204.42	8923.93	7598.79	10126.72	12939.92	5093.58	11028.89	5252.52	86986.57
7	Costanza	735.55	4482.74	9040.4	5358.1	7807.86	5688.85	2291.15	13314.54	7719.86	1946.5	4565.9	62951.45
8	Flanders		14795.77	14679.33	12535.23	5961.02	6647.57	13425.22	15833.84	10746.22	4006.77	9347.37	107978.34
9	Henderson	1949.3	5058.95	6957.29	815	2161.75	2303.41	6527.05	3295.12	2161.75	2303.41	2696.7	36229.73
10	Honeycut		193.88	4023.71	481.2	527.55	1548	193.88	2555.61	527.55	1548	193.88	11793.26
11	Kramer		4289.52	3592.03	4020.95	1715.9	1987.55	4289.52	4924.03	1715.9	1987.55	1814	30336.95
12	Peterson	432.34	9244.09	12170.44	4305.77	4853.6	1454.55	3516.93	15864.29	4119.5	4797.55	474.34	61233.4
13	Pierce	68	7541.3	16658.37	3311.47	8901.85	7661.15	5220.15	17618.63	3429.8	10832.7	7380.55	88623.97
14	Scott		3857.26	6281.51	2709.79	6496.35	3975.22	3857.26	5947.8	6496.35	3975.22	1284	44880.76
15	Grand Total	3666.39	60361.3	90026.41	43456.7	49041.35	44146.9	51118.6	100080.45	43702.05	47708.4	34591.98	567900.53

Figure 6.4: Pivot table summarized by month

The pivot table now is summarizing the data by month, where each column shows a different month. That is because you moved the date field to the Columns section of the PivotTable Fields window. Just to get an idea of the possibilities of a pivot table, Figure 6.5 shows what the pivot table would look like if the date field is moved to the Rows section of the PivotTable Fields window, below the Employee Last Name field.

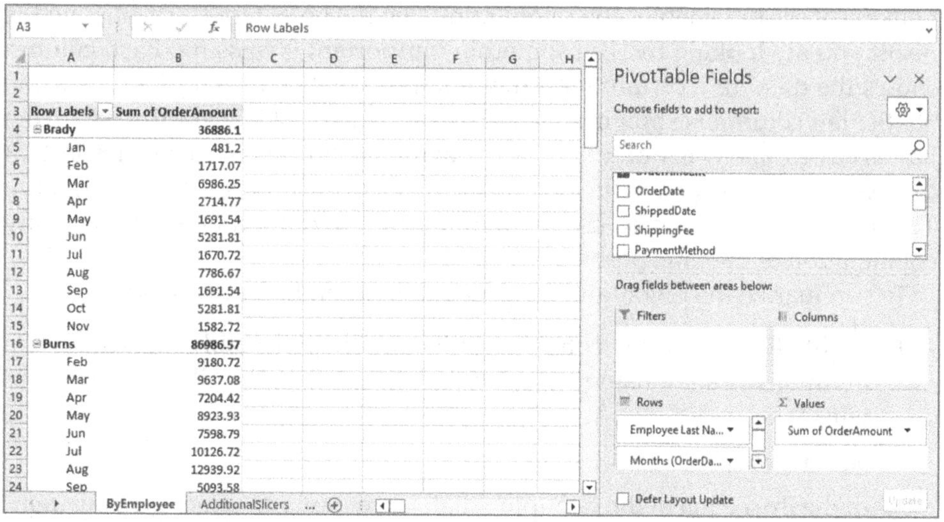

Figure 6.5: Pivot table summarized by last name and month

Figure 6.6 shows what the pivot table would look like if the date field is moved to the Rows section of the PivotTable Fields window, above the Employee Last Name. It all depends on how you want to see the data. For the rest of this section, make sure the date field is in the Columns section of the PivotTable Fields window.

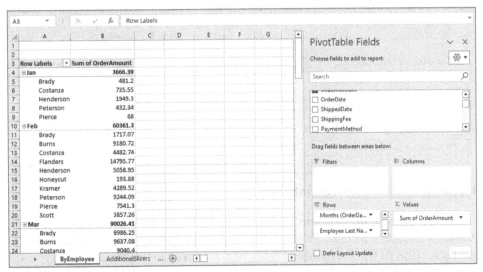

Figure 6.6: Pivot table summarized by month and last name

Summarizing a Pivot Table by More Than One Time Period

Looking at the pivot table, you might think that the pivot table is displaying the result you are looking for. But something important is missing. Each column shows the data for a certain month, no matter what year that month is from. So, the Jan column is showing the data from January 2022 and the data from January 2023, and every other year for that matter. So, it is especially important that we include the year in the pivot table to make the report more meaningful. The following steps can be used to summarize the date/time field using any combination of the time periods.

To summarize the pivot table by year and by month, follow these steps:

1. Right-click one of the column headers in the pivot table that displays a month. If you are using the sample data, right-click cell B4, which contains Jan.

2. Select Group.

3. In the By section of the Grouping dialog box, you can select as many items as you want just by clicking an item. For this example, check Months and Years and click OK.

The pivot table will now show the year and month, as shown in Figure 6.7.

Showing/Hiding the Totals for Each Time Period

In the example shown in the previous figures, notice how each year shows the totals for that year in a separate column. Sometimes you want to display the totals for each year, and sometimes you don't. To turn those totals on or off, right-click the year number, and select Subtotal Years. This is a toggle that will turn the totals on or off. The subtotals could potentially be available for years, quarters, months, days, hours, and minutes, if the pivot table is grouped by more than one of the available date/time periods.

B4			✕ ✓ ƒx	2022									
Sum of OrderAmount	Column Labels ▾												
	⊟ 2022					2022 Total	⊟ 2023						
Row Labels ▾	Jul	Aug	Sep	Oct	Nov		Feb	Mar	Apr	May	Jun	Jul
Brady		2714.77	1691.54	5281.81	1582.72	11270.84		2441.9	2714.77	1691.54	5281.81	1670.72
Burns	946	7204.42	5093.58	11028.89	5252.52	29525.41		3901.58	7204.42	8923.93	7598.79	9180.72
Costanza		6779.05	7719.86	1946.5	4565.9	21011.31	946.8	4485.25	5358.1	7807.86	5688.85	2291.15
Flanders	88	9011.88	10746.22	4006.77	9347.37	33200.24	3343	8804.17	12535.23	5961.02	6647.57	13337.22
Henderson		815	2161.75	2303.41	2696.7	7976.86		4958.37	815	2161.75	2303.41	6527.05
Honeycut		481.2	527.55	1548	193.88	2750.63		1949.3	481.2	527.55	1548	193.88
Kramer		4020.95	1715.9	1987.55	1814	9538.4		2688.95	4020.95	1715.9	1987.55	4289.52
Peterson		4839.87	4119.5	4797.55	474.34	14231.26	1420.95	5926.57	4305.77	4853.6	1454.55	3516.93
Pierce		12873.82	3429.8	10832.7	7380.55	34516.87	5482.15	12163.56	3311.47	8901.85	7661.15	5220.15
Scott		2709.79	6496.35	3975.22	1284	14465.36		3043.5	2709.79	6496.35	3975.22	3857.26
Grand Total	1034	51450.75	43702.05	47708.4	34591.98	178487.18	11192.9	50363.15	43456.7	49041.35	44146.9	50084.6

Figure 6.7: Pivot table summarized by year and month

Expanding/Collapsing Time Periods in the Pivot Table

Now that the pivot table is showing the data summarized by year and month, you may want to collapse each year to just show the total for that year and then re-expand the year to show all the months when you need to. There's a quick and easy way to do this.

The following date/time periods could potentially be expanded or collapsed if the pivot table is being grouped by more than one of the available date/time periods: years, quarters, months, days, hours, and minutes. For this example, you will collapse the years so the pivot table displays just the total for each year.

To expand/collapse a time period on a pivot table, follow these steps:

1. Right-click a year number in the pivot table. If you are using the sample data, right-click cell B4, which should contain "2022."

2. Select Expand/Collapse. This will show the choices shown in Figure 6.8.

3. Choose Collapse Entire Field. The pivot table will now show just the totals for each year, as shown in Figure 6.9. Each year can be individually expanded by clicking the plus sign icon to the left of each year number and then individually collapsed by clicking the minus sign icon to the left of each year number.

Using Slicers to Filter the Pivot Table by Date and Time

There are numerous ways to filter the pivot table using date and time fields, and this topic is discussed in Chapter 4. But when you add a date field to either the

Rows or Columns section of the PivotTable Fields window, you will get additional choices when you create slicers. You will now be able to create slicers based on the months, quarters, and years, or however you group your date/time field. Even if the date field is eventually removed from the Rows section or the Columns section of the PivotTable Fields window, additional slicers would still be available. In the following example, slicers will be added for the months, quarters, and years.

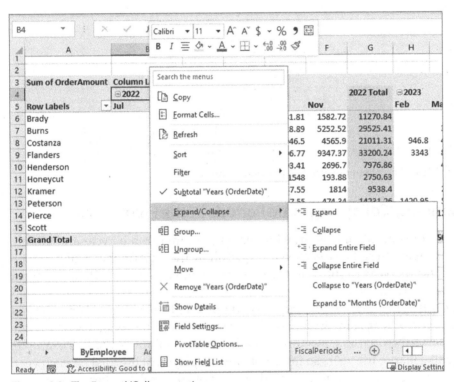

Figure 6.8: The Expand/Collapse options

To use the additional date slicers, follow these steps:

1. Select a pivot table that summarizes by a date/time field. If you are using the sample data, you can use the pivot table that is on the AdditionalSlicers sheet of the sample workbook.

2. Click the PivotTable Analyze tab.

3. Click Insert Slicer. You will see the Insert Slicers window, as displayed in Figure 6.10. Notice the choices at the bottom of the list, Months, Quarters, and Years. These additional slicers will appear in the Insert Slicers window only when a date field is currently in either the Rows or Columns section of the PivotTable Fields window or if a date field had been included in

either the Rows or Columns section of the PivotTable Fields window at some point for the current pivot table.

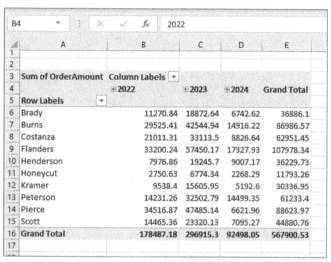

Figure 6.9: Pivot table collapsed by year

Figure 6.10: Additional slicers

4. Check the items you want. If you are using the sample spreadsheet, check Months, Quarters, and Years; then click OK.

5. You will see the slicer windows, as shown in Figure 6.11.

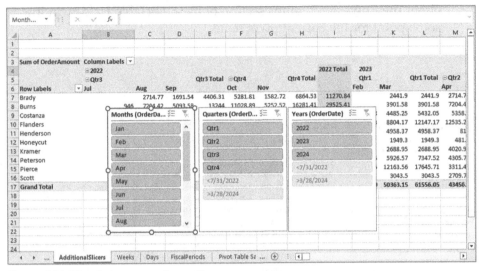

Figure 6.11: Month, quarter, and year slicers

6. Move the slicer windows where you want. You can now filter the pivot table by month, year, quarter, or whichever slicers you chose.

If you want the slicer to show only the date/time periods that contain data, then right-click the slicer and choose Slicer Settings. The Slicer Settings dialog box will display, as shown in Figure 6.12. Check Hide Items With No Data and click OK.

Figure 6.12: The Slicer Settings dialog box

Displaying Earliest and Most Recent Dates

Many times, in the business world, you might want to see the first time that a customer placed an order, the date of the most recent sale by a salesperson, or something similar. A pivot table can easily show the earliest (oldest) date or the most recent date. In the following example, the most recent date that each customer placed an order will be shown. Displaying the earliest date would work similarly.

To display the earliest date or the most recent date, follow these steps:

1. Select a pivot table. If you are using the sample data, select the pivot table that is on the Most Recent Order sheet of the sample workbook.

2. Drag a date field into the Values section of the PivotTable Fields window. If you are using the sample data, drag the OrderDate field into the Values section of the PivotTable Fields window. The pivot table will default to counts, as shown in Figure 6.13.

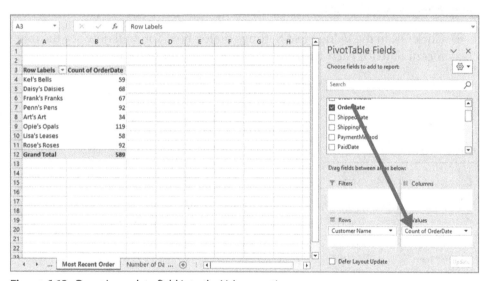

Figure 6.13: Dragging a date field into the Values section

3. Click the Count field in the Values section of the PivotTable Fields window and choose Value Field Settings. This will display the Value Field Settings dialog box, as shown in Figure 6.14.

4. Enter **Most Recent Date** in the Custom Name field.

5. Choose Min or Max from the Summarize Value Field By section. Max would show the most recent date, and Min would show the earliest date. For this example, I chose Max.

6. Click the Number Format button on the bottom of the dialog box.

7. In the Format Cells dialog box, choose Date for the Category, and then choose a date format. For this example, I chose 3/14/12. Click OK.

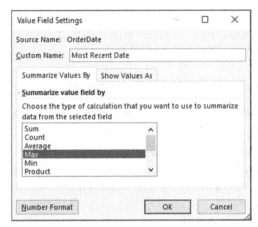

Figure 6.14: The Value Field Settings dialog box

8. Click OK in the Value Field Settings dialog box. You will now see the most recent date for each customer, as shown in Figure 6.15.

Figure 6.15: The most recent order date for each customer

Summarizing the Pivot Table by Number of Days

Earlier in the chapter, you learned how to summarize the data by day, month, quarter, and year. There are times when you want to summarize the data for a certain number of days grouped together. A seven-day period would make up a week, for example. Here's an interesting way to summarize the data by a certain number of days. In the following example, a seven-day period will be used.

To summarize the pivot table by a specified number of days, follow these steps:

1. Select a pivot table. If you are using the sample data, select the pivot table on the Number Of Days sheet of the sample workbook.

2. Drag a date field into the Columns section of the PivotTable Fields window. If you are using the sample data, drag the OrderDate field into the Columns section of the PivotTable Fields window. The pivot table will now be summarized by date, month, quarter, or year.

3. Right-click either the date, month, quarter, or year column heading on the pivot table. If you are using the sample data, right-click cell B4.

4. Choose Group. The Grouping dialog box will display, as shown in Figure 6.16.

5. On the By section, select Days and nothing else. The Number Of Days option at the bottom of the dialog box is now available. The Number Of Days option becomes available when Days is the only choice selected.

6. Change Number Of Days to 7 and click OK. The pivot table is summarizing the data by the number of days you selected, as shown in Figure 6.17.

Figure 6.16: The Grouping dialog box

	A	B	C	D	E	F	G
1							
2							
3	Sum of OrderAmount	Column Labels					
4	Row Labels	7/31/2022 - 8/6/2022	8/7/2022 - 8/13/2022	8/14/2022 - 8/20/2022	8/21/2022 - 8/27/2022	8/28/2022 - 9/3/2022	9/4/2022 - 9/10/2022 9,
5	Brady	208	1017.75			1489.02	432.34
6	Burns	946	5910.07	662.75	543.6	88	2031.88
7	Costanza	1853.29			3979.76	3688.75	1949.3
8	Flanders	2738.9	193.88	841	1495.75	10004.6	2074.41
9	Henderson	68	153	570		24	208
10	Honeycut		481.2				527.55
11	Kramer		2114.9		1906.05		481.2
12	Peterson	3143		1638.07	58.8	2676.9	
13	Pierce	10951.4		935.92	986.5	2810	
14	Scott		969.2	892.4	701.7	146.49	
15	Grand Total	19908.59	10840	5540.14	9672.16	20927.76	7704.68
16							
17							
18							

B4 ▾ 7/31/2022 - 8/6/2022

Figure 6.17: Pivot table showing summary by a number of days

This method does summarize the data by week. The only problem is that when you choose the Number Of Days setting, you are not able to group the pivot table further by other date periods, like you were able to do earlier in the chapter. In the next section, you will learn another way to summarize the data by week that can be grouped with other date periods.

Summarizing the Pivot Table Using Custom Date Calculations

So now that you have summarized your data by date, month, quarter, or year, you may want to break down the data in other ways using a date field. Many people want to separate the data by week, by the day of the week, or by fiscal period. To summarize the data in additional ways than what the pivot table provides, you will have to create calculations on the main data sheet and then expand the pivot table to include these new columns. This section will show you a few useful formulas to help you take full advantage of date fields on a pivot table.

Excel has many functions that provide additional analysis of date/time fields. You could use these functions to create formulas from dates that then can be used on the pivot table. These can be found by clicking the Formulas tab and then choosing the Date/Time category. Table 6.1 lists the Date/Time functions and what they do.

Table 6.1: Date/Time functions in Excel

FUNCTION NAME	DESCRIPTION
DATE	Converts the numbers for year, month, and day into a date field
DATEVALUE	Converts a text field containing a date value into a date field
DAY	Returns a number from 1 to 31 representing the day of a date
DAYS	Returns the number of days between two dates
DAYS360	Returns the number of days between two dates based on a 360-day year
EDATE	Adds or subtracts a number of months to a date to return another date
EOMONTH	Returns a date field that shows the last day of the month that is so many months away from a certain date
HOUR	Returns the hour of a time as a number from 0 (12 a.m.) to 23 (11 p.m.)
ISOWEEKNUM	Returns the ISO week number in a year for a given date

FUNCTION NAME	DESCRIPTION
MINUTE	Returns the minute of time as a number from 0 to 59
MONTH	Returns the month of a date as a number from 1 to 12
NETWORKDAYS	Returns the number of whole workdays between two dates
NETWORKDAYS.INTL	Returns the number of whole workdays between two dates and custom weekend parameters
NOW	Returns the current date and time
SECOND	Returns the second from a time as a number from 0 to 59
TIME	Converts the numbers for hour, minute, and second into a time field
TIMEVALUE	Converts a text field containing a time value into a time field
TODAY	Returns the current date
WEEKDAY	Returns a number from 1 to 7 identifying the day of the week of a date; as a default, 1 = Sunday
WEEKNUM	Returns the week number in the year
WORKDAY	Returns a date field with a number of workdays added to a date
WORKDAY.INTL	Returns a date field with a number of workdays added to a date with custom weekend parameters
YEAR	Returns the year of a date as a number
YEARFRAC	Returns the year fraction representing the number of days between two dates

Summarizing the Pivot Table by Week

Many organizations will want the data to be summarized by week. As shown earlier, a pivot table can summarize the data by date, month, quarter, and year, but not week. To summarize the data by week, you can use the built-in function called WEEKNUM, which will show a number from 1 to 53 for the week of a year for a date. It goes up to 53 because even though a year is made up of 52 weeks, the last couple days of the year could be in the 53rd week, because the year usually does not start on a Monday.

The WEEKNUM function is based on the calendar year. Once the WEEKNUM function is added to the list of data that drives the pivot table, the pivot table updates to include the new column. In the following example, the WEEKNUM function will be used to calculate the week in a year, and then you will see how to add that column to your pivot table. You can find an example of the WEEKNUM function in column R of the Formulas sheet of the sample workbook.

To include the week number in the pivot table, follow these steps:

1. Click a sheet that has the raw data that feeds a pivot table. If you are using the sample data, click the Pivot Table Sales sheet.

2. Click a cell in the row that contains the column headers. If you are using the sample data, click cell C1.

3. Use the Ctrl+Right Arrow keyboard shortcut to move to the last column on the right side of the data.

4. Click the next blank cell to the right of the pivot table on the header row. If you are in the sample data sheet, click cell R1.

5. Type **Weeknum** in the cell and press Enter. Now you should be in the next cell down.

6. Type **=WEEKNUM(XX)** in the cell and press Enter. **XX** is the cell on the same row that has the date. In the sample data, type **=WEEKNUM(C2)** and press Enter.

7. Copy that formula down to the rest of the column.

Now you need to make sure the pivot table includes the new column.

1. Select a sheet that contains a pivot table, and then select the pivot table. If you are using the sample data, click the pivot table on the Weeks sheet.

2. Click the PivotTable Analyze tab.

3. Click Change PivotTable Data Source, and then click Change Data Source again if the submenu appears. You will now see the Change Data Source dialog box, as shown in Figure 6.18.

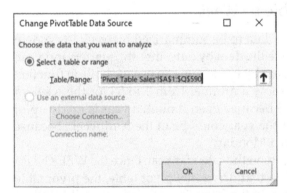

Figure 6.18: The Change PivotTable Data Source dialog box

4. Select the entire range by using the Ctrl+A keyboard shortcut. If you are using the sample data, the range should be 'Pivot Table Sales'!$A$1:$R$590.

Click OK. The Week Number is now near the bottom of the fields list of the PivotTable Fields window and can be used like any other field, including being able to be used in slicers.

5. Drag the Week Number field into the Columns section of the PivotTable Fields window. The pivot table now displays the week number, as shown in Figure 6.19. Now you can further summarize years, quarters, and months into weeks, or you can use the weeks any way you want to in the pivot table.

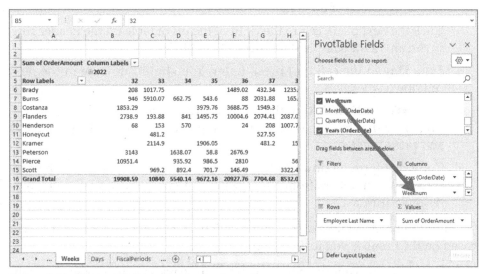

Figure 6.19: Pivot table displaying the week number

If you would like to show all weeks, even if they do not have data, then right-click one of the week numbers on the pivot table, choose Field Settings, click the Layout & Print tab, select Show Items With no Data, and click OK.

Using the Day of the Week in a Pivot Table

Another popular request is to be able to summarize the data by a certain day of the week, like Monday or Tuesday. To do this, you will need to create a formula using the WEEKDAY function, which returns a number from one to seven based on the day of the week of a date. As a default, when the WEEKDAY function returns the number 1, it means the date falls on a Sunday.

Once you have that number, you can use the INDEX function to look up the number in a small table and return the day of the week based on the number. Then, you would expand the pivot table to include these two new columns. You can find an example of the WEEKDAY function and the INDEX function in columns S and T of the Formulas sheet of the sample workbook. In the following example, the day of the week will be added to the pivot table.

To use the day of the week in a pivot table, start by creating a pivot table that displays data based on the day of the week using these steps:

1. Click a sheet that has the raw data that feeds a pivot table. If you are using the sample data, click the Pivot Table Sales sheet.

2. Click a cell in the row that contains the column headers. If you are using the sample data, click cell C1.

3. Use the Ctrl+Right Arrow keyboard shortcut to move to the last column on the right side of the data.

4. Click the next blank cell to the right of the pivot table on the header row. If you are in the sample data sheet, click cell S1.

5. Type **Day** in the cell and press Enter. You should now be in the next cell down.

6. Type **=WEEKDAY(XX)** in the cell and press Enter. XX is the cell on the same row that has the date. In the sample data, type **=WEEKDAY(C2)** and press Enter.

7. Copy that formula down to the rest of the column. Notice how the new column has numbers from 1 to 7, where 1 represents Sunday and 7 represents Saturday.

Now, you need to make a new column that will show the name of the day based on the number you just created.

1. Create a list on your spreadsheet that lists the days Sunday through Saturday. If you are using the sample data, you will see this list in column AA, as shown in Figure 6.20. If you have to type this list into your own spreadsheet, type **Sunday** in row 1 of a blank column and then type the rest of the names down the column. Having the word *Sunday* on row 1 will facilitate the INDEX function, because the WEEKDAY function will return the value of 1 when the date falls on a Sunday.

AA1	▾	⋮	✕
◢	Z	AA	
1		Sunday	
2		Monday	
3		Tuesday	
4		Wednesday	
5		Thursday	
6		Friday	
7		Saturday	

Figure 6.20: Days of the week

2. Click the cell to the right of the column heading "Day" and type **Day Name**; then press the Enter key. You should now be in the next cell down.

3. Enter the formula **=INDEX(*XX:XX,YY*)** and press the Enter key. *XX* is the column where the list of days is, and *YY* is the cell in the row that contains a date. If you are using the sample data, enter **=INDEX(AA:AA,S2)**.

4. Copy the formula down to the rest of the column.

Now you need to make sure the pivot table includes the new columns.

1. Select a sheet that contains a pivot table, and then select the pivot table. If you are using the sample data, click the pivot table on the Days Names sheet.

2. Click the PivotTable Analyze tab.

3. Click Change Data Source, and then click Change Data Source again if the submenu appears. You will now see the Change PivotTable Data Source dialog box.

4. Select the entire range by using the Ctrl+A keyboard shortcut. If you are using the sample data, the range should be `'Pivot Table Sales'! $A$ 1:$T$590`. Click OK.

5. The Day Name field is now near the bottom of the fields list of the PivotTable Fields window and can be used like any other field, including being used in slicers.

6. Drag the Day Name field into the Columns section of the PivotTable Fields window. The pivot table now displays the day name, as shown in Figure 6.21. Now you can further summarize years, quarters, and months into day names.

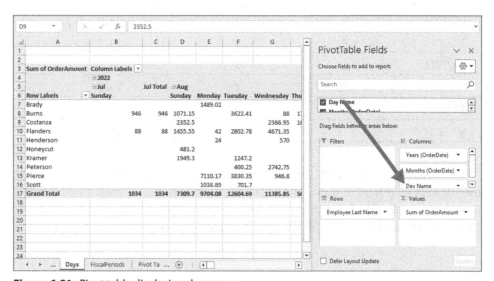

Figure 6.21: Pivot table displaying day names

If you would like to show all day names, even if they do not have data, then right-click one of the day names on the pivot table, choose Field Settings, click the Layout & Print tab, select Show Items With No Data, and click OK.

Using a Fiscal Period in a Pivot Table

Excel uses dates and date functions based on the calendar year, which of course begins on January 1 and ends on December 31. But many organizations work on a fiscal year that has a different start date and end date than a calendar year. There is no built-in function or option that allows you to define the fiscal year or the fiscal period in Excel, so you will have to set up formulas for the fiscal year or period, if you want the pivot table to represent a fiscal period.

In the following example, the fiscal year will start on July 1. Table 6.2 shows the fiscal month, fiscal quarter, and fiscal year for the different months in 2023, based on the fiscal year starting on July 1, 2023. This is just an example, and your own fiscal periods could vary.

Table 6.2: Fiscal periods based on fiscal start date of July 1, 2023

ACTUAL DATE	FISCAL MONTH	FISCAL QUARTER	FISCAL YEAR
7/1/2023	1	1	2023
8/1/2023	2	1	2023
9/1/2023	3	1	2023
10/1/2023	4	2	2023
11/1/2023	5	2	2023
12/1/2023	6	2	2023
1/1/2024	7	3	2023
2/1/2024	8	3	2023
3/1/2024	9	3	2023
4/1/2024	10	4	2023
5/1/2024	11	4	2023
6/1/2024	12	4	2023

To calculate fiscal month, quarter, or year, you will first need to isolate the month and year from a date. The MONTH function can be used to isolate the month, and the YEAR function can be used to isolate the year. Then, a table can be set up and the VLOOKUP function used to determine the fiscal month, quarter, and year based on the month of a date. The pivot table can then be expanded to include these columns.

This example gives you an idea of how to implement fiscal periods into a pivot table, based on the fiscal year starting on 7/1/2023. You will have to modify the steps for your own needs and your own fiscal periods, but these steps give you a good path to follow. The formulas needed are already contained in the sample workbook on the Formulas sheet. You will have to include similar formulas in your own workbook.

Click the Formulas sheet of the sample workbook. Select cell U2. Notice the formula in cell U2 uses the MONTH function to isolate the month from the date. The formula is as follows:

```
=MONTH(C2)
```

Click cell V2. It contains the formula for the fiscal month. It is using the VLOOKUP function. The formula is as follows:

```
=VLOOKUP(U2,AE:AG,2,FALSE)
```

Click cell W2. It contains the formula for the fiscal quarter, and it is another VLOOKUP function using the same table. The formula is as follows:

```
VLOOKUP(U2,AE:AG,3,FALSE)
```

Click cell X2. It contains the formula for the fiscal year, and it is another VLOOKUP function using the same table. The formula is actually as follows:

```
=YEAR(C2)-VLOOKUP(U2,AE:AH,4,FALSE)
```

This is because the fiscal year could be the year of the date on the current row, or 1 less than the year of the date on the current row, based on the month. The table used in the VLOOKUP formulas is in columns AE through AH to the right and is shown in Table 6.3. The first row of Table 6.3 shows the column of the worksheet. The first column of Table 6.3 shows the actual month of a date. The second column of Table 6.3 shows the fiscal month. The third column of Table 6.3 shows the fiscal quarter. The fourth column of Table 6.3 shows either a zero or a 1, so the fiscal years will be either the same year as contained in a date field or the year prior to the year contained in a date field.

Table 6.3: The table used in the VLOOKUP formulas to calculate fiscal periods

AE	AF	AG	AH
1	7	3	1
2	8	3	1
3	9	3	1
4	10	4	1
5	11	4	1

Continues

Table 6.3 (*Continued*)

AE	AF	AG	AH
6	12	4	1
7	1	1	0
8	2	1	0
9	3	1	0
10	4	2	0
11	5	2	0
12	6	2	0

You would need to set up these formulas and a similar table in your own workbooks to calculate the fiscal periods for your data. This method is certainly not the only way to calculate the fiscal month, quarter, and year, but it works. Now, you can include the columns in the pivot table.

NOTE For the formulas in this section to work, you will need to either enter them into the same cells as the sample data referenced or adjust the cells accordingly.

Now, you will need to expand the pivot table to include these columns. To include the fiscal periods in the pivot table, follow these steps:

1. Select a sheet that contains a pivot table, and then select the pivot table. If you are using the sample data, click the pivot table on the FiscalPeriods sheet.

2. Click the PivotTable Analyze tab.

3. Click Change Data Source, and then click Change Data Source again if the submenu appears. You will now see the Change PivotTable Data Source dialog box.

4. Select the entire range by using the Ctrl+A keyboard shortcut. If you are using the sample data, the range should be Formulas!$A$1:$X$590. Click OK. The Fiscal Month, Fiscal Quarter, and Fiscal Year fields are now near the bottom of the fields list of the PivotTable Fields window and can be used like any other field, including being able to be used in slicers.

5. Drag the Fiscal Month field into the Columns section of the PivotTable Fields window. The pivot table now displays the fiscal month, as shown in Figure 6.22. Now you can further summarize the pivot table by the fiscal periods.

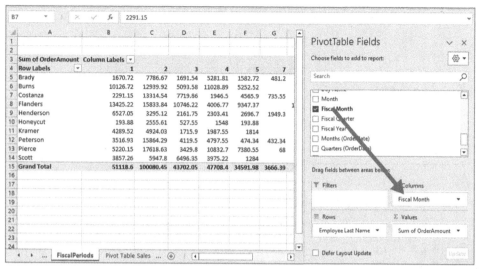

Figure 6.22: Pivot table showing fiscal month

Summary

In this chapter, you learned how to summarize the pivot table by second, minute, hour, day, month, quarter, and year, and any combination. You also learned how to use Excel's built-in functions to further summarize the pivot table by week, day name, and fiscal period.

In the next chapter, you will learn how to make a pivot table from more than one sheet.

Creating a Pivot Table from Multiple Spreadsheets

So far, all the pivot tables used in this book have come from one list of data, and in many cases, that is typical. But there will be times when different sheets have similar data or related data, so you will want to create the pivot table from multiple sheets or from multiple ranges within the same sheet. In this chapter, you will explore two different ways to generate a pivot table from more than one list of data. First, you will learn how to make a pivot table from lists that are similar to each other. Then, you will learn how to make a pivot table from lists that have different types of data but share a common field.

> **NOTE** For the examples presented in this section of the chapter, you can use the sample file called *MultipleSheets.xlsx* that is included with this book. You can find the sample files at www.wiley.com/go/GGRXL_PivotTables. Each section of this chapter will indicate which sheet to use from this workbook.

Creating a Pivot Table from Multiple Ranges Using the PivotTable Wizard

Let's say you have multiple sheets or multiple ranges on the same sheet that are structured in a similar way. Maybe the data on each sheet is a budget for each month, or for each district, for example. You may want to add these sheets together to get totals for a certain time period, for a region, or for something similar. The sheets could have some rows and columns in common, but they do not have to be structured the same way. They should, however, be somewhat similar.

The pivot table used in this example can use data that has column headers and row headers, unlike the other pivot tables used in this book, where only the columns headers were used. You want the pivot table to add the rows and columns from the different sheets together if they have the same name, but still account for the rows and columns that are in one sheet but not in others.

As an example, look at Figure 7.1, which contains the 2021 sheet for a company budget, and Figure 7.2, which contains the 2022 budget data. You can find these sheets in the sample workbook from the downloadable files for this chapter. Sheet 2022 of the sample workbook has the same rows and columns as sheet 2021, but with different budget amounts.

	January	February	March	April	May	June	July	Totals	% of Total
				Company Budget - 2021					
Sales	$88,866.00	$97,752.60	$107,527.86	$118,280.65	$130,108.71	$143,119.58	$157,431.54	$843,086.94	49.41%
Purchasing	$15,000.00	$16,500.00	$18,150.00	$19,965.00	$21,961.50	$24,157.65	$26,573.42	$142,307.57	8.34%
Research & Development	$17,000.00	$18,700.00	$20,570.00	$22,627.00	$24,889.70	$27,378.67	$30,116.54	$161,281.91	9.45%
Computer	$30,000.00	$33,000.00	$36,300.00	$39,930.00	$43,923.00	$48,315.30	$53,146.83	$284,615.13	16.68%
Warehouse	$14,000.00	$15,400.00	$16,940.00	$18,634.00	$20,497.40	$22,547.14	$24,801.85	$132,820.39	7.78%
Accounting	$15,000.00	$16,500.00	$18,150.00	$19,965.00	$21,961.50	$24,157.65	$26,573.42	$142,307.57	8.34%
Totals	$179,866.00	$197,852.60	$217,637.86	$239,401.65	$263,341.81	$289,675.99	$318,643.59	$1,706,419.50	

Figure 7.1: The 2021 company budget data (sheet 2021 from the sample workbook)

Now look at Figure 7.3, which contains company budget data for 2023, found in the 2023 sheet of the sample workbook. Notice that some of the row labels are different. The row that was called Research & Development in the 2021 and 2022 sheets is called R&D on the 2023 sheet. The 2023 sheet also has a new row called Website & Social Media. In real life, department names change over time, and new departments are created. The 2023 sheet reflects the updated department names.

Figure 7.2: The 2022 company budget data (sheet 2022 from the sample workbook)

Figure 7.3: The 2023 company budget data (sheet 2023 from the sample workbook)

These different sheets or ranges can be summarized in a pivot table using the PivotTable Wizard. The PivotTable Wizard is a legacy tool in Excel that at one point was a popular way to create a pivot table, but now is mostly outdated. The PivotTable Wizard still has at least one useful feature, namely, the Multiple Consolidation Ranges feature, which allows you to make a pivot table from multiple sheets or ranges that are structured in a similar way.

The PivotTable Wizard can be activated in two different ways. You can use a keyboard shortcut, or if that doesn't work, you can add an icon to the Quick Access Toolbar that will then open the PivotTable Wizard.

In this example, we want to include sheets 2021, 2022, and 2023 in a pivot table. The pivot table will go on a new, blank sheet.

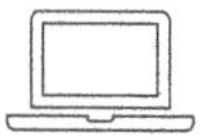

To use a keyboard shortcut to display the PivotTable Wizard, click a blank sheet of a workbook. If you are using the sample data, click the Totals sheet of the sample workbook. One way to activate the PivotTable Wizard is with a keyboard shortcut. Just press these keys one after the other, without holding them down. If you have a PC, press the **Alt** key, then press the **D** key, and finally press the **P** key. This should open the PivotTable and PivotChart Wizard dialog box, as shown in Figure 7.4.

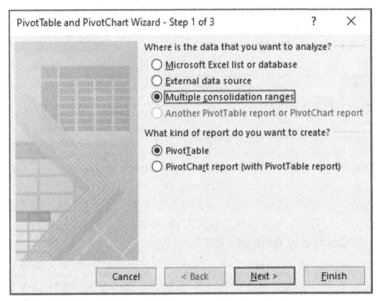

Figure 7.4: The PivotTable and PivotChart Wizard dialog box

If the keyboard shortcut didn't work, then you will have to add an icon on the Quick Access Toolbar that will then open the PivotTable Wizard.

To add an icon on the Quick Access Toolbar to display the PivotTable Wizard, follow these steps:

1. Click the File tab.

2. At the bottom of the menu in the left pane, either click the word *Options* or click the word *More*, and then click Options. You will now see the Excel Options dialog box.

3. Select Quick Access Toolbar on the left.

4. Click the drop-down menu where it says *Popular Commands* and choose All Commands.

5. Scroll down on the long list below the words *All Commands* and find PivotTable and PivotChart Wizard.

6. Select PivotTable and PivotChart Wizard by clicking it, and then click Add >> in the middle of the dialog box. The choice called PivotTable and PivotChart Wizard will then appear in the right column, as shown in Figure 7.5. Click OK.

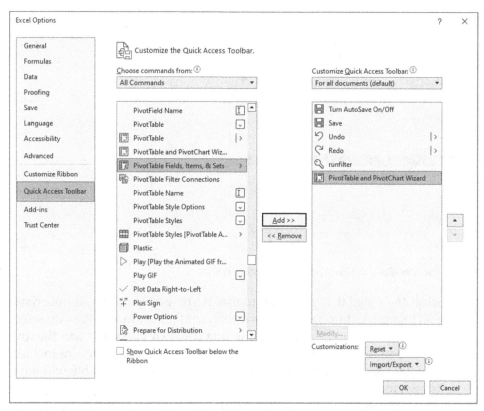

Figure 7.5: Adding the PivotTable and PivotChart Wizard to the Quick Access Toolbar

There will now be an icon for the PivotTable and PivotChart Wizard on the Quick Access Toolbar, which is the group of icons at the very top left of the Excel screen, above the tabs. Click that icon, and you will see the PivotTable and PivotChart Wizard dialog box, as shown in Figure 7.4.

Now that the PivotTable and PivotChart Wizard dialog box is open, you can summarize multiple sheets. In the following example, you are summarizing the company budgets for 2021, 2022, and 2023 shown earlier into a new pivot table.

1. Within the PivotTable and PivotChart Wizard dialog box, select Multiple Consolidation Ranges and click Next.

2. In the new dialog box, select Create A Single Page Field For Me, and click Next. You will see the dialog box called PivotTable and PivotChart Wizard – Step 2b of 3, as shown in Figure 7.6, but without the data added to the text boxes.

3. Click the field below the word *Range*. This will select the text box so that you can set the range.

4. Click the first sheet that you want to use in the pivot table. If you are using the sample data, click the 2021 sheet.

Figure 7.6: Step 2b of the PivotTable and PivotChart Wizard

5. Select the range that you want to use. If you are using the sample data, select range A3 through I10. It is important that the range that you select includes the column headers in the first row that you select and the row headers in the first column that you select. I purposely did not include the total row or column, because the consolidated pivot table will have its own totals.

6. Click Add. The range you selected should now appear in the All Ranges section of the dialog box.

7. Click the next sheet that you want to use in the pivot table. As a default, the same range that you used in step 5 will be used with the sheet you are currently on. You can either use the same range or select a different range. If you are using the sample data, click sheet 2022 and use the same range.

8. Click Add. The ranges you selected so far should now appear in the All Ranges section of the dialog box.

9. Repeat steps 7 and 8 for any additional sheets you want to use in the pivot table. If you are using the sample data, select sheet 2023, and click Add.

10. When you are done selecting ranges/sheets, click Next. This will take you to the next step in the PivotTable and PivotChart Wizard where you will be asked where you want to put your new pivot table.

11. If you want the pivot table to start on a certain cell, select that cell and click Finish. For this example, I chose cell A4. You will now see the pivot table, as shown in Figure 7.7.

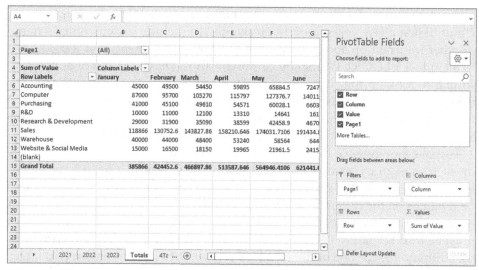

Figure 7.7: A pivot table made with the Multiple Consolidation Ranges option of the PivotTable and PivotChart Wizard

The new pivot table summarizes the multiple sheets. The rows that had the same names among the sheets were added together, but all rows were accounted for. If any of the individual sheets are updated, the pivot table can be refreshed, and then it will show the newest data from the individual sheets.

The Multiple Consolidation Ranges option within the PivotTable Wizard allows you to create a pivot table from sheets that are structured in a similar way. The next section introduces a way to make a pivot table come from multiple sheets that contain different types of data but have one field in common.

Creating a Pivot Table Using the Data Model

There will be times that the fields you want to use for a pivot table are spread across multiple sheets. Let's say we have one sheet that has a list of customers, for example. The sheet probably contains some kind of customer number or customer ID, which should be different for each customer. The sheet also contains the other fields for each customer, like the customer's name, address, city, and whatever other information you want to track for each customer.

In addition to the sheet that contains the list of customers, you have another sheet that shows a list of the orders or the sales. This sheet would probably contain a unique ID for each order and then the date of the order, the amount, and other fields that describe the order. Each order probably also contains the customer ID or the customer number for the customer that placed the order.

The order sheet may have the customer number, but not the customer's name. Up until just a few years ago, if you wanted to include the customer's name or other information about the customer in the order sheet, you would have to include a VLOOKUP function or maybe an INDEX function or something similar to look up the customer ID on the order sheet and gather the proper information from the customer sheet. You would need a separate VLOOKUP function for each field you want to get from the other sheet. Now you can make a pivot table from multiple sheets that have at least one common field.

To make a pivot table that includes fields from more than one sheet, the lists on each sheet must be formatted as a table. The sheets also must have a field in common. While it is not necessary that the common fields have the same field names on the different sheets, it is helpful when they do. The fields must have the same data type, so for example, they both must be text fields or both must be number fields. One of the fields also must be the unique identifier or the primary key for one of the tables. If you want to use more than two tables to create the pivot table, the multiple sheets do not have to all share the same exact field, but each sheet must have one field in common with one of the other sheets that are used to make the pivot table.

Theoretically, a pivot table can come from many sheets that are all formatted as tables. The connection between two sheets using the common fields is called a *join*, a *link*, or a *relationship*. These terms can be used interchangeably. When two or more formatted tables are used to make a pivot table and the sheets are linked on common fields, this creates a data model. In this section, you will learn how to create and manage a pivot table using a data model. This topic will be further explored in Chapter 8, "Improving a Pivot Table with Power Pivot."

For this example, a pivot table will be created using three sheets. First, a pivot table will be made from two sheets, and then the third sheet will be included. Using this technique, you could make a pivot table from many sheets.

Let's say you want to include fields from the Clients sheet, the Staff sheet, and the Sales sheet in a single pivot table. The Clients sheet includes the customer number, which is unique for each customer, and other fields for each customer. The Staff sheet contains the employee number and other fields for each employee. The Sales sheet contains the order number, which is unique for each order; the employee number of the employee who took the order from the customer; the customer number of the customer who placed the order; and other fields from the order. The three sheets are formatted as tables.

The Staff sheet and the Sales sheet both contain the employeeid, so that will be the common field that will link them. The Clients sheet has a field called companyid, which will link to the customerid field on the Sales sheet. You can see in Figure 7.8 that through these common fields, the tables can all be connected.

This is just an example to demonstrate this technique, which can be used on your own data, of course. Now that the data from the multiple sheets has been described, let's start to build a pivot table using the multiple sheets.

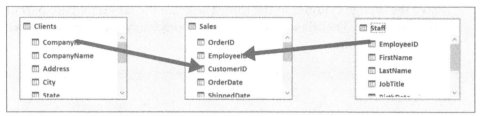

Figure 7.8   The common fields between the sheets

To build a pivot table from multiple sheets using the data model, follow these steps:

1. Click a cell within a formatted table. If you are using the sample data, click cell A1 of the Clients sheet.

2. Select the Insert tab.

3. Click the PivotTable icon on the left side of the ribbon. If the submenu comes up, click From Table/Range. You will now see the PivotTable From Table Or Range dialog box, as shown in Figure 7.9. The Table/Range name will show the name of the formatted table. This may or may not be the same as the sheet name.

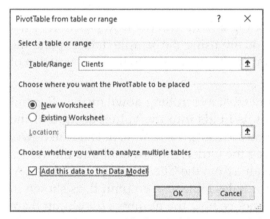

Figure 7.9: The PivotTable from Table or Range dialog box

4. Select the New Worksheet option.

5. Select the Add This Data To The Data Model checkbox and click OK. This will open a new sheet.

6. Click the All tab on the PivotTable Fields window. You will now see a list of the table names of the formatted tables in the workbook, as shown in Figure 7.10. You may see the table names listed twice. This can be confusing. If you see the table names listed twice, then use the table names that

have the orange cylinder in the icon. These are the tables that are part of the data model. The other tables without the orange cylinder are the names of formatted tables.

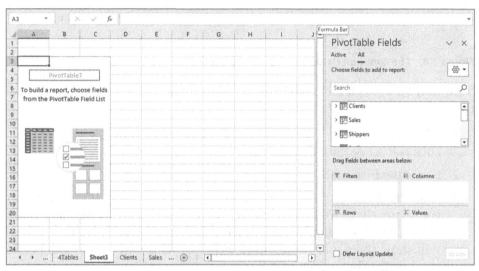

Figure 7.10: Creating a pivot table using the data model

7. Expand one of the tables and drag a field into the Rows section of the PivotTable Fields window. If you are using the sample data, expand the Clients table and drag the CompanyName field into the Rows section of the PivotTable Fields window.

8. Now add a field from a different table by scrolling down further. Expand another table and drag one of its fields into the Values section of the PivotTable Fields window. If you are using the sample data, scroll down, expand the Sales table, and drag the OrderAmount field into the Values section. Notice the CustomerName from the Clients table is in column A, and the OrderAmount from the Sales table is in column B, as shown in Figure 7.11. More importantly, notice how the numbers in column B are all the same numbers. That is because Excel does not yet know how the Clients table is related to the Sales table.

9. To create the relationship between the tables, first click the CREATE button in the yellow area of the PivotTable Fields window. If you don't see a yellow area, click the PivotTable Analyze tab, then click the Relationships icon toward the right side of the ribbon, and finally click New in the Manage Relationships window. You will now see the Create Relationship dialog box, as shown in Figure 7.12.

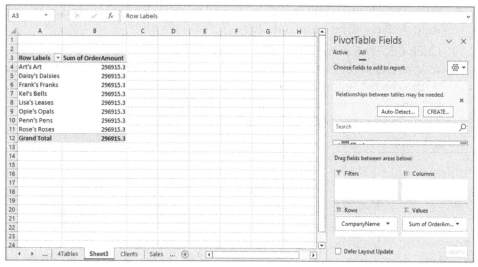

Figure 7.11: Pivot table using fields from two tables

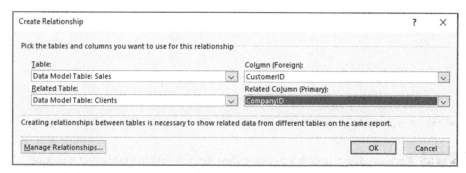

Figure 7.12: The Create Relationship dialog box

10. Click the Table drop-down menu. Choose one of the tables you used in the pivot table. You will want to choose the table where the common field is not the unique identifier for that table. If you are using the sample data, choose Data Model Table: Sales.

11. Click the Column (Foreign) drop-down menu. Choose the field that is the common field. If you are using the sample data, choose the CustomerID field.

12. Click the Related Table drop-down menu. Choose one of the tables you used in the pivot table. You will want to choose the table where the common field is the unique identifier for that table. If you are using the sample data, choose Data Model Table: Clients.

13. Click the Related Column (Primary) drop-down menu. Choose the field that is the common field. If you are using the sample data, choose the CompanyID field. The fields that you choose for Column (Foreign) and

Related Column (Primary) do not need to have the same field name, but they do have to be same data type.

14. Click OK. The pivot table should now show different numbers in each row, as shown in Figure 7.13, because Excel now knows which Orders go with which Customers because of the relationship. This is significant, because Excel now has some of the features of a relational database, like Microsoft Access, SQL Server, or Oracle.

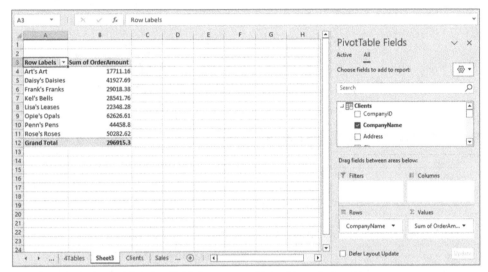

Figure 7.13: A pivot table using fields from two tables with a relationship

> **NOTE** A *primary key*, also called a *unique identifier*, is a field in a table that is unique for every record in the table, like a customer number in a customer table, for example. A foreign key is a field in another table that is linked to the primary key. The foreign key does not have to be unique in the related table. The primary key and the foreign key do not need to have the same field names, but they need to be the same data type.

Adding, Changing, or Deleting Relationships

There may be times when you want to add more relationships between different tables, change the existing relationships, or delete the existing relationships. The relationships can be managed on the PivotTable Analyze tab or the Data tab. Another way to manage table relationships will be covered in Chapter 8, "Improving a Pivot Table with Power Pivot."

To add, change, or delete relationships, follow these steps:

1. Click the PivotTable Analyze tab or the Data tab.

2. Click the Relationships icon. You will now see the Manage Relationships window, as shown in Figure 7.14. You will see the relationships that you have already set up, if there are any. From this dialog box, you can add, change, or delete relationships.

3. Close the Manage Relationships window when you are done with it.

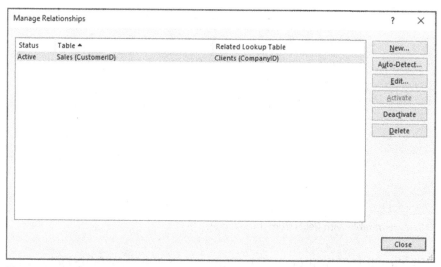

Figure 7.14: The Manage Relationships window

Adding Additional Tables into the Data Model

In the previous example, the CustomerName was used from the Clients table, and the OrderAmount was used from the Sales table. What if we wanted to also display the Employee Last Name in the pivot table? The Sales table has only the EmployeeID. To use the Employee Last Name, the Staff table will need to be included in the data model.

To include another table in the data model, follow these steps:

1. Click the All menu in the PivotTable Fields window.

2. Scroll through the fields list and expand the additional table that has a field you want to include. If you are using the sample data, expand the Staff table.

3. Drag the field you want to add into the Columns section of the PivotTable Fields window. If you are using the sample data, drag the LastName field from the Staff table into the Columns section of the PivotTable Fields window. The pivot table will now change, as shown in Figure 7.15. Notice how, in the example, the last name is shown on the pivot table for each column, but each row has the same numbers going across. This is because

Excel does not know how the Staff table fits into the mix. We have to create another relationship.

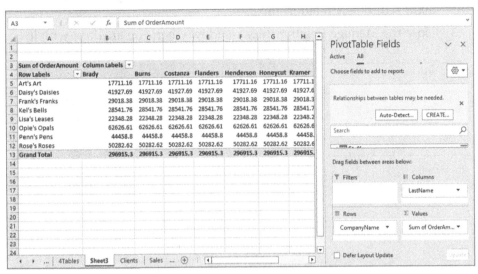

Figure 7.15: A pivot table with fields from three tables

4. Click the CREATE button in the yellow area in the PivotTable Fields window. If you don't see a yellow area, click the PivotTable Analyze tab, then click the Relationships icon toward the right side of the ribbon, and finally click New in the Manage Relationships window. You will now see the Create Relationship dialog box.

5. Click the Table drop-down menu. Choose one of the tables you used in the pivot table. You will want to choose the table where the common field is not the unique identifier for that table. If you are using the sample data, choose Data Model Table: Sales.

6. Click the Column (Foreign) drop-down menu. Choose the field that is the common field. If you are using the sample data, choose the EmployeeID field.

7. Click the Related Table drop-down menu. Choose one of the tables you used in the pivot table. You will want to choose the table where the common field is the unique identifier for that table. If you are using the sample data, choose Data Model Table: Staff.

8. Click the Related Column (Primary) drop-down menu. Choose the field that is the common field. If you are using the sample data, choose the EmployeeID field. The fields that you choose for the Column (Foreign) and the Related Column (Primary) do not have to have the same field, but they do have to be same data type.

9. Click OK and then close the Manage Relationships window. The pivot table should now show different numbers, as shown in Figure 7.16, because Excel now knows which Sales go with which Staff. The pivot table is now summarizing data from three different tables—Clients, Sales, and Staff.

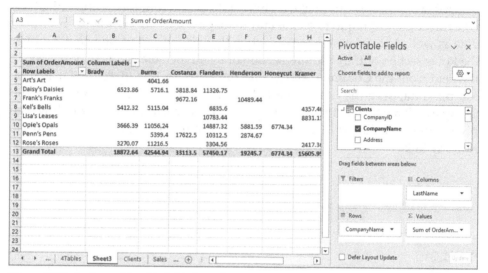

Figure 7.16: A pivot table with fields from three tables with relationships

Creating and Managing Sets

When the pivot table is created using the data model, there will be some similarities and some differences with pivot tables that are not made using the data model. For example, the PivotTable Fields window will operate the same way for both types of pivot tables. Another similarity is that the calculations that are available within the Value Field Settings dialog box will work the same way on pivot tables that come from the data model as they do on pivot tables that do not come from the data model. One big difference, however, is that the Calculated Fields and the Calculated Items that were demonstrated in Chapter 3, "Using Calculations in Pivot Tables," are not available in pivot tables made using the data model. The method to add your own calculations to a pivot table made using the data model will be covered in Chapter 8, "Improving a Pivot Table with Power Pivot."

Another difference is that a pivot table made using the data model can include a set, which is not available in pivot tables not made from a data model. A set allows you to pick and choose individual rows or columns that you want to display or not display on a pivot table. A set also allows you to re-order individual rows or columns within the pivot table. A set can be based on the fields contained in the Rows section or the Columns section of the PivotTable

Fields window. A set based on the row items will be available only when there is at least one field in the Rows section of the PivotTable Fields window, and a set based on the column items will be available only when there is at least one field in the Columns section of the PivotTable Fields window.

For this example, the same sheet that was used in the previous example will be used. This sheet should have a pivot table made from three different tables. Of course, the technique to create and manage a set will work with your own data as well. A set is more effective when there is more than one field in either the Rows section or the Columns section of the PivotTable Fields window. Move the field from the Columns section into the Rows section. If you are using the sample data, drag the LastName field from the Columns section below the CompanyName field in the Rows section in the PivotTable Fields window. The pivot table now should look like Figure 7.17. Now there are two fields in the Rows section.

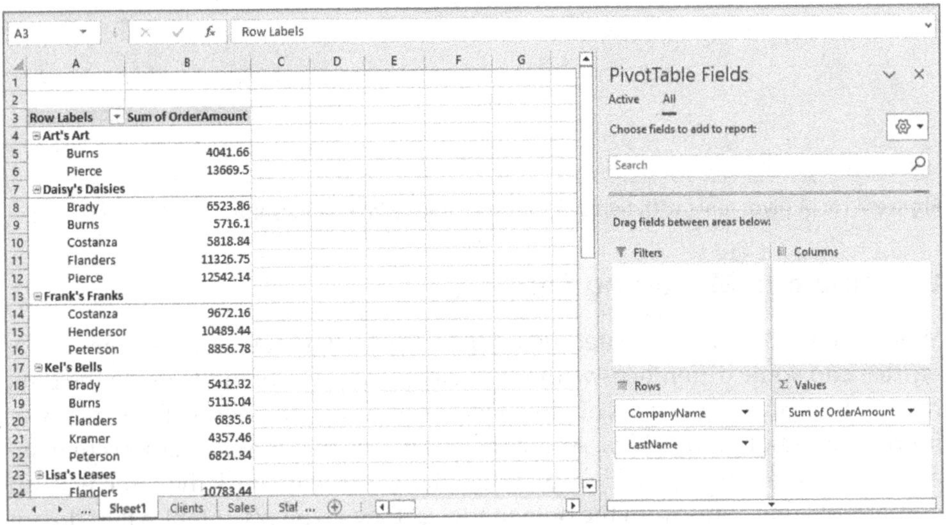

Figure 7.17: A pivot table with two fields in the Rows section

Notice that the employee last names are sorted alphabetically within each client. Let's say that for Art's Art, we want Pierce to show above Burns, but we want the employee last names to still be sorted alphabetically within each of the rest of the clients. This is the kind of situation that can be handled with a set. A normal sort would reorder the employees for all customers. A set will also allow you to remove an employee from one customer but keep the same employee in other customers. A normal filter would remove the employee from all customers.

To add a set, follow these steps:

1. Click a pivot table that was made a data model. If you are using the sample data, click Sheet1.

2. Select the PivotTable Analyze tab.

3. Choose the Fields, Items, & Sets icon toward the right side of the ribbon.

4. Choose Create Set Based on Row Items, which will be available only on pivot tables made from a data model that has at least one field in the Rows section of the PivotTable Fields window. The choice called Create Set Based on Column Items would be available only on pivot tables made from a data model that has at least one field in the Columns section of the PivotTable Fields window. You will see the New Set dialog box, as displayed in Figure 7.18. Notice how there is one row for each different Company Name/LastName combination, or whatever fields you have in the Rows section of the PivotTable Fields window.

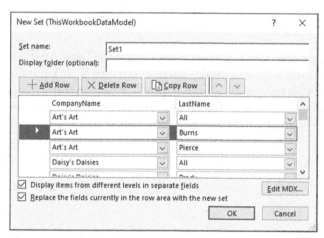

Figure 7.18: The New Set dialog box

5. Click the white space to the left of the item you want to move or delete. Notice how you can add a row, delete a row, copy a row, or use the green arrows to move the item up or down. If you are using the sample data, click the white space to the left of the row that has Art's Art for the CompanyName and Burns for the LastName.

6. Click the green down arrow to move that row down below the row that has Art's Art for the CompanyName and Pierce for the LastName.

7. Click OK. The pivot table will immediately change, as shown in Figure 7.19. Notice how the set is now in the Rows section of the PivotTable Fields window.

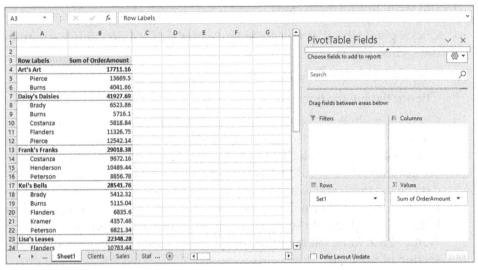

Figure 7.19: A pivot table with a set

Changing or Deleting a Set

To change the rows or columns that display in a set, click the PivotTable Analyze tab, then choose Fields, Items & Sets, and finally choose Manage Sets. You will now see the Set Manager dialog box, as shown in Figure 7.20. From this dialog box you can add, edit, or delete the sets. Choose the set you want and change it accordingly.

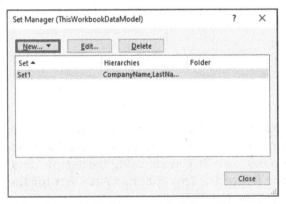

Figure 7.20: The Set Manager dialog box

To remove a set from the pivot table, drag the set from the Rows section or the Columns section to the fields section of the PivotTable Fields window. This will completely remove the set, and then you can move fields back into the various sections of the PivotTable Fields window as usual.

Summary

In this chapter, you learned two ways to make a pivot table using multiple sheets. One method used the PivotTable Wizard to make a pivot table from sheets that are structured in a similar way, and the other method used the data model to join tables that have a common field.

The next chapter will go even further with the data model by using the Power Pivot.

Improving a Pivot Table with Power Pivot

In the previous chapter, you learned to make pivot tables from more than one table using the data model. There's a lot more you can do with the data model. In this chapter, we will go further with the data model using Power Pivot.

Power Pivot is a set of tools designed to take your pivot tables and your data to the next level. With Power Pivot, you can create formulas in the powerful Data Analysis Expressions (DAX) language to further support and analyze the tables within the data model. Power Pivot can also create pivot tables from very large databases, much larger than what a regular Excel spreadsheet can handle. Power Pivot will allow you to pull data from multiple sources into the data model and then join the tables from different sources together to make pivot tables and pivot charts. Power Pivot also has a feature called a *key performance indicator* (KPI), which adds a visual element to a pivot table. Power Pivot can analyze your data in many more ways, but, for the purpose of this book, I will show how Power Pivot can be used to support pivot tables. This chapter will show you how to activate the Power Pivot add-in and how to use some of the Power Pivot features.

NOTE For the examples presented in this chapter, you can use the sample file called *powerpivot.xlsx* that is included with this book. You may also need the Access database called *States.accdb*. You can find the sample files at www.wiley.com/go/GGRXL_PivotTables. Each section of this chapter will indicate which sheets to use from this workbook.

Activating the Power Pivot Add-In

Power Pivot is an Excel add-in that must be activated before it can be used. When Power Pivot is activated, you will see a Power Pivot tab to the right of the Help tab. Once it is activated, the Power Pivot tab should appear every time you start Excel.

Power Pivot has been available for the PC desktop version of Excel since Excel 2013. It is not available in older versions of Excel, and as of this writing, it is not available on the Mac version of Excel or on Excel for the Web. The Mac version of Excel and Excel for the Web can utilize pivot tables made with the data model, but they can't access the additional features of Power Pivot.

To activate the Power Pivot add-in, following these steps:

1. Click the File tab.

2. At the bottom of the menu in the left pane, select Options. If necessary, select More and then Options. You will now see the Excel Options dialog box.

3. Click Add-ins on the left side of the Excel Options dialog box. You will see the Add-ins section of the Excel Options dialog box, similar to what is shown in Figure 8.1.

4. Click the Manage drop-down menu at the bottom of the dialog box and choose COM Add-ins.

5. Click Go. You will now see the COM Add-ins dialog box, as shown in Figure 8.2.

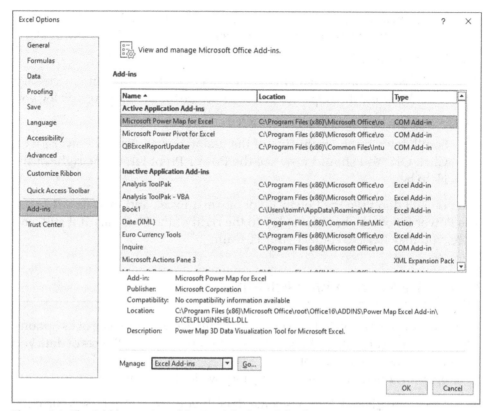

Figure 8.1: The Add-ins section of the Excel Options dialog box

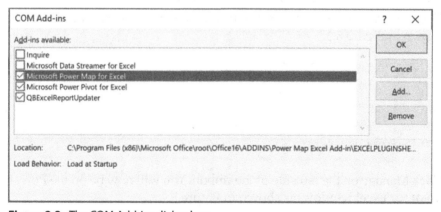

Figure 8.2: The COM Add-ins dialog box

6. Check Microsoft Power Pivot for Excel and leave the other checkboxes as they are and then click OK. You should now see the Power Pivot tab to the right of the Help tab.

Sometimes additional steps are needed to display the Power Pivot tab. If the Power Pivot tab isn't displaying, then continue with the following steps.

7. Click the File tab.

8. At the bottom of the menu in the left pane, select Options, or if necessary, select More and then Options. You will now see the Excel Options dialog box.

9. Select Customize Ribbon in the left pane.

10. Scroll down on the right side of the dialog box and check Power Pivot. Click OK. You should now see the Power Pivot tab to the right of the Help tab.

If you still don't see the Power Pivot tab, exit Excel, and then restart Excel. The Power Pivot tab should display to the right of the Help tab. If it still isn't there, you may have to contact your IT team.

Using the Power Pivot Add-In

Now that you have activated Power Pivot, it's time to explore some of its options. You will want to open a workbook that has several sheets with lists of data you want to include in a pivot table.

To open the Power Pivot for Excel window, do the following:

1. Open a workbook that has some data. If you are using the sample data, open the workbook called *PowerPivot.xlsx*. Notice the sample workbook has four sheets: Staff, Sales, Clients, and Shippers.

2. Click the Power Pivot tab. You will now see the Power Pivot ribbon, as shown in Figure 8.3.

Figure 8.3: The Power Pivot ribbon

3. Click Manage on the left side of the ribbon. You will now be on the Power Pivot for Excel window, as shown in Figure 8.4.

You may notice some tabs on the bottom of the Power Pivot for Excel window. If you are using the sample data, you will see the Clients, Sales, and Staff tabs, but you won't see the Shippers tab. The tabs that appear at the bottom of the Power Pivot for Excel window represent the tables that are part of the data model. When tables are in the data model, a pivot table can be made from them. Tables could have been added to the data model if you used Power Query to import data from other sources as described in Chapter 1, "Preparing the Data for an Excel Pivot Table." Another way to populate tables into the data model is if you made a pivot table using the data model as described in Chapter 7, "Creating a Pivot Table from Multiple Spreadsheets."

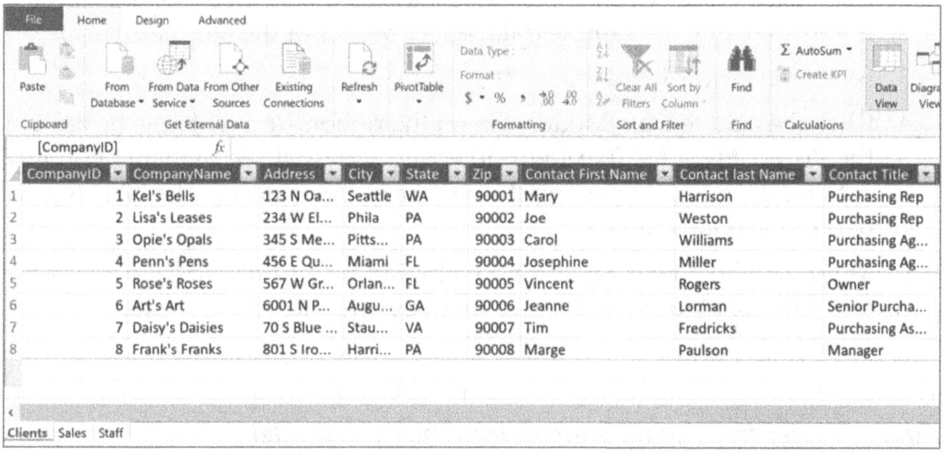

Figure 8.4: The Power Pivot for Excel window

Don't worry if you don't see any tables in the data model in your workbook yet. You will learn how to add tables to the data model in this chapter.

You won't be able to change the data in the Power Pivot for Excel window, but you will be able to refresh the data using the Refresh icon on the Home tab if the original data source changes. Each column can be sorted and filtered using the standard AutoFilters. Additional columns can be created with formulas, as you will learn in this chapter.

Adding Tables to the Data Model

Power Pivot allows you to add more tables to the data model either from Excel tables or from other sources. One of the huge advantages of Power Pivot is that it can handle very large databases. A normal Excel sheet can handle roughly 1,048,000 rows of data. Power Pivot can handle databases as big as two billion rows, which then can be made into pivot tables. If you have large databases that you want to import into Power Pivot, I recommend you use a computer with a fast processor and lots of memory. You can add tables to the data model from a formatted table in Excel as well as from other sources.

Adding Formatted Excel Tables into the Data Model

You can easily add data from the current Excel workbook into the data model. The data has to be formatted as a table.

To add an Excel table into the data model, do the following:

1. Close or minimize the Power Pivot for Excel window if it is still open.

2. Click a cell within a formatted table that is not yet part of the data model. If you are using the sample data, select cell A1 of the Shippers sheet.

3. Select the Power Pivot tab.

4. Click the Add to Data Model icon on the ribbon. You will now be back in the Power Pivot for Excel window, and you will see the table you just selected as one of the tabs on the bottom of the window. The table is now part of the data model.

5. Minimize the Power Pivot for Excel window and repeat these steps for any additional formatted tables that you want to add to the data model.

6. Save your work.

Adding Tables from Other Sources into the Data Model

In addition to being able to add tables from the current Excel workbook into the data model, many other data sources can be used as well. This is how you will be able to import larger databases into Power Pivot. These data sources include the following:

- Microsoft SQL Server
- Microsoft SQL Azure
- Microsoft Analytics Platform System
- Microsoft Access
- Oracle
- Teradata
- Sybase
- Informix
- IBM DB2
- OLEDB/ODBC
- Microsoft Analysis Services
- Microsoft Reporting Services
- Other Excel files
- Text files

Most databases are OLEDB/ODBC compliant, which means your IT team can probably set up an OLEDB or ODBC driver for your database. So, even if your database is not specifically in the previous list, there is probably a way to make the database accessible to Power Pivot.

In the following example, you will see the steps to import data from an Access database. The steps to import data from the other data sources would be similar. To import data from other databases, you will probably need support from your IT team. You should always remember to follow your company's guidelines when trying to access larger databases.

NOTE If you are using the downloaded book files, you can use the *States.accdb* sample file that is included for the following example.

To import data from an external data source into Power Pivot, do the following:

1. Use the same workbook as the previous example. If you are using the sample data, use the *PowerPivot.xlsx* workbook.

2. Select the Power Pivot tab.

3. Choose the Manage icon on the left side of the ribbon. You will be in the Power Pivot for Excel window.

4. Click the Home tab.

5. Click the From Other Sources icon in the Get External Data group of the ribbon. If you don't see this icon, you might need to first click the Get External Data icon and then click the From Other Sources icon. You will now see the Table Import Wizard dialog box, as shown in Figure 8.5.

6. Select a data source from the list and click Next >. If you are using the sample data, choose Microsoft Access from the list. You will now see the Connect To A Microsoft Access Database page in the Table Import Wizard dialog box, as shown in Figure 8.6.

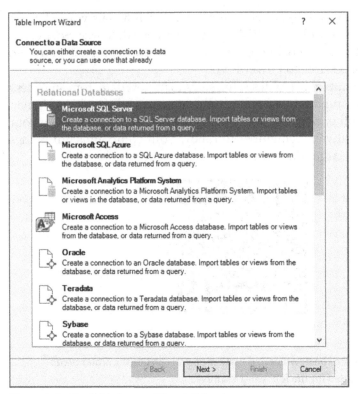

Figure 8.5: The Table Import Wizard dialog box

7. Click Browse and then use File Explorer to select an Access database. Click Open. If you are using the sample data, select the *States.accdb* Access database. If you chose another data source, the screen would ask for a server name or other information about your database. Your IT team can provide this additional information.

8. If the database you are using requires a username and password, then enter that information. If these are not required, then leave the boxes blank.

9. Click Next >. This will take you to the next step in the Table Import Wizard that will ask you to choose how to import the data.

10. Choose Select From A List Of Tables And Views To Choose The Data To Import. If you know the SQL language, you could select Write A Query That Will Specify The Data To Import, and then you would be able to use the SQL language to create your own query.

11. Click Next >. This will again take you to the next page of the Table Import Wizard where you will be asked to select specific tables and views.

12. Choose the tables you want to import into the data model. If you are using the sample data, choose the States table.

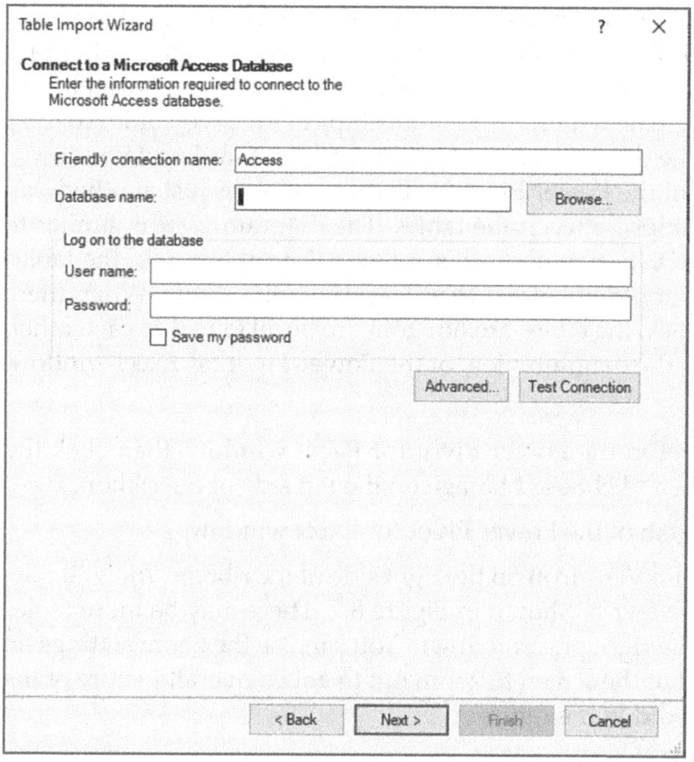

Figure 8.6: Connecting to a database

13. Click Finish. If you get a Security Warning window, click OK. You should get a window that says Success.

14. Close the Table Import Wizard dialog box.

15. Save your work.

You should see your new table as a tab at the bottom of the Pivot Table for Excel window. It is now part of the data model.

Joining Tables

Even though you now have multiple tables in the data model, there is another important step that is necessary before those tables can be made into a pivot table. The tables must be joined together on the common fields. Even tables from different data sources can be joined.

One way to join the tables is to close the Power Pivot for Excel window, select the PivotTable Analyze tab, and then click the Relationships icon, as described in Chapter 7, "Creating a Pivot Table From Multiple Spreadsheets." However, you can also join the tables from within the Power Pivot for Excel window using the diagram view window.

When joining tables, the field names do not have to be the same, but the fields must have the same data type. The relationships you create on the diagram view will show up within the Relationships of the PivotTable Analyze tab, and the relationships you create within the Relationships of the PivotTable Analyze tab will show up on the diagram view of the Power Pivot for Excel window.

The diagram view of the Power Pivot for Excel window is just another way to create the relationships between the tables. The diagram view is similar to the way Access and SQL Server and other relational databases join the tables together. Each table should be joined to at least one other table. When there are more than two tables, the tables are not going to be all joined to each other.

To join tables using the diagram view of the Power Pivot for Excel window, do the following:

1. If you are not yet in the Power Pivot for Excel window, then click the Power Pivot tab, and choose Manage on the left side of the ribbon.

2. Click the Home tab of the Power Pivot for Excel window.

3. Select the Diagram View icon on the right side of the ribbon. You will now see the diagram view, as shown in Figure 8.7. There may be more tables if you scroll to the right or scroll down. You can use the zoom settings on the bottom right of the screen to zoom out to get an overall picture of the data model, as I did in the figure.

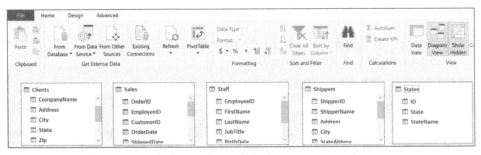

Figure 8.7: The diagram view, before tables are linked

4. You are looking for common fields. Select a field from one of the tables that is also in another table. Drag that field from the first table to the second table, placing it right on the corresponding field of the second table. For example, if you are using the sample data, you can drag the CompanyID from the Clients table onto the CustomerID of the Sales table since these are corresponding fields. Once you've made this connection, you will see a line added that shows the two tables have been joined. If you are using the sample tables, join the various tables together based on the field information shown in Table 8.1. When you have many tables, you may have to scroll around the Diagram view window to find the tables you are looking for. You can zoom out of the Diagram view on the bottom right

of the Diagram view window to get a bigger picture of the available tables in the data model.

Table 8.1: Common fields to join between the tables

FIRST TABLE	FIELD	SECOND TABLE	FIELD
Clients	CompanyID	Sales	CustomerID
Staff	EmployeeID	Sales	EmployeeID
Shippers	ShipperID	Sales	ShipperID
Clients	State	States	State

When you are done joining the tables together, the diagram view should look like Figure 8.8.

5. Save your work.

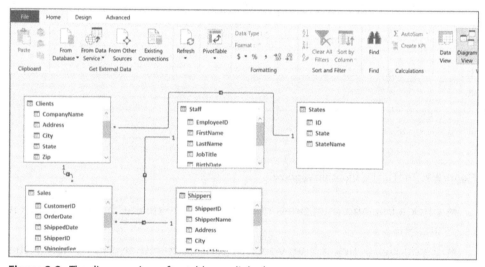

Figure 8.8: The diagram view, after tables are linked

Changing, Deleting, and Managing the Relationships

Your tables are now joined together on the common fields. While you are in Diagram view, here are some ways to change, delete, and manage the relationships:

- ▪ If you click or hover the mouse on a line, it will show you the fields that are used to join the tables together.
- ▪ Double-click a line to see the Edit Relationship dialog box, as shown in Figure 8.9. You could even choose different fields on the Edit Relationship dialog box, if needed. Close the Edit Relationship dialog box when you are done with it.

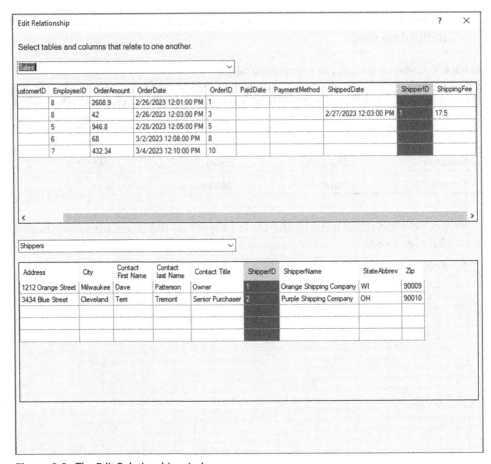

Figure 8.9: The Edit Relationship window

- Click a line and then press the Delete key to delete the relationship if necessary.
- If you right-click a line, you will be able to either edit or delete the relationship.

Creating a Pivot Table from the Power Pivot for Excel Window

Once tables are joined on the common fields, you are ready to make a pivot table from the multiple tables. You have learned several ways to create a pivot table in this book. You can also create a pivot table in the Power Pivot for Excel window.

To create a pivot table using the Power Pivot for Excel window, do the following:

1. Click the Home tab of the Power Pivot for Excel window.

2. Select the drop-down menu on the PivotTable icon on the ribbon. You will see the available templates, as shown in Figure 8.10. You can use any of the templates shown, but for this example choose PivotTable.

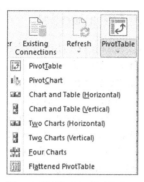

Figure 8.10: Available templates when creating a pivot table from the Power Pivot for Excel window

3. In the Create PivotTable dialog box, click OK. You will now be in a new sheet of the current workbook.

4. Click the All menu in the PivotTable Fields window. You will see the tables from the data model. If the table names are repeated, use the tables with the orange cylinders—they are the tables from the data model. Building the pivot table from multiple tables will be similar to the pivot table made from the data model used in Chapter 7, "Creating a Pivot Table from Multiple Spreadsheets," except the tables will already be joined together.

5. Drag the fields from the various tables into the sections of the PivotTable Fields window, as needed. If you are using the sample data, drag the CompanyName from the Clients table to the Rows section of the PivotTable Fields window and drag the OrderAmount from the Sales table to the Values section of the PivotTable Fields window. You should now see the pivot table, as shown in Figure 8.11.

6. Save your work.

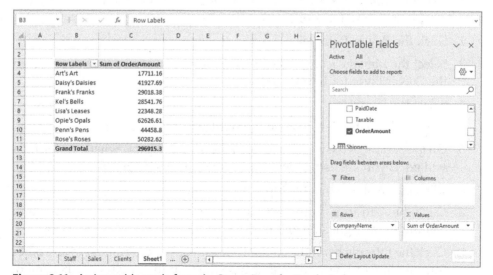

Figure 8.11: A pivot table made from the Power Pivot for Excel window

Adding Calculations to a Pivot Table Using the Data Model

Just like with any other pivot table, you will want to add, change, or delete the calculations that are on the pivot table that was made from the data model. The calculations in the Value Field Settings dialog box that were discussed in Chapter 3, "Using Calculations in Pivot Tables," will be available in a pivot table made from a data model. However, the calculated items and calculated fields, which were also mentioned in Chapter 3, will not be available on pivot tables made from a data model. You can create your own formulas in Power Pivot using Data Analysis Expressions (DAX) formulas. DAX formulas can be simple or complex and can be much more powerful than calculated fields and calculated items, and they can provide further analysis of the data.

For the purposes of this book, there are two types of DAX formulas, namely, calculated columns and measures. Calculated columns will be visible on a table on the data model as another column. They are similar to adding formulas to a normal list of data. Calculated columns can then be added to the pivot table like any other field.

Measures also use DAX formulas. They will not be visible in the data model, but measures can still be added to the pivot table. Measures are cumulative totals based on the entire table or several rows within the table, whereas calculated columns are based on one row within a table.

Adding a Calculated Column to a Table in the Data Model

In the following example, a sales tax calculation will be added to the sales table. Adding other calculations to a table would work in a similar way. Building a calculated column will be similar to creating a formula in an Excel spreadsheet.

Do the following to add a calculated column to a table:

1. Use the same workbook as the previous example. If you are using the sample data, use the workbook called *PowerPivot.xlsx*.

2. Click the Power Pivot tab.

3. Select the Manage icon on the left side of the ribbon. You will now be on the Power Pivot for Excel window.

4. Select the Home tab.

5. Choose the Data View icon on the right side of the ribbon.

6. On the bottom of the window, choose the tab of the table where the formula will go. If you are using the sample data, choose the Sales tab.

7. Click the Design tab at the top.

8. Click the Add icon on the left side of the ribbon. This will add a blank column to the right side of the table.

9. Click the formula bar if the cursor is not already there. Similar to any other formula in Excel, you can either type the formula or click the fx symbol

to see the available functions. As you type the formula, Excel will make suggestions. For this example, type **=[OrderAmount]*.07** and press the Enter key. You should see the new column on the right side of the table, as shown in Figure 8.12.

	ShippedDate	Shipp...	ShippingFee	PaymentMethod	PaidDate	Taxable	OrderAmount	Calculated Column 1	
1						N	2608.9	182.623	
2	2/27/2023 12:0...	1	17.5			Y	42	2.94	
3						Y	946.8	66.276	
4						Y	68	4.76	
5						N	432.34	30.2638	
6						Y	481.2	33.684	
7	3/7/2023 12:14:...	1	17.5			Y	1548	108.36	
8	3/9/2023 12:16:...	1				Y	2074.41	145.2087	
9	3/11/2023 12:1...	1				N	1760.11	123.2077	
10	3/11/2023 12:2...	2				N	153	10.71	
11	3/13/2023 12:2...	2	17.5			Y	626.4	43.848	
12	3/15/2023 12:2...	1				N	561	39.27	
13						N	1517.07	106.1949	
14	3/19/2023 12:3...	1				Y	662.75	46.3925	
15	3/21/2023 12:3...	1	17.5			N	1455.55	101.8885	
16	3/21/2023 12:3...	1				Y	437.7	30.639	

Figure 8.12: A table with a calculated column in the Power Pivot for Excel window

10. If you want to rename the column, right-click the column header, select Rename Column, type the new column name, and press Enter.

11. If you want to format the column, you can use the formatting icons on the Home tab of the Power Pivot for Excel window.

Your new column will automatically be available in the fields list of the PivotTable Fields window. Other calculated columns using the DAX language would be made in a similar way. Remember to save your work, and close or minimize the Power Pivot for Excel window.

NOTE The DAX language can be used to create very complicated formulas. To find a complete reference of the DAX language, visit learn.microsoft.com/en-us/dax/.

Adding a Measure into the Data Model

Another type of DAX formula that can be added to the data model is a measure. A measure is usually a cumulative total based on multiple rows and columns. Examples of a measure would be the earliest or most recent date that each customer placed an order, or the year-to-date sales for a customer. In the following example, the last time a shipment was made to each client will be displayed.

Do the following steps to create a measure:

1. Close or minimize the Power Pivot for Excel window if it is still open.

2. Click the sheet that has the pivot table made from a data model. If you are using the sample data, use the pivot table you made in the previous example, probably on Sheet1.

3. Select the Power Pivot tab.

4. Click the Measures icon on the left side of the ribbon then choose New Measure. This will display the Measure dialog box, as shown in Figure 8.13.

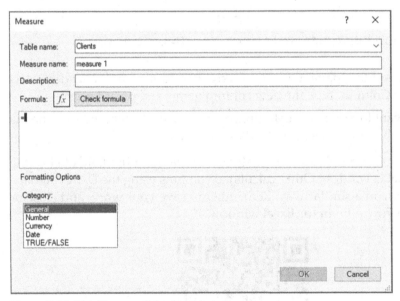

Figure 8.13: The Measure dialog box

5. Enter the table name. The table name is the table where the measure will be stored. For this example, click the drop-down menu to the right of Table Name and choose Clients.

6. In the Measure Name field, enter what you want for the measure name. For this example, enter **Last Ship Date**.

7. Enter a description or leave this field blank.

8. Click the fx icon to see a list of the available functions. You will see the Insert Function dialog box, as shown in Figure 8.14. You will see a list of DAX functions, some of which are available in normal Excel formulas, and many of which are available only in Power Pivot and Power BI, which also uses DAX expressions. As you click each function, it will give you a brief description of what the function does.

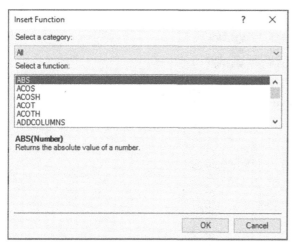

Figure 8.14: The Insert Function dialog box

9. Choose the function you want. In this example, scroll down and choose the LASTNONBLANK function.

10. Click OK. You will see the formula in the Measure window.

11. Click inside the parentheses of the formula and finish the formula. For this example, enter **Sales[ShippedDate]," ")** . The full formula should now be =LASTNONBLANK(Sales[ShippedDate]," ").

12. Choose a format from the bottom of the dialog box. For this example, I chose Date on the left and then 3/14/2001 from the Format drop-down menu on the right.

13. Click OK. The new field should be on the pivot table, as shown in Figure 8.15. If the field is not on the pivot table, then you can find the field in the fields list of the PivotTable Fields window in the table that you chose when you made the measure. The measure can be dragged into the Values section of the PivotTable Fields window like any other field.

You can modify a measure by clicking the Power Pivot tab, selecting the Measures icon on the left side of the ribbon, and then choosing Manage Measures, which will display the Manage Measures dialog box, as shown in Figure 8.16. From the Manage Measures dialog box, you can add, edit, or delete measures. Close the Manage Measures dialog box when you are done with it.

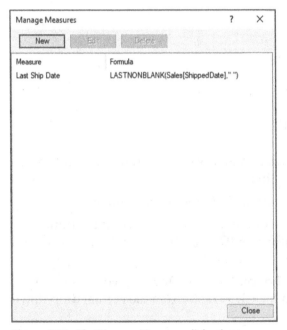

Row Labels	Sum of OrderAmount	Last Ship Date
Art's Art	17711.16	8/24/2023
Daisy's Daisies	41927.69	8/28/2023
Frank's Franks	29018.38	8/20/2023
Kel's Bells	28541.76	8/22/2023
Lisa's Leases	22348.28	8/28/2023
Opie's Opals	62626.61	9/1/2023
Penn's Pens	44458.8	8/30/2023
Rose's Roses	50282.62	9/1/2023
Grand Total	296915.3	9/1/2023

Figure 8.15: A pivot table with a measure

Manage Measures

New   Edit   Delete

Measure	Formula
Last Ship Date	LASTNONBLANK(Sales[ShippedDate]," ")

Close

Figure 8.16: The Manage Measures dialog box

Creating a KPI

Another great feature of Power Pivot is a KPI. It is a visual tool, somewhat similar to conditional formatting, which can show where an individual value falls within a column of numbers. To add a KPI, a measure has to be added first, because KPIs come from measures.

In the following example, a measure will be made that counts the number of orders for each client, and then a KPI will be made from it.

To create a measure and a KPI, do the following:

1. Use the workbook from the previous example.

2. Choose the Power Pivot tab.

3. Choose the Measures icon on the left side of the ribbon and then choose New Measure.

4. In the Measure dialog box, choose the table where you want the measure to be stored. If you are using the sample data, choose the Clients table.

5. For the measure name, enter **Count**.

6. For the formula, enter **=COUNT(Sales[OrderID])**.

7. Choose a format from the bottom of the dialog box. For this example, I chose Number, and then I enter **0** for the Decimal Places.

8. Click OK. The new measure should be on the pivot table.

    Now it is time to make a KPI using the measure that was just created. Do the following to add the KPI.

9. Choose the Power Pivot tab.

10. Choose the KPIs icon on the left side of the ribbon, and then choose New KPI. You will now see the Key Performance Indicator (KPI) dialog box, as shown in Figure 8.17.

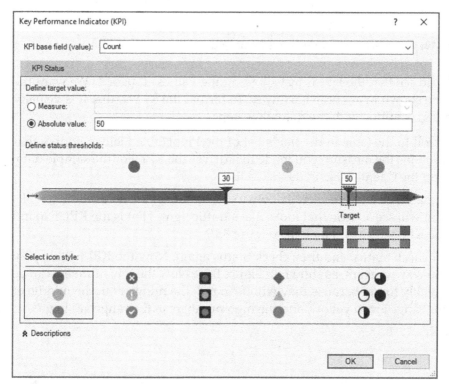

Figure 8.17: The Key Performance Indicator (KPI) dialog box

11. Click the drop-down menu for the KPI base field (value). You will see a list of the available measures. Choose the measure you want to use. If you are using the sample data, choose the Count measure.

12. You will want to reset the scale that you see in the middle of the dialog box. The scale can be based on another measure or a value. Choose Absolute Value, and enter a number to the right of Absolute Value and press Enter. For this example, enter **50** and press Enter. This should reset the scale. You can move the black filters back and forth on the scale to adjust where red ends and where yellow ends. For this example, drag the first black filter to 30 on the scale and the second black filter to 50 on the scale.

13. Choose the style you want and then click OK. The KPI will show up on the pivot table, as shown in Figure 8.18.

Row Labels	Sum of OrderAmount	Last Ship Date	Count	Count Status
Art's Art	17711.16	8/24/2023	18	-1
Daisy's Daisies	41927.69	8/28/2023	36	0
Frank's Franks	29018.38	8/20/2023	36	0
Kel's Bells	28541.76	8/22/2023	30	0
Lisa's Leases	22348.28	8/28/2023	30	0
Opie's Opals	62626.61	9/1/2023	60	1
Penn's Pens	44458.8	8/30/2023	48	0
Rose's Roses	50282.62	9/1/2023	48	0
Grand Total	296915.3	9/1/2023	306	1

Figure 8.18: A pivot table with a KPI, before formatting

You can see that the KPI is just showing the values -1, 0, or 1. We want the KPI to be shown in a more visual way. To format the KPI so that it is visually appealing, continue with the following steps.

14. Scroll to the table in the fields list of the PivotTable Fields window that contains the measure you made that drives the KPI. For the sample data, find the Clients table in the fields list.

15. Expand the table and scroll down to the bottom of the fields for that table. You will see an icon that looks like a traffic light. That is the KPI. Expand the KPI, which will look like Figure 8.19.

16. Uncheck Status, and then check Status again. Now the KPI will display the way we want, as shown in Figure 8.20. Now the low numbers can be quickly found because they will be in red, the numbers in the middle of the range are in yellow, and the high numbers in the range are in green.

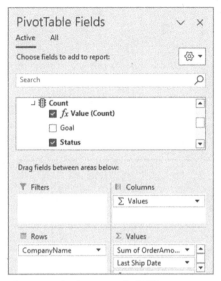

Figure 8.19: An expanded KPI

Row Labels	Sum of OrderAmount	Last Ship Date	Count	Count Status
Art's Art	17711.16	8/24/2023	18	●
Daisy's Daisies	41927.69	8/28/2023	36	◐
Frank's Franks	29018.38	8/20/2023	36	◐
Kel's Bells	28541.76	8/22/2023	30	◐
Lisa's Leases	22348.28	8/28/2023	30	◐
Opie's Opals	62626.61	9/1/2023	60	●
Penn's Pens	44458.8	8/30/2023	48	◐
Rose's Roses	50282.62	9/1/2023	48	◐
Grand Total	**296915.3**	**9/1/2023**	**306**	●

Figure 8.20: The pivot table with a KPI, after formatting

You can modify a KPI by clicking the Power Pivot tab, choosing the KPIs icon, and then choosing Manage KPIs, which will display the Manage KPIs dialog box, as shown in Figure 8.21. From the Manage KPIs dialog box, you can add, edit, or delete KPIs. Close the Manage KPIs dialog box when you are done with it.

Summary

In this chapter, you learned how to activate the Power Pivot add-in, how to add tables to the data model from different data sources, how to join tables together, how to create DAX formulas, and how to create and display KPIs on the pivot table made with a data model.

Figure 8.21: The Manage KPIs dialog box

In the next chapter, you will create a user-friendly dashboard by using many of the components you have learned from this book along with a few other features too.

Pulling It All Together: Creating a Dashboard from Pivot Tables

Throughout this book, you have learned how to get your data ready to be made into a pivot table, how to create and format a pivot table, how to add calculations, how to sort and filter the pivot table, and how to create charts from a pivot table. In this chapter, we will tie everything together to make a user-friendly, interactive, informative dashboard.

A dashboard can consist of any combination of pivot tables, charts, sorts, filters, slicers, timelines, text, graphics, and really any other object available in an Excel spreadsheet. You can use your imagination to make your own dashboard any way you want it to be. The end result of a dashboard should be easy to use, visually appealing, and interactive, and it should show the results that the user is looking for. It should also be flexible to grow and change, as the user's needs will change. This chapter shows a specific example to give you an idea of the possibilities of what you can do with a dashboard. You can then take it from there. First, I will show you a finished dashboard, and then you will learn how to build a similar dashboard.

> **NOTE** For the examples presented in this chapter, you can use the sample files called *FinishedDashboard.xlsm* and *DashboardBase.xlsx* that are included with this book. You can find the sample files at `www.wiley.com/go/GGRXL_PivotTables`.

Looking at a Finished Dashboard

Let's take a look at the sample dashboard shown in Figure 9.1. Using the sample files that come with the book, open the file called *FinishedDashboard.xlsm*. When you open the sample file, you see the dashboard as shown in the figure.

> **NOTE** The file called *FinishedDashboard.xlsm* contains macros that make some of the features of the dashboard work. When you open this file, you may get a message on top of the spreadsheet below the ribbon that asks if you want to enable the content. If you see this message, click the Enable Content button. This will make all of the features work correctly in the workbook.

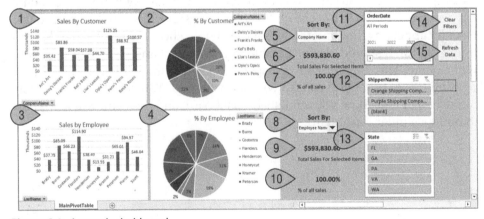

Figure 9.1: A sample dashboard

Let's take a look at the components of the dashboard (with numbers corresponding to Figure 9.1).

1. Column chart showing sales by customer

2. Pie chart showing percent of sales by customer

3. Column chart showing sales by employee

4. Pie chart showing percent of sales by employee

5. Drop-down menu allowing the user to pick the sort order for the customer charts

6. Total sales for the customer based on the current filter

7. Percent of overall sales for the customer based on the current filter

8. Drop-down menu allowing the user to pick the sort order for the employee charts

9. Total sales for the employee based on the current filter

10. Percent of overall sales for the employee based on the current filter

11. Timeline based on the order date

12. Slicer based on the shipper's name

13. Slicer based on the state

14. A button to clear the filters to show all data

15. A button to easily refresh the charts if the original data changes

The user can filter the customer charts by company using the AutoFilter on the customer chart, and the user can filter the employee charts by employee name using the AutoFilter on the employee charts. The slicers and timelines can be used for more filters. The slicers and the timeline will update all charts. The user can sort the charts using the drop-down menus, which are form objects called *combo boxes*. The buttons on the right side of the window are form objects called *command buttons*. The form objects will be covered a little later in the chapter.

Notice how the only sheet that you see at the bottom is the MainPivotTable sheet. Also notice that you don't see the pivot tables that are driving the dashboard. The column headers, row headers, formula bar, and gridlines are also not showing. These items have been hidden from view to improve the appearance of the dashboard. For the rest of this chapter, you will learn how to create a similar dashboard.

Creating Your Own Dashboard

Now, let's build a similar dashboard. Some of the steps are topics that were already covered in the book, and some will be new.

Close the *FinishedDashboard.xlsm* workbook, and open the *DashboardBase* *.xlsx* workbook from the sample files that come with the book. Of course, these examples will work with your own workbook as well.

In the sample workbook, the data for the pivot tables comes from the four sheets: Staff, Sales, Clients, and Shippers. The tables are joined together on the common fields, creating a data model, as discussed in Chapter 7, "Creating a Pivot Table from Multiple Spreadsheets."

When you click the MainPivotTable sheet, you will see three pivot tables. One is a summary for each customer, one is a summary for each employee, and one is a summary (a grand total) for all orders, which will be used to calculate the percentage of total for all sales. The bottom pivot table (the summary of all orders) will not be affected by any of the slicers or timelines. It will remain static unless the data changes. You can click each pivot table to see the fields for that pivot table in the PivotTable Fields window. Each pivot table is managed independently. These are simple pivot tables that are used to drive the dashboard. Your dashboard may need several pivot tables to achieve the desired results of the dashboard, and your pivot tables can be simple or more complex.

Adding Charts to Your Dashboard

We will start the dashboard by adding some charts to the dashboard. For this example, there will be a column chart and a pie chart for each pivot table. Of course, when you make your own dashboard with your data, you can use whatever chart types you need and as many charts as you need.

To add the charts to the dashboard, do the following:

1. Click the pivot table that you want to make a chart from. If you are using the sample data, click cell A3 of the MainPivotTable sheet in the DashboardBase workbook. This cell is within the customer pivot table.

2. Select the PivotTable Analyze tab.

3. Choose the PivotChart icon on the right side of the ribbon. This will display the Insert Chart dialog box.

4. Choose the chart type you want. For this example, I chose the Column chart.

5. Click OK. The chart should be displayed. Move, resize, and format the chart as needed. I recommend you at least change the chart title and add the data labels. See Chapter 5, "Making the Pivot Table More Visual with Charts," for tips about formatting the chart.

6. Repeat the steps for the charts that you want for your dashboard. For this example, I added a column chart and a pie chart for the customer pivot table and for the employee pivot table. Your dashboard should look something like Figure 9.2.

7. Save your work.

Figure 9.2: Pivot tables and charts

Adding Slicers and Timelines to Your Dashboard

The charts have the AutoFilters for the fields that are on the chart, but your dashboard may require more filters. This is where the slicers and timelines come in. Slicers and timelines were covered in Chapter 4, "Sorting and Filtering the Pivot Table." For this example, a slicer is added for the state, another slicer is added for the shipper's name, and a timeline is included so the user can choose a date range.

Do the following to add slicers to the dashboard:

1. Click a pivot table. If you are using the sample data, click cell A3 of the MainPivotTable sheet.

2. Choose the PivotTable Analyze tab.

3. Select the Insert Slicer icon near the middle of the ribbon. You will see the Insert Slicers dialog box.

4. Click the All tab at the top of the Insert Slicers dialog box. Choose as many slicers as you want for your dashboard. For this example, I chose the State field from the Clients table and the ShipperName field from the Shippers table.

5. Click OK. You will now see the slicers on the window. Move, resize, and format the slicer windows as needed.

6. Save your work.

You may also want to add a timeline so the user can choose a date range for your dashboard.

To create a timeline, do the following:

1. Click a pivot table. If you are using the sample data, click cell A3 of the MainPivotTable sheet.

2. Choose the PivotTable Analyze tab.

3. Select the Insert Timeline icon near the middle of the ribbon. You will see the Insert Timelines dialog box.

4. Choose as many timelines as you want for your dashboard. For this example, I chose the OrderDate field from the Sales table.

5. Click OK. You will now see the timeline on the window. Move, resize, and format the timeline window as needed.

6. Save your work.

Right now, the slicers and timeline update only the pivot table that you used to create the slicers and the timeline. For the dashboard, we want the slicers and timeline to update multiple pivot tables and therefore the charts.

To make the slicers and timeline update multiple pivot tables, do the following:

1. Right-click a slicer or a timeline window.

2. Choose Report Connections.

3. Check the pivot tables that you want the slicer or timeline to update. For this example, I checked PivotTable1 and PivotTable3.

4. Click OK.

5. Repeat these steps for the other slicer and timeline windows, and then save your work.

Your dashboard should now look something like Figure 9.3.

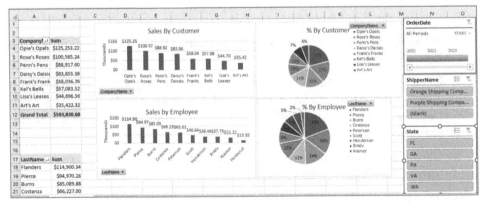

Figure 9.3: Pivot tables, charts, slicers, and timeline

Displaying Totals and Percent of Totals

The charts currently show the subtotals for each customer or each employee. What if you wanted to see the totals based on the filtered data for each chart and also the percent of the overall total for all of the sales instead? This will be a great use of the GETPIVOTDATA function we learned in Chapter 3, "Using Calculations in Pivot Tables."

Do the following to use the GETPIVOTDATA function to create calculations:

1. Click a blank cell away from the charts and pivot tables. For this example, I chose L4.

2. Type in a = to start a formula.

3. Click the total for one of your pivot tables. For this example, I chose cell B12, which is the total for the customer pivot table. This will give you a formula that should be

   ```
   =GETPIVOTDATA("[Measures].[Sum of OrderAmount]",$A$3).
   ```

   Press the Enter key.

The formula that was just entered calculates the total; however, it would also be good to show the percentage of total sales. This can be done by taking the number that was just created and dividing it by the number for all sales, which will produce the percent of total sales. This is the purpose of the third pivot table in the sample data sheet. We can add this by following these steps:

1. Click the cell below the cell you just created. For this example, I selected cell L5.

2. Type in a = to start a formula.

3. Click the number you just created in cell L4.

4. Type in the / for division.

5. Click the total for the pivot table that contains the grand total. For this example, I chose cell A30. The formula should be

   ```
   =L4/GETPIVOTDATA("OrderAmount",29).
   ```

   Press the Enter key. This will give you a decimal number.

6. Format the number you just created as a percentage.

7. Repeat these steps to make similar calculations for the other pivot tables, if needed, and then save your work.

Your pivot table should now look something like Figure 9.4.

Working with Form Controls, Macros, and VBA Code

So far in this chapter, you have applied many of the skills you learned in previous chapters to create a decent dashboard. It is now time to take the dashboard to the next level with form controls, macros, and a little bit of Visual Basic for Applications (VBA) code.

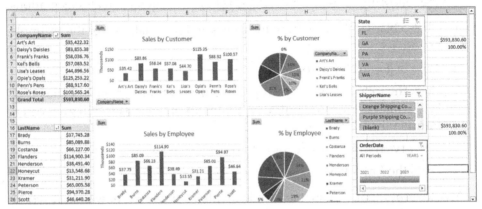

Figure 9.4: A dashboard with totals

Form controls are objects that can be added to an Excel spreadsheet to make the spreadsheet easier to use and more interactive. Form controls can also be made to run a macro that will make the form control more functional.

A macro is a way to automate steps in the Excel spreadsheet. Macros consist of lines of Visual Basic code, or VBA. Macros can be recorded or entered manually. When macros are recorded, the VBA code is entered into the macro automatically.

Most people create a macro by recording the macro. Experienced programmers can add or change the VBA code manually, which then can greatly enhance the functionality of an Excel workbook. For the purposes of this book, you will see how to create form controls, how to record a macro, and how to associate the macro with the form controls. To access form controls and macros, you have to first enable the Developer tab.

> **NOTE**　All of the pivot tables and dashboards that have been made up to this point in the book should work on Excel for the Web. Once you add macros to the workbook, however, the macro-enabled workbooks will not work on the Excel for the Web. If you want to have automated routines that will work on Excel for the Web, you will have to use Office Scripts instead of VBA Macros. Office Scripts can be recorded like macros but use a different programming language that is called Office Scripts.

The Developer Tab

Even though some macro commands can be found on the right side of the View tab of the ribbon, the Developer tab will give you more flexibility with macros and VBA code. The Developer tab will also give you access to form controls. Once you activate the Developer tab, it will show up every time you start Excel until you deactivate it.

To turn on the Developer tab, do the following:

1. Click the File tab.

2. At the bottom of the menu in the left pane, choose Options, or choose More and then choose Options. You will now see the Excel Options dialog box.

3. Select the Customize Ribbon tab.

4. On the right side of the Excel Options dialog box, check Developer, as shown in Figure 9.5. Notice the choice above Developer called Automate, which is how you would access the Office Scripts as mentioned in the previous note.

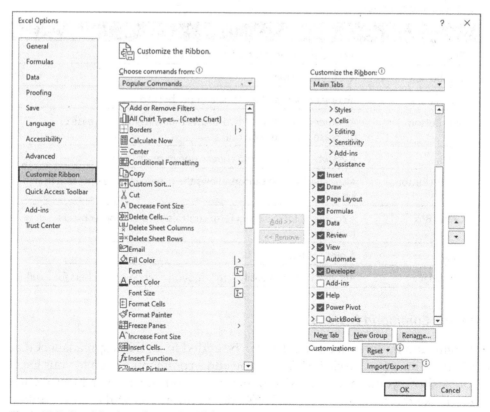

Figure 9.5: Excel Options, Customize Ribbon settings

5. Click OK. You should now see the Developer tab to the right of the View tab.

6. Select the Developer tab. You should now see the ribbon, as shown in Figure 9.6.

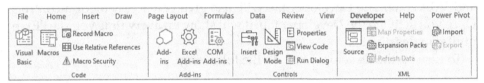

Figure 9.6: The ribbon of the Developer tab

Many of the choices on the ribbon for the Developer tab mention macros, Visual Basic, and code. Macros can be created and managed independently of form controls. For the purposes of this book, I will show you how the macros interact with the form controls to enhance the dashboard.

The form controls are accessible from the Insert icon within the ribbon on the Developer tab. Each form control can be made to run a macro. Table 9.1 describes what the form controls do.

Table 9.1: Form controls

CONTROL	DESCRIPTION
Button	A clickable object that will run a macro when clicked
Combo Box	A drop-down menu
Check Box	An object that can be checked or unchecked
Spin Button	An object consisting of two arrows that will either increase or decrease the value of a cell
List Box	A list where the user can choose one or more items
Option Button	Also called a radio button, allows the user to choose one item from a list
Group Box	A container for the other form controls used to group objects together
Label	A piece of text
Scroll Bar	Allows the user to easily scroll through a range of numbers for a cell

Adding Command Buttons

A command button is a button that can be added to an Excel spreadsheet that will run a macro when clicked. When you add a command button to your Excel spreadsheet, you can use an existing macro, or you can create a macro when you make the command button. Let's add a button that will clear the filters from both pivot tables, and another button that will refresh the pivot tables with any new data.

Do the following to add a command button to clear the filters for the pivot tables:

1. Use the slicers or AutoFilters to apply a filter to the pivot tables.
2. Click a blank cell away from the charts and the pivot tables.
3. Click the Developer tab.
4. Choose the Insert icon on the ribbon. You will see the form controls, as shown in Figure 9.7. Notice how there are two categories, Form Controls and ActiveX Controls. The Form Controls can all be set up to run macros. The ActiveX Controls can be more flexible than the Form Controls, but the ActiveX Controls require that the VBA code be entered manually. We will use the controls in the Form Controls category.

Figure 9.7: Form controls

5. Choose the first control on the first row. It is a button, also called a command button.
6. Click a blank spot of the workbook. You will now see the Assign Macro dialog box, as shown in Figure 9.8. From this dialog box, you can choose an existing macro from the list if there are any. Alternatively, you can type in the VBA code manually by choosing New, or you can record a new macro by choosing Record.

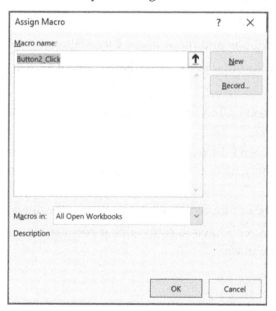

Figure 9.8: The Assign Macro dialog box

7. For this example, choose Record. You will now see the Record Macro dialog box, as shown in Figure 9.9.

Figure 9.9: The Record Macro dialog box

8. Give your macro a name by filling in the box below Macro Name. If you change the macro name from the default, your new name cannot contain any spaces.

9. In the Store Macro In drop-down menu, choose This Workbook.

10. Click OK. You are now recording the macro. Any step that you do within the Excel spreadsheet will be recorded into the macro.

11. Select any cell within a pivot table.

12. Choose the PivotTable Analyze tab.

13. Choose the Clear icon on the ribbon and then choose Clear Filters.

14. Repeat steps 11 through 13 for the other pivot tables that you want to clear.

15. Click the Developer tab.

16. Choose the Stop Recording icon on the left side of the ribbon. You will now see a button on the sheet.

17. Right-click the button and choose Edit Text to change the text of the button. Type Clear Filters. You may have to resize the button so all of the text fits.

18. Click away from the button. The button can now be used to clear the filters.

19. To change or move the button, you have to right-click it because if you click the button, it will run the macro.

Another process to automate for the user is to be able to refresh the pivot tables if the original data changes. You can do this with another command button. Do the following to add a button to refresh the pivot tables:

1. Click the Developer tab.

2. Choose the Insert icon on the ribbon. You will see the form controls.

3. Choose the first control on the first row. It is a button for a command button.

4. Click a blank spot of the workbook. You will now see the Assign Macro dialog box.

5. For this example, choose Record. You will now see the Record Macro dialog box.

6. Give your macro a name by filling in the box below Macro Name. If you change the macro name from the default, your new name cannot contain any spaces.

7. In the Store Macro In drop-down menu, choose This Workbook.

8. Click OK. You are now recording the macro. Any step that you do within the spreadsheet will be recorded into the macro.

9. Select any cell within a pivot table.

10. Choose the PivotTable Analyze tab.

11. Choose the drop-down menu under the Refresh icon on the ribbon and then choose Refresh All.

12. Click the Developer tab.

13. Choose the Stop Recording icon on the left side of the ribbon. You will now see a button on the sheet.

14. Right-click the button and choose Edit Text to change the text of the button. Type Refresh Data.

15. Click away from the button. The button can now be used to refresh the pivot tables.

16. If you want to change or move the button, you have to right-click it because if you click the button, it will run the macro.

Saving a Workbook with a Macro

When you created the buttons in the previous examples, you also recorded macros at the same time. Now that the workbook contains macros, the workbook must be saved a certain way so that the macros are also saved. If you do not save the workbook as a macro-enabled workbook, you will lose your macro.

To save a workbook with a macro, do the following:

1. Click the Save icon. You will see the Microsoft Excel dialog box, as shown in Figure 9.10. The correct choice on this window is No.

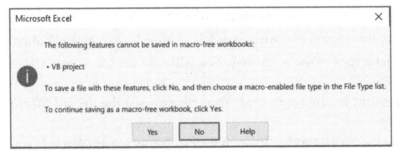

Figure 9.10: The Microsoft Excel dialog box

2. Click No. Click Browse in the Save As column, if necessary. You will now see the Save As dialog box, as shown in Figure 9.11.

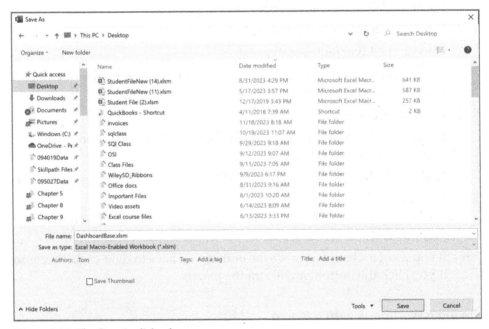

Figure 9.11: The Save As dialog box

3. Click the drop-down menu for the Save As Type choice.

4. Choose Excel Macro-Enabled Workbook (*.xlsm) from the list.

5. Choose Save. This will make a separate copy of the workbook, with an *.xlsm* file extension.

Adding a Combo Box

The dashboard that you have now is pretty similar to the dashboard that was demonstrated at the beginning of this chapter. Now, a drop-down menu will be added that will allow the user to choose how the charts will be sorted. The drop-down menu is a form control that is a called a combo box. The combo box needs a list of items somewhere on the spreadsheet. If you are using the sample workbook, scroll over to cell AA1. You will see a list of two items, as shown in Figure 9.12. If you are using your own data, type in a similar list in your workbook starting in cell AA1, and then another list starting in cell AC1. Of course, you can use any cells in your own workbook, but these specific cells will make the next examples work properly.

AA	AB	AC	AD
Company Name	1	Last Name	1
Sum		Sum	

Figure 9.12: The lists for the combo box

Follow these steps to create a combo box:

1. Click the sheet with your dashboard.

2. Select the Developer tab.

3. Click the Insert icon on the ribbon.

4. Choose the second icon on the top row of form controls. This should be the combo box (▤).

5. Click a blank cell of the spreadsheet. The combo box will be on the sheet, but it probably has to be resized. Drag the bottom sizing handle up so the combo box fits in one cell.

When you click the drop-down menu on the combo box, nothing happens yet. You have to format the control and also assign a macro. All of the other form controls would need to be set up in a similar way to make them work properly as well.

To set up the combo box, do the following:

1. Right-click the combo box. If you see a submenu that just has three choices, right-click the combo box very quickly to see the full menu.

2. Choose Format Control. You will see the Format Object dialog box, as shown in Figure 9.13.

3. Choose the Control tab.

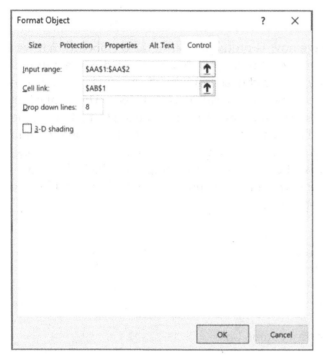

Figure 9.13: The Format Object dialog box

4. Click the space to the right of Input Range. Enter **AA1:AA2** or select cells AA1:AA2.

5. Click the space next to Cell Link and enter **AB1** or select AB1.

6. Click OK.

7. Click away from the combo box.

The drop-down menu on the combo box works, but nothing happens when you choose an item from the drop-down menu. To make the combo box do something when you choose an item, you need to assign a macro to the combo box. This method will work with the other form controls as well. Some macros can be recorded, and some macros have to be manually typed in. Because this macro has some programming logic, it has to be typed. The sample code for this combo box has been included in cells AG1 through AG14 of the MainPivotTable sheet in the sample workbook. That code is also shown in Listing 9.1. There is additional code in cells AN1 through AN14 that will be used in the combo box for the employee pivot table that will be added to the dashboard a little later in this chapter.

Listing 9.1: Customer combobox code

```
' Cell AB1 is populated from the linked cell in the combo box
' If the user chooses Company Name from the combo box, cell
'     AB1 will have the value of 1
```

```
' If the user chooses Sum from the combo box, cell AB1 will have
'       the value of 2

If Range("Ab1") = 1 Then ' Sort by Customer Name
  ActiveSheet.PivotTables("PivotTable1").PivotFields( _
    "[Clients].[CompanyName].[CompanyName]").AutoSort xlAscending, _
    "[Clients].[CompanyName].[CompanyName]"
Else ' Sort by Sum
  ActiveSheet.PivotTables("PivotTable1").PivotFields( _
    "[Clients].[CompanyName].[CompanyName]").AutoSort xlDescending, _
    "[Measures].[Sum of OrderAmount]", ActiveSheet.PivotTables
("PivotTable1"). _
    PivotColumnAxis.PivotLines(1), 1
End if
```

NOTE For a full reference of the VBA code, visit `https://Learn.microsoft` `.com/en-us/office/vba/api/overview`.

Do the following to add the macro into the combo box:

1. Right-click the combo box.

2. Choose Assign Macro.

3. Click New. You will now be in the Microsoft Visual Basic for Applications window, as shown in Figure 9.14. Normally, you would type in the VBA code here. The sample code for this combo box is included in cells AG1 through AG14 in the MainPivotTable sheet in the sample workbook, or if the sample workbook is not available, you can enter the code from Listing 9.1 manually and jump to step 8.

4. Minimize the Microsoft Visual Basic for Applications window. On the sample spreadsheet, highlight cells AG1 to AG14.

5. Right-click cell AG1 and select Copy.

6. Move your mouse to the Excel icon on the taskbar at the bottom of the screen and reopen the Microsoft Visual Basic for Applications window.

7. Paste the code in. The window now should look like Figure 9.15.

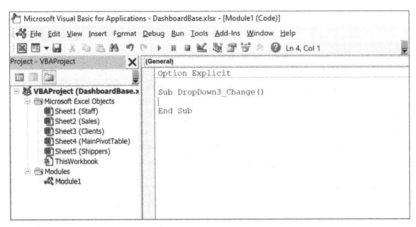

Figure 9.14: The Microsoft Visual Basic for Applications window

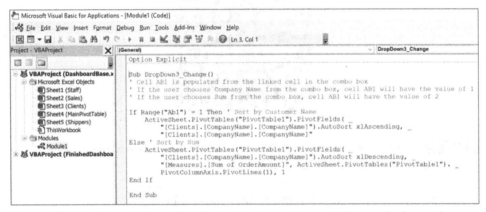

Figure 9.15: The Microsoft Visual Basic for Applications window with the combo box code

8. Close the Microsoft Visual Basic for Applications window.

9. Click away from the combo box and then save your work.

Now when you make a selection from the combo box, the charts for the customer should be sorted accordingly.

You will now set up a second combo box to sort the charts for the employee pivot table. The code for this combo box is in cells AN1 through AN14 in the sample workbook. It is also shown in Listing 9.2

Listing 9.2: Employee combo box code

```
' Cell AD1 is populated from the linked cell in the combo box
' If the user chooses Last Name from the combo box, cell AD1
'    will have the value of 1
' If the user chooses Sum from the combo box, cell AD1 will have
'    the value of 2
```

```
If Range("Ad1") = 1 Then ' Sort by Customer Name
  ActiveSheet.PivotTables("PivotTable3").PivotFields( _
    "[Staff].[LastName].[LastName]").AutoSort xlAscending, _
    "[Staff].[LastName].[LastName]"
Else ' Sort by Sum
  ActiveSheet.PivotTables("PivotTable3").PivotFields( _
    "[Staff].[LastName].[LastName]").AutoSort xlDescending, _
    "[Measures].[Sum of OrderAmount]", ActiveSheet.PivotTables
("PivotTable3"). _
    PivotColumnAxis.PivotLines(1), 1
End If
```

To create and set up the employee combo box, do the following:

1. Click the sheet with your dashboard.

2. Select the Developer tab.

3. Click the Insert icon on the ribbon.

4. Choose the second icon on the top row of form controls. This should be the combo box.

5. Click a blank cell of the spreadsheet. The combo box will be on the sheet, but it probably has to be resized. Drag the bottom sizing handle up so the combo box fits in one cell.

6. Right-click the combo box. If you see a submenu that just has three choices, right-click the combo box very quickly to see the full menu.

7. Choose Format Control. You will see the Format Control dialog box.

8. Choose the Control tab.

9. Click the space to the right of Input Range. Type in **AC1:AC2** or select cells AC1:AC2.

10. Click the space next to Cell Link and type in **AD1** or select AD1.

11. Click OK.

12. Click away from the combo box.

The drop-down menu on the combo box works now, but nothing happens when you choose an item from the drop-down menu. To make the combo box do something when you choose an item, you need to assign a macro to the combo box. The sample code for this combo is included in cells AN1 through AN14 of the MainPivotTable sheet in the sample workbook as well as in Listing 9.2. Do the following to add the macro into the combo box:

1. Right-click the combo box.

2. Choose Assign Macro.

3. Click New. You will now be in the Microsoft Visual Basic for Applications window. The sample code for this combo box is included in cells AN1

through AN14 of the MainPivotTable sheet in the sample workbook. If the sample workbook is not available, you can enter the code manually from Listing 9.2 and jump to step 8.

4. Minimize the Microsoft Visual Basic for Applications window. On the sample spreadsheet, highlight cells AN1 to AN14.

5. Right-click cell AN1 and select Copy.

6. Move your mouse to the Excel icon on the Taskbar at the bottom of the screen and reopen the Microsoft Visual Basic for Applications window.

7. Paste the code in. The window now should look like Figure 9.16.

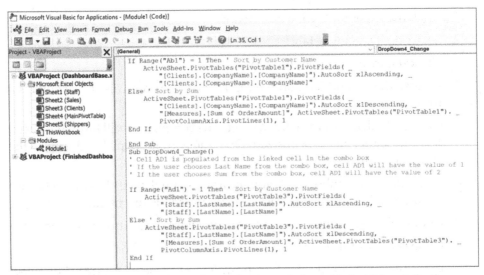

Figure 9.16: The Microsoft Visual Basic for Applications window with the VBA code for the second combo box

8. Close the Microsoft Visual Basic for Applications window.

9. Click away from the combo box and save your work.

When you make a selection from the combo box, the charts for the employee should be sorted accordingly.

Adding Finishing Touches to Your Dashboard

Your dashboard looks good: it is interactive, and it displays the results based on what the user selects. Remember, the finished dashboard presented at the beginning of the chapter did not show the actual pivot table, and the only sheet that was being shown was the sheet that contained the dashboard. The column headers, row headers, gridlines, and formula bar were also hidden. These will be good steps you can take to finalize the dashboard. Before you do these final steps, make sure everything is working on your dashboard, and make sure all objects on the dashboard are formatted the way you want.

Hiding Sheets

You may want to hide the other sheets of the workbook so that the only thing the user sees is the dashboard. This is great for users who just want to run the dashboard to get certain results. Once the sheets are hidden, we also want to make sure that the user cannot unhide the sheets.

To hide a sheet, do the following:

1. Right-click any sheet at the bottom of the workbook, except the MainPivotTable sheet, and then select Hide.

2. Repeat step 1 for any sheet you want to hide, leaving only the sheet that contains the dashboard.

Now, let's make it so the sheets cannot be unhidden. You do this by protecting your workbook. To protect your workbook, proceed with the following steps:

1. Click the Review tab.

2. Click the Protect Workbook icon. You will see the Protect Structure and Windows dialog box, as shown in Figure 9.17.

3. Type in a password that you make up and then click OK.

4. On the next window, type in the same case-sensitive password, and click OK.

5. Save your work.

Your spreadsheet is now protected. Nobody will be able to unhide the sheets unless they know the password.

Figure 9.17: The Protect Structure and Windows dialog box

Hiding the Pivot Table, Gridlines, Column Headings, and the Formula

You also may want to hide the pivot table by hiding the columns where it is contained so that the only thing the user can see is the dashboard. You can also make it so the user cannot unhide the columns containing the pivot table.

To hide the pivot tables, do the following:

1. Highlight all columns of the spreadsheet containing your dashboard and related data. For the sample workbook, highlight from column A to column AD.

2. Right-click one of the highlighted cells.

3. Select Format Cells.

4. In the Format Cells dialog box, choose the Protection tab. You will see the Format Cells dialog box, as shown in Figure 9.18.

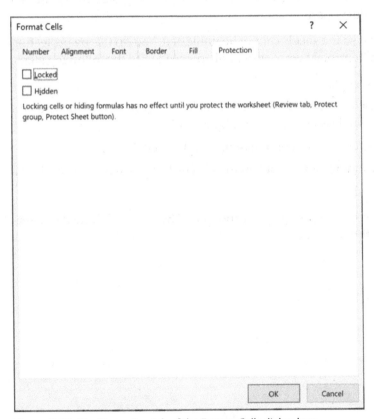

Figure 9.18: The Protection tab of the Format Cells dialog box

5. Uncheck the Locked box.

6. Click OK.

7. Click any cell so that the columns are no longer selected.

8. Highlight the columns containing the pivot table only. In the sample workbook, highlight columns A and B.

9. Right-click one of columns and then select Hide. Your pivot tables are no longer visible.

You may want to hide the gridlines, the row and column headers, and even the formula bar on your dashboard. You can easily do this by clicking the View tab and then unchecking the boxes for Gridlines, Headings, and Formula Bar, as shown in Figure 9.19.

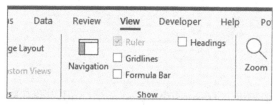

Figure 9.19: The View tab

While your pivot tables are no longer visible, the user can still unhide the columns and access them. To protect the pivot tables from being accessed, do the following:

1. Click the Review tab.

2. Select the Protect Sheet icon. You will see the Protect Sheet dialog box, as shown in Figure 9.20. Any box that is checked means that feature will still be available when the sheet is protected.

3. Check the following boxes:

   ▪ Select Locked Cells

   ▪ Select Unlocked Cells

   ▪ Insert Columns

   ▪ Insert Rows

   ▪ Sort

   ▪ Use AutoFilter

   ▪ Use PivotTable And PivotChart

4. Type in a password that you make up in the space at the top of the dialog box.

5. Click OK.

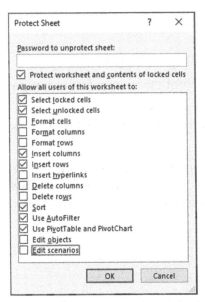

Figure 9.20: The Protect Sheet dialog box

6. On the next screen, type in the same case-sensitive password and click OK.

7. Save your work.

The user will no longer be able to unhide the hidden columns unless they know the password, but everything else should still work. You now have a beautiful, interactive, user-friendly dashboard.

Summary

In this chapter, you learned how to create a user-friendly dashboard using many of the components from previous chapters of the book. You also learned how to add form controls to the dashboard.

You now have the tools to manage your data; create and format pivot tables; add calculations to the pivot table; add sorts, filters, and charts to the pivot table; and summarize the pivot table by dates and times. You also learned several ways to make pivot tables from multiple sheets and to create great dashboards from your pivot tables.

Thank you for reading this book. I truly hope it helps you get great results from your data with pivot tables. I wish you much success!

Index